On the Gunline

U.S. Navy and Royal Australian Navy Warships off Vietnam, 1965–1973

During the Vietnam War, 270 U.S. Navy and four Royal Australian Navy warships served at various times on the gunline. Within this armada were the battleship *New Jersey*, ten cruisers, 212 destroyers, fifty destroyer escorts, and the inshore fire support ship *Carronade*. When necessary, naval guns poured out round after round, until their barrels overheated and turned red, exterior paint blistered, and rifled-barrel liners were worn smooth. Allied troops locked in battle with North Vietnamese Army or Viet Cong troops in South Vietnam were grateful for artillery support from the sea. When North Vietnam launched the Easter Offensive across the DMZ in 1972, eight to ten ships in line, abreast, often firing simultaneously and around the clock, delivered desperately needed fire support. At one point, over forty cruisers and destroyers were serving together on the gunline. Warships conducting SEA DRAGON and LINEBACKER operations – naval bombardment of military targets along the coast of North Vietnam – came under fire on a number of occasions. Runs in to within five miles of a hostile shore, to strike Vinh, Haiphong, and other targets, often preceded duels with shore batteries. Most such action occurred at mission completion as ships zigzagged, while racing seaward at high speed to clear the coast, to throw off the aim of enemy gunners. This book highlights the grit, determination, and heroism of young men – many who would likely have preferred the laid-back lifestyle of the 1960s, were it not for their country's call to arms.

Photographs; maps and diagrams; appendices; a bibliography; and an index to full-names, places and subjects add value to this work.

To the officers and men of the U.S. Navy and Royal Australian Navy who served aboard the battleship *New Jersey*, cruisers, destroyers, and destroyer escorts on the gunline off Vietnam

CAMPAIGNS
1. Vietnam Advisory Campaign (15 March 1962-7 March 1965)
2. Vietnam Defense Campaign (8 March-24 December 1965)
3. Vietnamese Counteroffensive (25 December 1965-30 June 1966)
4. Vietnamese Counteroffensive (1 July 1966-31 May 1967) Phase II
5. Vietnamese Counteroffensive (1 June 1967-29 January 1968) Phase III
6. Tet Counteroffensive (30 January-1 April 1968)
7. Vietnamese Counteroffensive (2 April-30 June 1968) Phase IV
8. Vietnamese Counteroffensive (1 July-1 November 1968) Phase V
9. Vietnamese Counteroffensive (2 November 1968-22 February 1969) Phase VI
10. Tet 69/Counteroffensive (23 February-8 June 1969)
11. Vietnam Summer-Fall 1969 (9 June-31 October 1969)
12. Vietnam Winter-Spring 1970 (1 November 1969-30 April 1970)
13. Sanctuary Counteroffensive (1 May-30 June 1970)
14. Vietnamese Counteroffensive (1 July 1970-30 June1971) Phase VII
15. Consolidation I (1 Jul 1971-30 Nov 1971)
16. Consolidation II (1 Dec 1971-29 Mar 1972)
17. Vietnam Ceasefire Campaign (30 Mar 1972-28 Jan 1973)

On the Gunline

U.S. Navy and Royal Australian
Navy Warships off Vietnam,
1965–1973

Cdr. David D. Bruhn, USN (Retired)
and
STGCS Richard S. Mathews, USN (Retired)

HERITAGE BOOKS
2019

HERITAGE BOOKS

AN IMPRINT OF HERITAGE BOOKS, INC.

Books, CDs, and more—Worldwide

For our listing of thousands of titles see our website
at
www.HeritageBooks.com

Published 2019 by
HERITAGE BOOKS, INC.
Publishing Division
5810 Ruatan Street
Berwyn Heights, Md. 20740

International Standard Book Number
Paperbound: 978-0-7884-5895-8

Heritage Books by Cdr. David D. Bruhn, USN (Retired)

Battle Stars for the "Cactus Navy":
America's Fishing Vessels and Yachts in World War II

Enemy Waters:
Royal Navy, Royal Canadian Navy, Royal Norwegian Navy,
U.S. Navy, and Other Allied Mine Forces Battling the
Germans and Italians in World War II
Cdr. David D. Bruhn, USN (Retired) and Lt. Cdr. Rob Hoole, RN (Retired)

Eyes of the Fleet:
The U.S. Navy's Seaplane Tenders and Patrol Aircraft in World War II

Ingram's Fourth Fleet:
U.S. and Royal Navy Operations Against German Runners,
Raiders, and Submarines in the South Atlantic in World War II

MacArthur and Halsey's "Pacific Island Hoppers":
The Forgotten Fleet of World War II

Home Waters:
Royal Navy, Royal Canadian Navy, and U.S. Navy
Mine Forces Battling U-Boats in World War I
Cdr. David D. Bruhn, USN (Retired) and Lt. Cdr. Rob Hoole, RN (Retired)

Nightraiders:
U.S. Navy, Royal Navy, Royal Australian Navy, and
Royal Netherlands Navy Mine Forces Battling the
Japanese in the Pacific in World War II
Cdr. David D. Bruhn, USN (Retired) and Lt. Cdr. Rob Hoole, RN (Retired)

On the Gunline:
U.S. Navy and Royal Australian Navy Warships off Vietnam, 1965–1973
Cdr. David D. Bruhn, USN (Retired) and
STGCS Richard S. Mathews, USN (Retired)

We Are Sinking, Send Help!:
The U.S. Navy's Tugs and Salvage Ships in the African,
European, and Mediterranean Theaters in World War II

Wooden Ships and Iron Men:
The U.S. Navy's Ocean Minesweepers, 1953–1994

Wooden Ships and Iron Men:
The U.S. Navy's Coastal and Motor Minesweepers, 1941–1953

Wooden Ships and Iron Men:
The U.S. Navy's Coastal and Inshore Minesweepers,
and the Minecraft that Served in Vietnam, 1953–1976

Contents

Photos and Illustrations

Maps and Diagrams

Photo Contents

Vietnam sunset.
USS *Oklahoma City* (CLG-5) Western Pacific 1971-72 cruise book

Foreword

David Bruhn's *Gunline* presents a comprehensive and illustrative study of the contribution during the Vietnam War of the U.S. and Australian surface warships and sailors that operated along the coasts of North and South Vietnam. Quite often the subjects that first come to mind with regard to naval actions in the conflict are the bombing campaigns conducted by the aircraft carriers of Task Force 77 and the river patrols and riverine assaults by U.S. Naval Forces, Vietnam. But as Bruhn has demonstrated in this admirable work, U.S. battleship *New Jersey* (BB-62), the cruisers, destroyers, and other surface combatants of the Seventh Fleet and the Royal Australian Navy's destroyers played a major role in the war. His prodigious research has documented the involvement of the surface forces that battled North Vietnamese coastal guns in Operation Sea Dragon, provided naval gunfire support to allied ground troops locked in battle with Viet Cong guerrillas in South Vietnam, intercepted enemy trawlers attempting the seaborne infiltration of war materials in Operation Market Time, and protected the maritime evacuations from South Vietnam in 1975. Bruhn enlightens the reader about the sacrifices made by American and Australian sailors to enemy and friendly fire, shipboard accidents, and serving in the often storm-tossed South China Sea. The author does not shy away from controversial episodes such as Marcus Aurelius Arnheiter's command of USS *Vance* (DE-387) and the HMAS *Melbourne* (R-21) collision with *Frank E. Evans* (DD-754). Appendices identify personnel casualties suffered by Seventh Fleet ships, the surface combatants that served in Vietnamese waters, and awards earned by the Australian naval contingent. In short, this volume should be the first stop for anyone wanting to know the full story of the American and Australian sailors who "went in harm's way" along the combat-wracked shores of Vietnam.

Edward J. Marolda, Former Director of Naval History (Acting) and Senior Historian of the Navy

Foreword

I am delighted to contribute a foreword to *On the Gunline* by David Bruhn. His latest book describes in detail the operational activities of some 270 U.S. Navy and four Royal Australian Navy (RAN) warships that served on the 'gunline' during the Vietnam War. The book gives an excellent overview of the war from the maritime perspective and provides the reader with a clear and comprehensive understanding of the impact the navy made in support of the troops ashore.

Within the context of the war, the RAN contribution was modest compared to the significant resources deployed by the U.S. Navy. This contribution however, in response to U.S. requests, was valuable because it filled a gap in specific U.S. Navy shortages. Australia's contributions to the war grew incrementally from the first commitment of Army advisers to fielding a Task Force and air and naval units. Australia was the only allied nation to provide naval support to the U.S. during the Vietnam War.

In late 1966, the Australian Government directed Defence to consider an increased force commitment to the war in Vietnam. From the naval perspective, the provision of one of the new Guided Missile Destroyers (DDG) recently arrived from the U.S. and fully compatible with the U.S. Navy logistical system was straight forward. The U.S. had made it clear that a clearance diving team able to undertake explosive ordnance disposal duties would be welcome. This request was quickly endorsed given the significant dividend such a deployment would bring and the fact that such a capability was immediately available.

Following discussions between commander in chief Pacific Fleet, Adm. Roy L. Johnson and the RAN chief of Naval Staff, Vice Adm. Alan W. R. McNicoll in February 1967, the RAN agreed to provide a destroyer on a rotational basis under the operational command of the Seventh Fleet and a clearance diving team (CDT3) under the operational control of the U.S. Commander Naval Forces Vietnam. A RAN destroyer was provided to Seventh Fleet on a rotational basis from March 1967 to September 1971, involving nine deployments at six to seven-month intervals. RAN warships provided naval gunfire support and also participated in Operation Sea Dragon.

CDT3 operated within Operation Market Time (Task Force 115) and was fully integrated within the US Navy EOD Group in Vietnam (CDT3 was known as EODMUPAC Team 35). Eight teams were deployed between February 1967 and May 1971, totaling eight officers and 41 sailors, rotating through the war zone at approximately seven-month intervals. The two (i.e. destroyer and CDT) comprised the RAN Force Vietnam.

In response to a U.S. request for flying support, Australia announced in July 1967 it would provide a detachment of RAN aircrew and support personnel. Named the Royal Australian Navy Helicopter Flight Vietnam (RANHFV), it was assigned to the U.S. Army 12th Combat Aviation Group which provided rotary-wing support for forces in III Corps Tactical Zone. From October 1967 it was incorporated into the 135th Assault Helicopter Company flying helicopters in both utility and gunship configurations. Each flight consisted of pilots, gunners, aircrew and maintenance, and support personnel. Some 200 personnel in four annual contingents were deployed from September 1967 to June 1971 and, flying in support of the South Vietnamese, unquestionably saw the most intense combat of any RAN personnel in the war.

The Australian naval forces proved an outstanding success in the operations in which they took part, and attracted the warmly expressed appreciation from their U.S. counterparts. This is reflected by the award of five U.S. Navy Unit Commendations to the RAN—two to HMAS *Perth*, one to HMAS *Hobart*, and two to CDT3.

As an example of U.S. Navy appreciation for RAN participation, Capt. Guy R. Griffiths commanding officer HMAS *Hobart* forwarded the following message from commander Seventh Fleet, Vice Adm. John J. Hyland, USN, as he left for return to Australia: "While operating with the Seventh Fleet, *Hobart* has drawn well deserved praise from all echelons of command both afloat and ashore…. Your aggressive response to all missions has been unsurpassed. Your outstanding performance in the face of enemy fire in Sea Dragon and in support of First Marine Division has been a tribute to exceptionally strong leadership, exemplary training and a strong cohesive spirit. By continuing the long tradition of the navies of our two countries working together for a common cause you have made a definite and highly significant contribution to the mission of the free world forces in Southeast Asia…."

The three DDGs (*Hobart*, *Perth* and *Brisbane*) fitted in seamlessly with the USN whose confidence in their operational abilities meant they regularly assumed the duties of Commander Task Unit, demonstrating the high level of integration the RAN achieved. With *Perth* and *Hobart* scheduled for maintenance, the *Daring*-class HMAS *Vendetta* was selected in late 1968 to relieve *Brisbane* and deployed in September 1969. During the ensuing seven months, *Vendetta* performed credibly in a role for which she had been specifically designed—naval gunfire support— and proved to be a more than adequate replacement for a DDG on the gunline. To keep *Vendetta* operational within a U.S. support organisation tested the RAN's logistic system but confirmed the RAN's ability to successfully operate with the USN.

Vietnam provided the RAN with an excellent opportunity to deploy its surface ships in a high tempo operational environment, which tested both crew and equipment serviceability and reliability. The navy passed the test with flying colours and contributed positively to the enduring relationship the RAN has with the U.S. Navy.

With its comprehensive coverage of the maritime war in Vietnam *On the Gunline* offers a valuable and interesting analysis of naval operations off Vietnam. Such an analysis will contribute to longer term strategic thinking on the use of naval forces in the future.

Commodore Hector Donohue, AM RAN (Rtd)

Foreword

Commodore Donohue has done an admirable job of describing the Royal Australian Navy's participation in Naval Gunfire Support (NGFS) operations during the Vietnamese conflict, and Dr. Marolda provides a fine overview of ten years of naval gunfire support, anti-infiltration, and coastal surveillance operations. Rather than echo their work, I want to briefly describe my personal experiences aboard USS *Parsons* (DDG-33) off the coast of South Vietnam during the North Vietnamese Easter Offensive, March through May 1972.

Parsons was at Yokosuka, Japan, preparing for a radar picket assignment in the Sea of Japan when a flash message arrived in late March 1972. It directed us to get under way as soon as possible and proceed at best speed to the Gulf of Tonkin. The North Vietnamese Easter offensive—launched out of the DMZ, the Central Highlands, and the approaches to Saigon in South Vietnam—had begun. South Vietnamese forces in close proximity to the DMZ were being driven back and were in great danger of being overrun. They desperately needed artillery support. Commander Bruhn describes this offensive in vivid detail.

In March 1972, Destroyer Squadron 15 was composed of *Parsons*, and four World War II *Gearing*-class destroyers—*Rowan* (DD-782), *Gurke* (DD-783), *Richard B. Anderson* (DD-786), and *Bausell* (DD-845). *Parsons* was newer, a *Forrest Sherman* destroyer commissioned in 1959, and converted to guided missile configuration. For NGFS purposes, she retained a single 5"/54 gun mount, forward, of her original three mounts. She was also the squadron flagship.

The gunline ran parallel to the coastline, about 4,000 yards offshore. The North Vietnamese Army (NVA) used QL1, the principal highway south from the DMZ, for movement of troops and supplies, and it was within easy range of our guns. Ships conducting gunfire were assigned circular stations about 2,000 yards apart and designated by color code, Red, Yellow, Green, etc. The gunline commander (normally an embarked squadron commander) received and passed fire missions to the ships. When they were available, he also put the ships in contact with spotters for called fire.

In the early stages of the NVA offensive, ARVN (South Vietnamese Army) units ashore lost cohesion and often lacked artillery support. With air support initially disrupted by cloud cover, eight to ten ships in line, abreast, often firing simultaneously and around the clock, delivered desperately needed fire support. At one point, over forty cruisers and destroyers were serving on the gunline.

For nearly ninety days during the Easter Offensive, *Parsons* was either on the gunline or assigned carrier plane guard duties. We wore out our barrel liner and went alongside a tender at anchor in Da Nang to replace it. We fired over 5,000 rounds of NGFS, but were very FRUSTRATED. For effective NGFS, a ship needs a reliable gun. Our crew was well-trained and the fire control system behaved beautifully. Our SINGLE gun was our Achilles heel. Even at the best of times the Mk 42 5"/54 was a complex gun system: micro switches, limit stops, cams and other components had to work perfectly for the gun to hoist, load, and fire. Every ship with these type of mounts had some reliability issues, but our problem was self-inflicted. Early on the gunline, we had to flood the gun barrel because of a hang fire, hot gun situation. Unfortunately, the breechblock was not fully raised, and saltwater penetrated the innards of the mount. Salt water and electronics don't mix well—ever. Herculean effort by the Gunner's Mates restored partial dependability over time, but it was never the same again.

There was a standby station, Station Black, on the gunline, farther offshore. When a ship's gun failed, it was ordered to Station Black to repair it. *Parsons* spent a lot of time there. If there was no prospect for immediate repair, ships were exiled to a carrier escort assignment until they had a ready gun.

Our sense of pride took a real beating. We were a generation newer than the other four destroyers in the squadron, we were the flagship, and we had the 3-D radar and the guided missile system. We were the Proud, Powerful *Parsons*. Unfortunately, our single, balky gun often consigned us to Station Black or inhaling stack gas and jet exhaust behind a carrier. Our squadron mates mounted 5"/38 guns, first introduced in 1934. They may not have had the range we did, but they kept on shooting, shooting, and shooting.

Gun reliability aside, *Parsons'* single gun limited our NGFS missions. We were judged not able to safely participate in Linebacker operations against North Vietnam. While the other squadron destroyers had after mounts, necessary for self-protection against shore battery fire when clearing the coast, we did not. The other destroyers struck against Vinh, Haiphong, and other targets in the north; we kept the peace at Station Black.

It was very satisfying during the Easter Offensive to know we were mostly firing at real military targets that posed a substantial and immediate threat to our Vietnamese allies, with spotters to call the fall of shot. Other missions were not spotted and had no identified target. *Parsons* was frequently assigned harassment and interdiction missions, firing at random times and targets within a one-square-kilometer area. These areas were uninhabited and without any military value. They may have kept the North Vietnamese awake, but we doubted it, and thought they were, a great waste of ammunition.

Commander Bruhn has delivered a superb, comprehensive treatment of the important role that NGFS played during the Vietnamese war. I doubt if there is a destroyer sailor who served then who did not participate in the delivery of Naval Gunfire. I hope you enjoy this quick-paced and engrossing read.

Capt. Steven C. Saulnier, USN (Retired)
Senior Advisor River Assault and Interdiction Division 44,
  Hai Quan Viet Nam, 1970-1971
Commanding Officer, USS *Fletcher* (DD-992), 1980-1982
Commander, Destroyer Squadron Thirteen, 1988-1991

Acknowledgements

The masterful painting *Sea Dragon Operation off Vinh* by renowned maritime and aviation artist Richard DeRosset graces the cover of this book. The fine art depicts the USS *Epperson* and *Mansfield* taking fire from North Vietnamese shore batteries, following a run in by the destroyers to within five miles of the coast in the vicinity of Vinh. Following engagement of shore targets, the practice of ships engaged in such operations was to zigzag while retiring to seaward at flank speed in an effort to avoid enemy fire. Richard has created over 900 paintings and murals during his illustrious career, but this one had special meaning as he served aboard *Epperson* in the early 1970s.

Seaman Richard DeRosset, USN
USS *Paul Revere* (APA-248) Western Pacific 1974 cruise book

Many thanks to Commodore Hector Donohue and Chief Petty Officer Fire Controlman Russell Graystone for providing information and photographs pertaining to the service of Royal Australian Navy destroyers on the gunline during the Vietnam War. Commodore Donohue, AM RAN (Retired), was kind enough to pen a foreword for the book. He began his career in the RAN in 1955 as a seaman officer and subsequently sub-specialized as a clearance diver and torpedo and anti-submarine officer. His service in the RAN included command of the destroyer escort HMAS *Yarra* and the guided missile frigate HMAS *Darwin*. Ashore, he held a number of senior positions in Defence policy and force development prior to retirement in mid-1991.

Lt. Hector Donohue, RAN
Courtesy of Hector Donohue

Chief Petty Officer Graystone, RAN (Retired), joined the service at age 15, in January 1969. He made his first deployment at age 16 in 1970. Termed FESR (Far East Strategic Reserve); it involved the deployment and integration of Australian and New Zealand forces under British command for the regional defense of the southwest Pacific. Graystone spent much of his career at sea, assigned to the destroyer escorts HMAS *Derwent* and *Stuart*, as well as the destroyer *Vampire*, missile destroyer *Brisbane*, and patrol boat *Attack*. He retired in January 1989. Graystone is webmaster of the Gun Plot website (www.gunplot.net).

Turning to the American side, Dr. Edward J. Marolda is one of two other esteemed individuals who were kind enough to pen forewords, reflecting their unique perspectives and adding richness to the book. Dr. Marolda served as the Acting Director of Naval History and Senior Historian of the Navy. In 2017 the U.S. Naval Historical Foundation honored him with its Commodore Dudley W. Knox Naval History Lifetime Achievement Award. Marolda has written scores of books and articles. An expert on Vietnam, he taught courses at Georgetown University in Washington, D.C. on the Vietnam War and on the Cold War in the Far East. Before embarking on his laudable historian career, Marolda was a U.S. Army officer and served in Vietnam.

1st Lt. Edward Marolda, USA, in Vietnam. He served with the 538th Transportation Company, 64th Quartermaster Battalion, and later the 7th Transportation Battalion, based at Long Binh northeast of Saigon.
Courtesy of Edward Marolda.

Retired U.S. Navy Captain Steven S. Saulnier also reviewed the book and wrote a foreword. Possessing much knowledge of fleet operations as a result of diverse experience gained during a very distinguished career, his perspective was particularly useful. His sea duty began following graduation from the U.S. Naval Academy with service aboard the Navy's first snorkel submarine USS *Irex* (SS-482), commissioned on 14 May 1945, and culminated with his command of Destroyer Squadron Thirteen.

In the interim, he earned two master's degrees from Stanford University, before receiving orders to the guided missile destroyer *Fox* (DDG-13), which served on the gunline. Subsequent duty in Vietnam included senior advisor to River Assault and Interdiction Division 77/River Interdiction Division 44, operations officer aboard the USS *Parsons* (DDG-33), and executive officer of USS *Gurke* (DD-783). Saulnier's later service included command of the destroyer USS *Fletcher* (DD-992), assignment as surface operations officer of Carrier Group One, and Pentagon duty including head of Congressional Policy and Coordination of the Navy staff.

Lt. Steven C. Saulnier, USN, while serving as Damage Control
Officer aboard the guided missile destroyer USS *Fox* (DLG-33).
USS *Fox* Western Pacific 1968 cruise book

I am indebted to retired Navy Captain Philip M. Palmer, who assisted me with both this book, and a previous one as well. *Wooden Ships and Iron Men: The U.S. Navy's Coastal and Inshore Minesweepers, and the Minecraft That Served in Vietnam, 1953-1976* includes Palmer's engrossing account of the role that USS *Meadowlark* (MSC-196) played in the prelude to the Bay of Pigs Invasion of Cuba. One passage from his account follows:

> In early 1961 we were sent along with *Parrot* to Guantanamo Bay, Cuba, for service in the Swan Island patrol.... We knew nothing about the assignment when we sailed from Charleston.... We knew nothing of the planned invasion at the Bay of Pigs and, certainly, were unaware that we had any role in such an event.

Formal photograph of Comdr. Philip M. Palmer, taken in Washington, DC, prior to his reporting to command of Naval Magazine, Subic Bay. Courtesy of Philip M. Palmer

Following his command of *Meadowlark*, a 144-foot coastal minesweeper, Palmer was drafted into the nuclear power program in mid-career by Adm. Hyman G. Rickover. He then served as main propulsion assistant aboard the nuclear-powered aircraft carrier *Enterprise*, during which she was involved in Tonkin Gulf operations. Capping a remarkably diverse, and successful career, Palmer later served as the charter navy officer System Acquisition Manager for the AEGIS

(Weapon System) Shipbuilding Project from 1977-1979. He retired in 1984.

Capt. Robert Kermen, USNR (Retired), also read the manuscript and provided comments based on his diverse duty as an enlisted man in Vietnam. This duty included that of gunner aboard the armored troop carrier *ATC-112-7* (with River Division 112), as a Journalist Third Class aboard the gun cruiser USS *St. Paul* (CA-73), and assignment ashore working for the historian on commander, Naval Forces Vietnam's staff.

Cdr. Ron Swart, USN (Retired) has lent his expertise to other books by the author and did so again. After achieving the rank of Mineman Chief Petty Officer, he was commissioned to Ensign (LDO Surface Ordnance). Subsequently, he served three tours as a Mobile Mine Unit commanding officer, two tours on the Mine Warfare Command staff, as chief staff officer to commander, Mobile Mine Assembly Group, and finally as commander, Mobile Mine Assembly Group.

Michael Halldorson, who served aboard the destroyer USS *Hopewell* (DD-681) from June 1964 to January 1967, provided insights about duty in Vietnam. He reflects back on his time aboard her as a junior enlisted man in his aptly titled book, *Navy Daze: Coming of Age in the 1960s Aboard a Navy Destroyer*, published in 2016.

Canadian George Duddy, a retired professional engineer, clarified details about the heroic efforts of a U.S. Marine Corps and Army officer to blow up the Dong Ha railroad bridge, north-northwest of Quang Tri.

I am particularly grateful to my coauthor, Richard Mathews. Rick and I first met in 1979 when I reported aboard the destroyer *Leftwich* (DD-984) in San Diego. I came to her from the frigate *Miller* (FF-1091) on the East Coast. I was only aboard *Leftwich* for thirteen months before finishing my enlistment and leaving the Navy to attend college. Serving in the same division, he as a Sonar Technician First and I as a Second, we were kindred souls.

The Navy was then still in the doldrums, following an unpopular war, and the resultant reductions in funding and force levels. I do not recall there being many stories about the Vietnam War, if any, told by old hands to younger sailors. I did not know that Mathews had spent so much time off Vietnam until I read his biography for this book.

Finally, a crisp salute to Lynn Marie Tosello, editor of *On the Gunline* and several of my past books. She is a pleasure to work with and to converse with about Navy-related material and other topics. Possessing a very sharp mind and keen eye, in addition to the eloquence of prose one would expect of someone versed in letters, she adds much to accounts of standing out to sea and sailing in harm's way.

Preface

Very often most of the crew had NO idea of what we were doing on the gunline. Infrequently, the CO would get on the 1MC and describe a recent action and mention the number of bunkers taken out or the KIAs [enemy casualties] we got. Most of the rest of the time we just did our assigned tasks leaving the actual details of what was going on to the wardroom [the officers on board]. This is one of the reasons I would really like to have detailed ship's histories of the Benner *and the* Robison. *I've always wondered what the ribbons I earned actually mean.*

I suppose an interested sailor could have gone up to CIC [the ship's combat information center] and poked around a bit to find out more information or could have tried to find out from a shipmate in the know, but I don't think this happened very much. I did hear the gunner's mates talk from time to time about the number and kind of shells fired that day. But that's about it.

—Coauthor Richard Mathews, STGCS(SW), USN Retired, recalling
his service as a mid-grade sonar technician aboard the destroyer
USS *Benner* (DD-807), and guided-missile destroyer
USS *Robison* (DDG-12) during the Vietnam War.

Photo Preface-1

5-inch/54 guns of the destroyer USS *Mullinnix* (DD-944) fire at enemy positions in South Vietnam, both day and night, 30 October 1966.
National Archives photograph #USN 1118703

Two hundred sixty-nine U.S. Navy warships served at various times on the 'gunline' during the Vietnam War. Among this armada of Seventh Fleet units were the battleship *New Jersey*, 10 cruisers, 208 destroyers, and 50 destroyer escorts. A breakdown of these fleet units by ship class is provided in the table. Almost all of the ships remained under the direct control of the Seventh Fleet while deployed to the war zone off Vietnam. A few destroyers and destroyer escorts were assigned at times to Operation MARKET TIME, a coastal surveillance force of ships and aircraft established to interdict the smuggling by sea of arms and munitions to the Viet Cong in South Vietnam.

U.S. Navy Battleship, Cruiser, Destroyer, and Destroyer Escort Classes (1 battleship, 10 cruisers, 208 destroyers, and 50 destroyer escorts)

Battleship/Cruiser Classes	#Ships	Destroyer Classes	#Ships
Iowa-class BB	1	*Allen M. Sumner*-class DD	34
Baltimore-class CA/CAG	4	*Fletcher*-class DD	30
Cleveland-class CLG	4	*Forrest Sherman*-class DD	16
Des Moines-class CA	1	*Gearing*-class DD	87
Long Beach-class CGN	1		
Guided Missile Destroyer Classes		**Destroyer Escort Classes (3 guided missile DEGs)**	
Bainbridge-class DLGN	1	*Bronstein*-class DE	1
Truxton-class DLGN	1	*Brooke*-class DEG	3
Belknap-class DLG	9	*Claud Jones*-class DE	4
Charles F. Adams-class DDG	15	*Courtney*-class DE	4
Farragut-class DLG	7	*Edsall*-class DER	14
Leahy-class DLG	7	*Garcia*-class DE	5
Mitscher-class DDG	1	*Knox*-class DE	19

BB:	battleship	DD:	destroyer
CA:	heavy cruiser	DE:	destroyer escort
CAG:	guided-missile heavy cruiser	DEG:	guided-missile ocean escort
CGN:	nuclear-powered cruiser		
CLG:	guided-missile light cruiser	DER:	radar picket destroyer escort
DDG:	guided-missile destroyer		
DLG:	destroyer leader		
DLGN:	nuclear-powered destroyer leader		

The table does not include other Market Time units that were occasionally called upon to conduct naval gunfire support missions. These included Navy fast patrol craft ("Swift boats") and Coast Guard cutters armed with 81mm mortars, and Navy ocean minesweepers with 40mm guns. Such action usually resulted from a requirement to provide urgent gunfire support to a friendly unit under attack. Infrequently,

Market Time vessels were assigned pre-planned gunfire missions in support of ground operations near the coast.[1]

Map Preface-1

I, II, III, and IV Corps Tactical Zones, Republic of Vietnam

RAN DESTROYERS ON THE GUNLINE

The Royal Australian Navy provided a destroyer on a rotational basis to the Seventh Fleet for service on the gunline—four in total from March 1967 to September 1971. The destroyers carried out naval gunfire support in all four of the Corps Tactical Zones (identified on the preceding map and discussed later in the book).[2]

Photo Preface-2

Aboard the guided missile destroyer HMAS *Hobart*, Vice Adm. John J. Hyland, USN (commander U.S. Seventh Fleet) is welcomed by Rear Adm. Richard I. Peek, RAN (commander of the Australian Fleet). Both flag officers were visiting the *Hobart* on the occasion of the first Australian warship to serve with the USN during the Vietnam War. Australian War Memorial photograph NAVY13307

The first RAN destroyers to deploy to Vietnam were the *Charles F. Adams*-class guided missile destroyers HMAS *Hobart*, *Perth*, and *Brisbane*. Armed with two 5-inch/54 caliber gun mounts that fired a 76-lb high-explosive projectile, they were capable of firing 40 rounds per minute at targets out to and beyond fourteen nautical miles in most conditions.

The *Daring*-class destroyer *Vendetta* also served on the gunline. Her six 4.5-inch guns were capable of providing accurate and rapid fire to nine nautical miles at a rate of 16 rounds per gun per minute.[3]

HMAS *Hobart* and *Perth* were also actively involved in Operation SEA DRAGON—the bombardment of North Vietnamese military targets and interdiction of supply routes and logistic craft along the coast of North Vietnam. These operations, extending from the Demilitarized Zone northward to the Red River Delta, lasted from April 1967 until suspended in November 1968. The two destroyers came under fire on a number of occasions. *Perth* was hit once during her first deployment and *Hobart* suffered two killed and seven wounded when she was mistakenly hit by missiles fired from a U.S. Air Force jet aircraft. *Hobart* was awarded a U.S. Navy Unit Commendation in recognition of her exemplary service in Vietnam; *Perth* earned both the U.S. Navy Unit Commendation and the U.S. Meritorious Unit Commendation.[4]

OVERVIEW OF NAVAL GUNFIRE SUPPORT (NGFS)

Naval gunfire support (NGFS), also known as shore bombardment, is the use of naval artillery to provide fire support for amphibious assault and other troops ashore operating within their range. Naval gunfire can be direct or indirect. When targets are visible from the ship, naval guns are able to put out a rapid, accurate volume of direct fire on such targets. The ship lays its guns directly on the target, and conducts its own firing and spotting procedures. When targets are not visible from the ship, ground or air observation of the fall of shot is necessary for adjustment. Ships can deliver accurate, effective fire on "indirect fire" targets through the use of ground or air observers.[5]

The mobility of ships permit flexibility in the employment of naval gunfire, by offering a wide choice in the selection of firing positions for the execution of fire missions. At one extreme, the battleship *New Jersey* was able to conduct shore bombardment behind armor plate while evading enemy fire by maneuver. At the other end of the spectrum, shallow draft, gunfire support vessels could move in closer to shore, or even inshore, and engage enemy defenses at short range.[6]

The selection of ships for a particular mission was often determined by their guns. In Vietnam, the 16-inch guns of the *New Jersey*, and 8-inch guns of the heavy cruiser *St. Paul*, were ideal for use against enemy batteries, heavy fortifications, and installations for which destruction and penetration were desired. Their greater ranges also made them excellent deep supporting weapons. The rapid rate of fire and relatively small pattern size of the 5-inch guns of the smaller cruisers and destroyers were well suited for the neutralization and destruction of most targets in close support of friendly troops.[7]

Photo Preface-3

The destroyer USS *Theodore E. Chandler* (DD-717) prepares to direct gunfire at enemy targets ashore. A Navy spotter, flying tandem in an Army "bird dog" will call and control the mission over Vietnam. Photo taken 20 November 1966.
National Archives photograph #USN 1119104

The above guidelines pertained to prearranged gunfire missions, those planned prior to an amphibious landing or to support an attack ashore to cover known or suspected enemy troops or installations. In the case of "Targets of Opportunity" or an urgent "Call Fire," the ship most suited or, in some cases, the only one available, would employ its heaviest caliber guns. Troops under attack were undoubtedly grateful for the 3-inch gunfire of a destroyer escort, at relatively modest ranges. Target of opportunity fire was delivered on targets, the location of which previously was unsuspected or unknown. Urgent calls for fire, resulted from friendly forces requesting fire on a specific target(s)—normally enemy forces in close proximity.[8]

The tactical purposes of naval gunfire included: supporting fires, close and deep; counterbattery fire; harassing fire; and interdiction fire. Close supporting fires were normally in immediate support of ground troops ashore. Deep supporting fires were delivered to supplement close supporting fires by neutralizing in the rear, reserves, weapons, and command and control, and communication systems. Counterbattery fire was used to neutralize or destroy enemy batteries. Harassing fire was undertaken to interfere with enemy rest and recuperation, the repair of equipment/installations, and replenishment of food, water, and ammunition. Interdiction fire was employed to deny the enemy use of particular areas, routes of approach, and transport functions.[9]

Before leaving this primer on NGFS, an overview of gun projectiles is in order. The below types of projectiles were, however, not common to every size and type of naval gun:

- High capacity (HC): Designed especially for use in shore bombardment, by providing a relatively high-explosive content at the expense of armor-piercing qualities. HC was effective for both neutralization and destruction.

- Anti-aircraft common (AAC): Large high-explosive (HE) content and an expansive bursting radius (35 to 50 yards).

- Armor piercing (AP): Designed to pierce armor plate before detonating, through the use of a base-detonating delay-action fuze, a heavy nose, and a relatively small HE-content for the weight of the shell.

- Common (C): Compromise between high-capacity and armor-piercing projectiles with respect to bursting charge and penetrative ability.

- White phosphorous (WP): Designed for screening but also offered substantial incendiary and anti-personnel capabilities against exposed troops.

- Illuminating (Ill): Used for illumination at night in order to assist in adjustment of fire of both naval guns and troop weapons, to facilitate friendly troop activities, and to render infiltration by the enemy more difficult.[10]

U.S. NAVY PERSONAL AND UNIT AWARDS

Combat Action Ribbon   Navy Unit Commendation   Meritorious Unit
(CR)   (NUC)   Commendation (MUC)

Readers eager to find out more about a particular warship that served on the gunline between 1965-1973, may refer to Appendix A. The lengthy table lists all 269 ships in alphabetical order, with an associated summary of the numbers of Combat Action Ribbons, Navy Unit Commendations, and Meritorious Unit Commendations earned during this period. Nearly all are for Vietnam service. There are exceptions, however, since some ships engaged in other notable activities.

The 312-foot, 1900-ton destroyer escort USS *McMorris* (DE-1036) was one such exception. Powered by four Fairbanks-Morse diesel engines to a modest top speed of only a little over 20 knots, her armament was equally modest, two 3-inch/50 single-barrel, rapid fire mounts, and two trainable Mk 32 torpedo tube mounts. She, and the other three *Claud Jones*-class DEs, served in Vietnam, but only she received unit awards. In addition to being the 'first' destroyer escort to fire shore bombardment in support of troops in South Vietnam, *McMorris* received a Meritorious Unit Commendation for Spring & Summer 1970 & April-May 1972. The MUC was for special operations unrelated to Vietnam service.[11]

Photo Preface-4

Destroyer escort USS *McMorris* (DE-1036) off Oahu, Hawaii, 10 March 1972; she is displaying "Spooky" electronics arrays fitted in this class of DE. Naval History and Heritage Command photograph #NH 82940

The Meritorious Unit Commendation was established by the Secretary of the Navy on 17 July 1967. It was awarded to units which distinguished themselves by either valorous or meritorious achievement considered outstanding, but to a lesser degree than required for the Navy Unit Commendation. The MUC could be awarded for qualifying actions or achievement either in combat or noncombat situations.

The more prestigious Navy Unit Commendation, dating back to its inception in 1944, was awarded to qualifying units that distinguished themselves by outstanding heroism in combat against a hostile foreign force or for extremely meritorious service not involving combat but in support of military operations.

The Combat Action Ribbon, a military decoration of even higher precedence, was instituted on 17 February 1969. Qualifying Navy, Marine Corps, and Coast Guard personnel must have been in a ground or surface combat fire-fight, or action during which they were under enemy fire, and their performance under fire must have been satisfactory. Initially, the ribbon was for service in combat from 1 March 1961 and thereafter. On 5 October 1999, the award was made retroactive to 7 December 1941.

TOP TWENTY-SIX WARSHIPS BASED ON NUMBERS OF COMBAT ACTION RIBBONS EARNED (1965-1973)

The table below identifies the twenty-six cruisers and destroyers that received the most combat action ribbons for Vietnam duty, which may promote vigorous discussion among some readers. Many good and true sailors believe that their ship was the best among its peer group, based on quantifiable and/or personal criteria. A former *Joseph Strauss* sailor might argue that she was the "top gun," if you consider ship size versus combat action—it being the only "tin can" among the top six ships. Cruiser sailors could assert that their heavier guns put more "hot steel" on target, and *Stoddard* sailors could highlight that their World War II vintage *Fletcher*-class DD earned eleven combat action ribbons—surely a more notable achievement.

Lest some believe that such loyalty, decades later, does not exist, I offer the following. Coauthor Mathews, upon seeing that the *Robison* had made the list, quickly asserted that *Benner* (the other destroyer he served aboard on the gunline) was equally deserving.

The dates in the following table reflect when the ships were originally commissioned. Some ships were later decommissioned for conversion, and recommissioned before being placed back in service.

Twenty-six Cruisers and Destroyers that received the most Combat Action Ribbons in the Vietnam War

CR	MUC	NUC	Ship/Commissioning Date		Ship Class
21	1	2	*Newport News* (CA-148)	29 Jan 49	*Des Moines*
16	1	1	*Joseph Strauss* (DDG-16)	20 Apr 63	*Charles F. Adams*
14	4	1	*St. Paul* (CA-73)	17 Feb 45	*Baltimore*
14		2	*Boston* (CA-69/CAG-1)	30 Jun 43	*Baltimore*
13	2	1	*Oklahoma City* (CLG-5)	22 Dec 44	*Cleveland*
11	2		*Canberra* (CAG-2)	14 Oct 43	*Baltimore*
11		2	*Stoddard* (DD-566)	15 Apr 44	*Fletcher*
9	2	1	*Berkeley* (DDG-15)	7 Feb 62	*Charles F. Adams*
9		2	*Providence* (CLG-6)	15 May 45	*Cleveland*
9	2		*Benjamin Stoddert* (DDG-22)	21 Mar 63	*Charles F. Adams*
9	1	1	*Turner Joy* (DD-951)	3 Aug 59	*Forrest Sherman*
8	3	2	*Edson* (DD-946)	3 Apr 59	*Forrest Sherman*
8	3	1	*Ozbourne* (DD-846)	5 Mar 46	*Gearing*
8	3		*Hull* (DD-945)	3 Jul 58	*Forrest Sherman*
8	3		*Morton* (DD-948)	26 May 59	*Forrest Sherman*
8	2	1	*Goldsborough* (DDG-20)	9 Nov 63	*Charles F. Adams*
8	2		*Allen M. Sumner* (DD-692)	26 Jan 44	*Allen M. Sumner*
8		2	*Waddell* (DDG-24)	28 Aug 64	*Charles F. Adams*
8		1	*Blue* (DD-744)	20 Mar 44	*Allen M. Sumner*
8	1	1	*Hollister* (DD-788)	29 Mar 46	*Gearing*
7	3	1	*Cochrane* (DDG-21)	21 Mar 63	*Charles F. Adams*
7	2	1	*Hamner* (DD-718)	12 Jul 46	*Gearing*
7	1		*Bausell* (DD-845)	7 Feb 46	*Gearing*
7	1		*Buchanan* (DDG-14)	7 Feb 62	*Charles F. Adams*
7	1	1	*Robison* (DDG-12)	28 Oct 61	*Charles F. Adams*
7			*Ingersoll* (DD-652)	17 Aug 43	*Fletcher*[12]
250	40	24			

Many of the combat action ribbons received by these and other ships were earned off the coast of North Vietnam dueling enemy shore batteries during Operations SEA DRAGON (April 1967-November 1968) and FREEDOM TRAIN/LINEBACKER (March-October 1972). The others were for duty on the gunline off South Vietnam, and for less frequent actions which occurred while assigned to other duties, including the escort of aircraft carriers in the Tonkin Gulf.

Although the book's title generally refers to shore bombardment by the battleship *New Jersey*, cruisers, destroyers and destroyer escorts off Vietnam; other Seventh Fleet tasks were also carried out by destroyers and destroyer escorts, in particular. These included Taiwanese Strait patrol duty, and assignment to Task Force 130 (Manned Spacecraft Recovery Force Pacific) for the recovery of Apollo astronauts and their space capsules. The term "on the gunline" originally referred to shore bombardment assignments off South Vietnam. Later, as noted above, this fleet shorthand was also associated with a ship participation in Operations Sea Dragon and Freedom Train/Linebacker.

It must be highlighted that the number of ships, 269, cited by the authors as having served "on the gunline" could easily be contested by Vietnam veterans. As previously noted, some smaller Navy and Coast Guard ships and craft assigned to Operation MARKET TIME were infrequently called upon to provide naval gunfire in defense of friendly ground troops under attack. Moreover, some units, such as the Inshore Fire Support Ship USS *Carronade* (LFR-1), served on the gunline in addition to more common participation in inshore operations. It could also be argued that some nuclear- and conventionally-powered missile cruisers included in the 269 total ships, did not serve on the gunline at all—their primary duty being to screen carriers in the Tonkin Gulf by functioning as PIRAZ ships.

Popular jacket patches among sailors that served in Vietnam (Tonkin Gulf Yacht Club) and on Market Time operations

AIRCRAFT CARRIERS RELOCATED SHOREWARD

With the commencement in February 1965 of Operation ROLLING THUNDER (the large-scale sustained bombing of North Vietnam), participating aircraft carriers operated from a location in the Gulf of Tonkin designated 'Yankee Station.' Initially Yankee Station was about 400 miles off the coast of North Vietnam, in part to keep the carriers beyond the range of North Vietnamese aircraft. This distance required long over-water flights, many needing mid-air refueling, and greatly restricted the number of sorties flown per day.[13]

The solution was to move Yankee Station closer to the intended targets, about 150 miles offshore. However, the new location made the carriers vulnerable to air attack, and it became very important for the task force commander to know if there were any hostile aircraft mixed in with friendly air traffic. An air defense concept, termed Positive

Identification Radar Advisory Zone (PIRAZ), was established, which called for stationing ships about 30 miles off the mainland to attain radar coverage of the air space over North Vietnam.[14]

The PIRAZ ships were to be positioned between the land targets and carriers to monitor and keep track of all air traffic in the area. In addition to being armed with surface-to-air missile systems, these ships would be under the protective umbrella of the carrier's fighter aircraft, and could call in an interceptor at any time. Additionally, because of the possibility of North Vietnamese torpedo boats so close to the mainland, each PIRAZ ship was to have an accompanying destroyer, termed a 'shotgun,' as added protection against these threats.[15]

NEW TECHNOLOGY MOSTLY SUCCESSFUL, BUT...

In 1956, the heavy cruisers USS *Canberra* and *Boston* were fitted with Terrier surface-to-air missile systems, replacing their after triple 8-inch gun turrets. The high-angle guns of the U.S. Navy's cruisers and destroyers, putting out a concentrated barrage of fire, had been sufficient against piston-engined aircraft. However, newly introduced highspeed Soviet jet aircraft, armed with missiles, presented a threat that even the most sophisticated gunfire control system could not meet.[16]

However, Terrier missiles required considerable magazine space, making the system unsuitable for smaller ships. Consequently, the smaller Tartar missile was developed and began going to sea in 1960 aboard *Charles F. Adams*-class destroyers. The earlier Terriers and Tartars had a range of around 10 nautical miles, with a later Terrier design increasing to 20 nautical miles. To provide longer range or 'area defense' against air attacks, the 60-nautical-mile-range Talos was later fielded and fitted in a number of cruisers. The nuclear-powered cruiser USS *Long Beach* was credited with using Talos to destroy two Soviet-built MiG fighter aircraft off North Vietnam in 1968.[17]

One embarrassment in newly fielded technology was DASH. This small helicopter was developed to find Soviet submarines acquired on sonar and attack them with torpedoes before the subs could close the ship employing it to within range of their anti-ship weapons. A number of destroyers were modified to carry two small radio-controlled, unmanned Drone Anti-Submarine Helicopters with the addition of a hangar and flight deck. Despite extensive trials, which included using some helicopters for spotting gunfire, the DASH system did not prove reliable. There were a number of reasons for this, one was that the helicopter, once airborne, was susceptible to jamming of its radio control system.[18]

Mathews remembers witnessing aboard the destroyer *Benner*, the loss of one of her diminutive helicopters:

> I remember Lt. (jg) Tracy at the small control panel of our DASH drone ASW helicopter one day. With his hand on the joystick he watched the bird fly off the ship. He turned it and then turned it back and it headed for the horizon. Then a look of panic came across his face. "It won't come back, it won't come back!" We watched as it disappeared from view and I believe he said, "One hundred and eighty thousand dollars!" His hand was still on the joy stick!

Photo Preface-5

A drone anti-submarine helicopter (DASH) under the control of Lt. (jg) Mark S. Barg, aboard the USS *Nicholas* (DD-449), off the coast of Oahu, Hawaii, 10 February 1965. National Archives photograph #USN 1111342

Within three years of extensive fleet deployment, more than half of the DASH helicopters were out of operation. Aboard the USS *George L. MacKenzie* (DD-836), her hangar and landing deck were neither sizable enough, nor strongly built enough, to service manned aircraft after this occurred, so the destroyer suddenly had a fine movie theater.[19]

ODE TO DESTROYERS AND SAILORS GENERALLY

A destroyer is a lovely ship,
Probably the nicest fighting ship of all.

Battleships are a little like steel cities or great factories of destruction. Aircraft carriers are floating flying fields. Even cruisers are big pieces of machinery, but a destroyer is all boat.

In the beautiful clean lines of her, in her speed and roughness, in curious gallantry, she is completely a ship, in the old sense.

—John Steinbeck

USS *Lloyd Thomas* (DD-764) Western Pacific 1972 Cruise book

There is a certain blend of courage, integrity, character, and principle which have no satisfactory dictionary name but has been called different things at different times in different countries. Our American name for it is "guts."

—Louis Adamic (1899-1951)

Perhaps the most valuable result of all education is the ability to make yourself do the things you have to do, when it ought to be done, whether you like it or not.

—Thomas Huxley

I never found naval men at a loss. Tell them to do anything that is not impossible, and depend on it, they will do it ... their manner of life creates in them a self reliance, which you seldom find in men of other professions.

—The Duke of Wellington 1769

Photo Preface-6

Navy Recruiting Poster by Howard Chandler Christy, issued in 1917.
Naval History and Heritage Command photograph #NH 63193-A-KN

"Tin can" (destroyer) sailors are a special breed, one that takes great pride in their ships and vocation. One public display of such pride could be witnessed in the late 1970s at Norfolk, Virginia, when a particular destroyer was in port. Walking down the pier, one's eyes were drawn to the ship's ASROC launcher, adorned with a painting of a famous 1917

Navy recruiting poster. The associated modified slogan read, "If I were a man, I'd ride a FRAM."

By the early 1960s, vast numbers of *Fletcher*-, *Allen M. Sumner*-, and *Gearing*-class destroyers built during World War II were in dire need of repair and modernization. Fiscal restraints made the construction of an entire new fleet impractical, so selected hulls were extensively modified under the FRAM (Fleet Repair and Modernization) program. Sailors called the modified destroyers "FRAM cans," "can" being a contraction of "tin can," Navy jargon for a destroyer or destroyer escort.

In a representative modernization of one *Gearing*-class destroyer, the *George K. MacKenzie*'s "upper works" were stripped at the Brooklyn Navy Yard and rebuilt along different lines using lighter weight materials. One of her three 5-inch turrets and all secondary anti-aircraft armament disappeared; her torpedo tubes amidships were replaced by ASROC (an anti-submarine rocket-launcher); and two triple-torpedo tubes were added to the 01 level, forward of the remodeled bridge. Gone were her antiquated anti-submarine weapons ("K" guns, hedgehog batteries, and "roller racks" of "ash cans") which destroyers had carried since World War I. A hangar and raised platform dominated the waist of the ship, providing facilities for two DASH helicopters.[20]

With apologies to cruiser sailors, the bulk of this book is devoted to describing operations of "tin cans," destroyers and destroyer escorts. There is a chapter dedicated to the battleship *New Jersey*, and another to the Inshore Fire Support Ship *Carronade*, because of the uniqueness of these ships. However, by virtue of their sheer numbers, the "cans" warrant the most attention. Unfortunately, even within this category, it is only possible to provide details for a sampling of the destroyers and destroyer escorts that served on the gunline. Hopefully, readers will take solace in the fact that the crews of many ships shared similar experiences on the gunline and during liberty port visits. It's the authors hope that the backdrop presented herein will help bring to the fore fond memories of sailing the deep and of runs ashore with shipmates.

To this end, the postscript provides a pictorial of shipboard life and scenes from common liberty ports. The photographs used are from ships' cruise books. Although many are of low quality, taken with low cost cameras available to average sailors, they reflect that period of time. Not surprisingly, the photographs in the cruise books of admirals' flagships were of much higher quality, suggesting they were taken by photographer's mates. Some of the photographs were of viewscapes and other features of liberty ports not typically visited by Seventh Fleet ships.

To illustrate a few of the differences between fleet flagships and a destroyer or destroyer escort, the authors offer two photographs of the USS *St. Paul*, the Navy's last all gun heavy cruiser, and one of Mathews enjoying some solitude in his "rack," the one place a sailor could call his own aboard the USS *Benning*, a *Gearing*-class destroyer.

Photo Preface-7

Personnel of different departments facing off in a tug-of-war aboard the *St. Paul* (CA-73). Capt. Hugh Good Nott, her commanding officer, is serving as the referee. Nott had been a chief quartermaster on submarines in World War II, before receiving an officer's commission in 1945. He previously commanded the submarines *Stickleback* (SS-415) and *Grayback* (SS-574), and the repair ship *Delta* (AR-9).
Courtesy of Capt. Robert J. Kermen, USNR (Retired)

Photo Preface-8

Admirals' flagships like the USS *St. Paul* offered amenities not available on the much smaller destroyers. The heavy cruiser had a full band which played during under way replenishments at sea, as well as at ship's functions, such as barbecues on the fantail. Courtesy of Capt. Robert J. Kermen, USNR (Retired)

Photo Preface-9

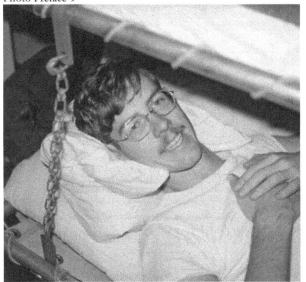

Sonar Technician Third Class Richard Mathews enjoying some "rack time" aboard the USS *Benner* (DD-807), circa 1969-1970. Courtesy of STGCS(SW) Richard Mathews, USN (Retired)

FROM OUR AUSSIE FRIENDS

The following poems, published in HMAS *Perth*'s onboard newspaper, were provided complements of Commodore Hector Donohue, AM RAN (Retired)

I THOUGHT I SAW A WBLC

I thought I saw a WBLC [North Vietnamese water borne logistics craft],
A bearing down on me,
Instead it was a fishing junk,
A heading out to sea.
Then suddenly, as it went past,
Its sides came down you see,
Exposed a flaming aperture
A pointing straight at me.
It opened up its guns at us
But we were quick to learn,
We opened up our throttles wide
And did a big "U" turn
Now the gunboat was fast
But not a patch on us,
The term I think applicable,
We left him in our dust.
Then came the Gunnery Officer's turn,
To make his claim for fame,
To show them some true marksmanship
And give the *Perth* a name
Alack, alas it came to pass
We never were to fire.
As we were supposed to open up,
The Gun Plot caught on fire.
The moral of this story is
Ever so plain to see,
If you sight a WBLC
For God's sake head to sea.

—Anonymous, *Perth* Pundit, Dec 1967

The following verse in a subsequent *Perth* Pundit caused a few laughs:

Wrap me up in my flak jacket and helmet
And send me deep down below.
Where the bombs and shrapnel can't reach me,
In the frig flat, where all the cowards go.
Anonymous, Perth Pundit Dec 1967
("frig flat" is an Aussie term for a ship's refrigerator flat which is located low down in the ship.)

If we wished, we could tune our transistor radios to Radio Hanoi, especially during the night hours, and have a laugh whilst listening to Hanoi Hannah spread disinformation (propaganda) about the war. Her subsequent account of the action on 18 October 1967 would have the listener believe: "The brave gunners of the People's Republic of North Vietnam had badly damaged the Australian ship *Perth* and killed many of its sailors. Go home Australian sailors: this immoral and illegal war is not in your interests." Of course, this was an open invitation for one of our resident poets to pen the following:

Hanoi Hannah so they say,
Claims that we are all from Long Bay
And we've been freed out here on bail
Rather than sit back there in jail.
Well maybe most of us have fears,
But at least we are all volunteers,
And believe in what we're fighting for,
Although we often curse this war.

—Anonymous, *Perth* Pundit February 1968

1

Into the Lion's Den

A daring raid into strongly defended enemy territory.... The enemy has once again been reminded of the mobility of the fleet.

—From the front page of a *New York Times* article
reporting on the Battle of Haiphong Bay.[1]

Photo 1-1

Heavy cruiser USS *Newport News* (CA-148), March 1970.
National Archives photograph K-81521

Shortly before midnight on 27 August 1972, the USS *Newport News*, while flinging salvos from her 8-inch guns at enemy shore targets inside Haiphong Harbor, detected three North Vietnamese *Komar*-class patrol boats moving at top speed. The *Newport News* was leading a daring attack on North Vietnam's major port, assisted by three other surface units (identified below along with their commanding officers.) The last heavy cruiser built for the U.S. Navy, she had been named for the city in which she was constructed, Newport News, Virginia. Her keel was laid at Newport News Shipbuilding & Dry Dock Co. on 1 October 1945, and she was commissioned on 29 January 1949.[2]

Ship	Comm./ Decomm.	Commanding Officer
USS *Newport News* (CA-148) *Des Moines*-class	29 Jan 49/ 27 Jun 75	Capt. Walter Franklin Zartman
USS *Providence* (CLG-6) *Cleveland*-class	15 May 45/ 31 Aug 73	Capt. Paul Coy Gibbons Jr.
USS *Robison* (DDG-12) *Charles F. Adams*-class	9 Dec 61/ 1 Oct 91	Comdr. Robert Lawrence Lage
USS *Rowan* (DD-782) *Gearing*-class	31 Mar 45/ 18 Dec 75	Comdr. Robert Franklin Comer

Screened by the destroyer *Rowan*, the *Newport News* had been radically maneuvering on easterly courses, and would soon run out of sea room. To the east, a short distance ahead, lay the île de Norway archipelago; to the northeast the coast of Cat Ba; and to the north, the shoals and minefields of Haiphong. It wasn't known if the Soviet-built P-6 (NATO designation, Komar) patrol boats had torpedoes or missiles or both. The boats had used the cover of darkness and the karst islands of the Dao Cat Ba archipelago to mask their presence from radar, and were now moving to close off the only escape route.[3]

Embarked aboard the *Newport News* was commander, Seventh Fleet, Vice Adm. James L. Holloway III, USN. Two weeks earlier, he had received tasking from the Joint Chiefs of Staff to plan for a naval gunfire strike, code named LION'S DEN, against military facilities in the Haiphong-Cat Ba area. The targets were to include the airfield at Cat Ba, military barracks, coastal defense guns, ammunition dumps, and radars. Haiphong lay about three hundred miles north of the front lines, and as the major North Vietnamese port, heavily used by Communist China and Soviet Union shipping, had always been heavily defended.[4]

Photo 1-2

Against a backdrop of karst islands, a CH-53D Sea Stallion helicopter sweeps the bay in Hon Gay, North Vietnam, on 18 March 1973, as part of Operation END SWEEP. National Archives #USN 711571

Moreover, following extensive aerial mining by the Seventh Fleet of the channels and approaches to the port of Haiphong on 8 May 1972, the North Vietnamese had considerably strengthened the defenses in the Haiphong area. These defenses now included search and detection radars, coast watcher networks, coastal defense guns, gun-control radar, surface-to-air missile sites, and fire-control direction centers to coordinate gun and missile use. Intelligence briefers advised that there would be no air threat. The enemy aircraft in the area were day fighters with no ability to attack ship targets at night. It was also thought that torpedo- or missile-equipped high-speed patrol craft would not pose a threat, because no fast patrol boats had been detected in the Haiphong area in several months. It appeared that coastal defense artillery would constitute the only real threat to the ships.[5]

ENEMY ARTILLERY RUDIMENTARY, BUT ...

Seventh Fleet cruisers and destroyers conducting gunfire support on a daily basis generally had a low regard for the danger posed by North Vietnamese shore batteries. When the fall of shot came close, a ship simply moved farther away or changed course and speed, and the shore battery gunners had to recalculate their fire-control problem. The North Vietnamese guns being used for coastal defense were field artillery pieces—deadly against fixed targets but not designed to track moving ones. The technique of field artillery was to fire a few rounds at a fixed point, observe the fall of shot, and then adjust the fire in range and azimuth until the rounds consistently hit the desired point. Fortunately, it typically took more time for a battery to get "registered on the target," than a Naval Gunfire Support ship might be stationary. Of course, there was always the possibility of a luck shot.[6]

Admiral Holloway was well aware that if one of his ships were to become immobilized within range of a shore battery, it would take only a few minutes before the artillery would be hitting it consistently. To bring the targets at Haiphong and Cat Ba within range of the ships' guns, the bombardment group would have to close the shoreline to well within range of the enemy's coastal artillery emplacements. Although their guns might lack accuracy, the sheer volume of fire from the large number of defense sites would increase the chances of a ship being hit.[7]

SELECTION AND PREPARATION OF SHIPS

The four bombardment ships selected for Lion's Den were designated Task Unit 77.1.2.   Captain John Renn, commander, Destroyer Squadron 25, aboard the guided-missile destroyer *Robison*, was the officer in tactical command for the operation. *Robison* was to team with the *Providence*, a 6-inch gun and missile cruiser; while the World War II *Gearing*-class destroyer *Rowan* would join the heavy cruiser *Newport News*. The *Rowan* was selected for the mission because of a one-of-a-kind weapons system aboard the ship. A field modification had converted her anti-submarine warfare rocket launcher to a Shrike anti-radiation missile launcher. Shrike was an air-to-ground missile used by carrier aircraft against the North Vietnamese gun and missile control radars. The Shrike homed on electronic signals emanating from an active enemy radar. The *Rowan* surface ship weapon system would be getting its first test in the Lion's Den.[8]

The elements of Task Unit 77.1.2 were pulled from the gunline off Quang Tri Province and dispatched to the Gulf of Tonkin to top off magazines and bunkers from the fleet oilers and ammunition ships on station there. (Most of the guns and ammunition then being used for shore bombardment were the same as those employed in World War II: 5-inch/38, 6-inch/47, and 8-inch/55.) The *Newport News* loaded more than one thousand rounds of 8-inch ammunition. Then the ships proceeded north independently at twenty-five knots to rendezvous about seventy miles southeast of Haiphong.[9]

Map 1-1

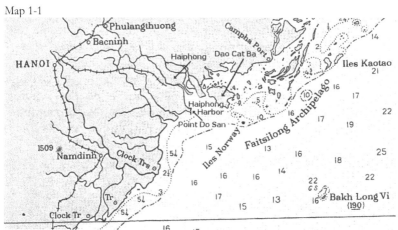

Hanoi/Haiphong area of North Vietnam
USS *Canberra* (CAG-2) Western Pacific 1967-1968 cruise book

The four ships were to arrive individually in the rendezvous area and to maneuver independently on random courses until after dark, when they would be unobservable by any local fishing craft that might be in the area. At 2000, the ships would form up in a column with *Rowan* as guide and proceed at twenty-five knots for the Point Do Son light (spelled Do San on the map), which marked the entrance to the Haiphong Channel. The light remained operational as a navigational aid for the duration of the war. Its obvious purpose was to help guide munitions-laden cargo ships from China, the Soviet Union, and other Communist bloc countries to the wharves of Haiphong. After the port was mined on 8 May 1972, the flow of war materiel through it ceased. Yet the light remained on, a fortunate eventuality for Task Unit 77.1.2 as it maneuvered around the shallows, shoals, and mined areas in the approaches to Haiphong.[10]

About ten miles off the coast, the *Providence* and *Robison* were to depart to close their assigned targets, which were generally southwest of Cat Ba. The *Rowan* and *Newport News* would continue on their north-northeast course to the entrance of the Haiphong Channel and after turning to an eastern course, conduct a firing run just outside of the five-fathom curve (30-foot water depth). The *Newport News*, with the biggest guns of the force, was assigned the most important targets. These included the fuel dump and vehicle storage at Cat Ba Airfield, the Do Son radar, Haiphong SAM sites, the Cat Ba military supply dump, fire-control radars and coastal gun batteries. Several of these targets were at the extreme range of her 8-inch guns, and would require the cruiser to penetrate the Haiphong Harbor approaches as far as her twenty-seven-foot draft would allow.[11]

The rendezvous of the four warships occurred on schedule, and there was no evidence of detection by local fishing or commercial craft during the approach to the objective area. At 2200, General Quarters was sounded aboard the *Newport News*, sending her crew to battle stations in preparation for the night's mission. As the heavy cruiser raced north at twenty-six knots to approach the turn point for her firing leg, the Do Son light appeared on time and in its proper place.[12]

NAVAL GUNS OPEN ON SHORE TARGETS

Photo 1-3

USS *Newport News* (CA-148) firing a salvo from her forward 8-inch gun turret, during Operation SEA DRAGON, 12 October 1967.
National Archives photograph #USN 1128303

At 2321, the *Newport News* came right to a heading of 070 on her firing course, and Captain Zartman gave the order to commence firing. The shore batteries immediately began to return fire. The North Vietnamese guns were not using flashless powder, and their muzzle blasts could be clearly seen as aim points for the ship's counterbattery fire. Flashes from numerous gun positions to the north lit up a full 45-degree arc of the horizon off the cruiser's port bow. Enemy rounds were falling in the vicinity, not too close, but splashes were clearly visible to sailors stationed topside to report the fall of shot.[13]

At 2330, the *Newport News* came a little further right to a course of 091 to run parallel to the five-fathom curve, which was only a mile or two north. *Providence* and *Robison*, on the cruiser's starboard quarter, had commenced their firing runs; *Rowan*, up ahead, was banging away with her 5-inch guns against coastal defenses and had launched two Shrikes at radar sites.[14]

Photo 1-4

Guided missile destroyer USS *Robison* (DDG-12) berthed at Sasebo, Japan.
USS *Robison* Western Pacific 1972 cruise book

Stepping out onto the port bridge to better observe the action, commander, Seventh Fleet, was afforded a clear view of the North Vietnamese coast with the muzzle flashes from the shore batteries and the explosions of ship projectiles. Cones of tracer fire rose ten thousand feet into the sky, coming from the anti-aircraft batteries at Cat Ba, Haiphong, and Hanoi, firing at Navy planes in the area. At the apex of each cone of tracers was a Navy plane attacking a target or transiting the area for an armed reconnaissance of major supply routes from China.[15]

At 2333, the order "Cease fire, cease fire" came over the speakers in the mounts, and the *Newport News'* guns fell quiet. The *Rowan* had completed her mission five minutes earlier and had been detached and cleared to depart the objective area. The *Providence* and *Robison* had also finished up their bombardment duties and were retiring to the south. As the admiral stepped back inside the pilothouse, Captain Zartman informed him that all the *Newport News* assigned targets had been covered and that several secondary explosions had been noted at Cat Ba Airfield and the ammunition dump. As he was speaking, a dungaree-clad sailor serving as a battle phone talker reported, "Captain, Combat reports a surface target, designated Skunk Alfa, at ten thousand yards bearing 088, heading for us at high speed." ("Skunk" is Navy brevity code for "hostile surface contact.")[16]

RAPID ACTION REQUIRED

Captain Zartman quickly issued a stream of orders, Skunk Alfa was designated a hostile threat, all gun batteries were directed to take the target under fire, and *Rowan* ordered to rejoin the *Newport News*. Skunk Alfa, which had been visually identified with night observation devices as a P-6 class Soviet-made fast attack craft, was located five miles distant near a collection of small karst islands extending south of Cat Ba, a site well suited for an ambush. The rocks and pinnacles dead ahead were making it difficult for the fire-control radars to lock on the patrol boat. Even if this were not the case, the ship's forward guns could not fire because the firing circuits for the 8-inch guns cut out at low angles of fire over the bow to avoid destroying an electronics antenna that had recently been installed on the fo'c'sle.[17]

Newport News came hard right to unmask her battery, and all of the cruiser's port-side guns began firing as rapidly as they could be loaded. Within minutes, Skunk Alfa appeared to be on fire and trying to escape on a northerly course. Concurrently, CIC (ship's combat information center) reported two more Skunks with the same characteristics as Alfa, eight miles dead ahead, moving from left to right. As the cruiser's guns swung around to take this new threat under fire, the antenna on the fo'c'sle again prevented their use. The quickest maneuver to counter the threat would be to turn to port, and engage the fast craft with gunfire on the starboard side. However, this action would take the *Newport News* toward shoal water and not the open sea to the south.[18]

No matter, there was little choice. As the ship heeled over in a tight port turn, the cruiser's 5- and 3-inch batteries had their first crack at the enemy. Despite rapid continuous fire, the P-6s continued to come. Their zigzagging approach through the many ship-sized karst islands confused the cruiser's radars, and tracking by optics was hampered by the darkness of the night and the many islets. Soon, a new challenge was presented the gun crews. Several "star shells" (illumination rounds) fired by the *Rowan* had detonated prematurely. Instead of silhouetting the P-6s from above, the parachute flares hung at a low altitude between the ships and the enemy, screening them behind the glare.[19]

FOURTH ENEMY FAST ATTACK CRAFT REPORTED

Newport News had been steering easterly and southeasterly courses to keep skunks Bravo and Charlie under continuous fire with all batteries, and would soon run out of sea room. When a report was received from *Providence* that a fourth fast patrol boat had been detected, Admiral Holloway decided to call for some help from Navy tactical air. Picking up a UHF radio handset mounted on the bulkhead in the pilothouse, he transmitted a voice message on a guarded (monitored) circuit:

> Attention any Seventh Fleet Aircraft in the vicinity of Haiphong. This is Blackbeard [commander, Seventh Fleet's personal call sign] on board *Newport News* with a shore bombardment force in Haiphong Harbor. We are engaged with several enemy surface units and need illumination to sort things out. Any aircraft in the area give me a call on guard. What we really need are high-power flares. Blackbeard out.[20]

Almost immediately came a response from Raven 44, the flight leader of two A-7 Corsair attack aircraft carrying out an armed reconnaissance flight north of Hanoi, "We have flares and Rockeye on board. I can see all the shooting down there. I wondered what was going on. I am overhead and ready to help." Holloway instructed Raven 44, to light up the area with flares, report on what he could see, and stand by for further orders.[21]

Almost immediately, the entire seascape of the Haiphong Harbor approaches was almost blindingly lit by a million-candlepower flare. Raven 44 reported that he had the *Newport News* in sight with an accompanying destroyer and could see a cruiser and a destroyer to the east. He also spotted two North Vietnamese fast attack boats closing the *Newport News*. With the targets now clearly visible, the heavy cruiser's guns increased their rate of fire to the maximum, as the aircraft carried out a coordinated attack. While one A-7 Corsair dropped a flare, the other attacked with Rockeye—a weapon that distributed a cluster of lethal bomblets in an oblong pattern over a large area.[22]

It was almost impossible to miss a ship with Rockeye, even a small craft moving at high speed, and under the continuing flare illumination, the Rockeye and ships' gunfire finished off three of the Skunks, but not until the closest one had approached to within three thousand yards. At 2342 the *Newport News* and *Rowan* ceased fire; the battle was over. In the seventeen-minute firefight, the two warships had fired 294 rounds at the P-6s, sinking skunks Bravo, Charlie, and Delta. The remaining Alfa, out of range, on fire and limping north, was about to be eliminated by the two Corsairs. The aircraft were from Attack Squadron VA-93. Lt. (jg) William W. Pickavance was the flight leader, with Lt. (jg) Patrick D. Moneymaker as his wingman. Both would retire from the Navy with the rank of Rear Admiral.[23]

The next morning Task Unit 77.1.2 was disestablished, and the *Newport News, Rowan, Providence,* and *Robison* continued south to the Gulf of Tonkin to top off powder and projectiles and prepare to go back on the gunline. At that time in the war, all gun-armed major combatants were taking their turns on the gunline. Even the Seventh Fleet flagship, the missile cruiser *Oklahoma City* (CLG-5), was providing shore fire support with her 6-inch battery every three or four days.[24]

2

Destroyer Escort Radar Picket Ships Ordered to Vietnam

Three days after leaving Pearl, we would arrive on Station One near Attu, "box" [patrol] an area for four days, then move down to the next station. I believe there were seven stations in all. Each DER [radar picket ship] would replace the next down the line. The ship coming out of Pearl took Station One, while the DER on the last station was released.

After 27 days on the DEW [Distant Early Warning] line we would head for Pearl, some of us so low in fuel we had to stop at Midway to refuel, especially during the winter picket months of December through March, where our four Fairbanks Morse Diesels were all on the line for propulsion.

The cold, foggy winter months spawned the roughest seas I have ever experienced. One of the DERs lost her large radar screen aft. We called it the "bed spring" because it was shaped like one. Our topside aluminum superstructure creaked and even split at the welded seams.

—Alan Cranny, a former crewman aboard a radar picket ship, describing
duty on patrol stations along a mid-ocean line, monitoring aircraft
within range of radar and potentially Soviet-launched missiles.[1]

On 25 March 1965, the destroyer escort radar picket ships—USS *Brister* (DER-327), *Forster* (DER-334), and *Vance* (DER-387)—departed Pearl Harbor, bound for Vietnam. The three sister ships were former World War II era destroyer escorts. Powered by four Fairbanks-Morse diesel engines producing 6,000 hp, the DEs could make 21 knots with a range of 9,100 nautical miles at an economical 9 knots.[2]

Radar picket ships had been developed as a result of bitter lessons learned at Okinawa in World War II, where devastating kamikaze attacks demonstrated to the Navy the need for an early warning system for its fleets. The Navy first modified several *Buckley*-class DEs by adding more powerful radar equipment at the expense of armament, but the ships proved unsuccessful. The onset of the Cold War and the threat of Soviet nuclear missiles spurred the conversion of thirty-four *Edsall*-class destroyer escorts to radar picket ships. *Brister*, *Forster*, and *Vance* were part of this group.[3]

PEDIGREE OF THE RADAR ESCORT SHIPS

In the 1950s, Cold War tensions ran high and so did a 3000-mile long network of radar stations north of the Arctic Circle, maintained by the U.S. and Canada for providing early warning of the approach of Soviet planes or missiles. To expand this defense network, the U.S. Navy was assigned the task of extending the DEW (Distant Early Warning) line seaward through the use of lines of radar picket ships on patrol.[4]

Photo 2-1

Destroyer Escort Radar picket ship USS *Vance* (DER 387) under way, November 1967. U.S. Navy photo #DER-387-809X1-11-67

The former DEs—fitted with additional radar equipment, reclassified as destroyer escort radar picket ships (DERs), and ordered to duty in the Atlantic and Pacific—soon found themselves on long, lonely patrols constantly alert for Soviet aggression. Though possessing only modest armament, two 3-inch/50 single gun mounts, the DERs boasted a full suite of radio gear and radar equipment. Shipyard modifications included enlarging the ships' nerve centers—Combat Information Centers—to handle data fed by the new air search, height-finding, and surface search radar. To operate/maintain this equipment required increased manning. To accommodate them, the center portion of the main deck was enclosed and a superstructure added to provide more and spacious living quarters for the crew.[5]

Initially assigned to patrol-station duty on the DEW line, fourteen of the destroyer escort radar picket ships would later serve in Vietnam. They, and their length of service as DERs, are identified in the table.

Destroyer Escort Radar Picket Ships that served in Vietnam

Ship	DER Service	Ship	DER Service
Brister (DER-327)	1956-1968	*Koiner* (DER-331)	1955-1969
Camp (DER-251)	1956-1971	*Kretchmer* (DER-329)	1956-1973
Falgout (DER-324)	1955-1969	*Lowe* (DER-325)	1955-1968
Finch (DER-328)	1956-1969	*Newell* (DER-322)	1957-1968
Forster (DER-334)	1956-1971	*Savage* (DER-386)	1955-1969
Haverfield (DER-393)	1955-1969	*Vance* (DER-387)	1956-1969
Hissem (DER-400)	1955-1970	*Wilhoite* (DER-397)	1955-1969

ESCORT SQUADRON 5 ESTABLISHED IN SEATTLE

Established on 30 July 1955
Comdr. John C. Spencer, squadron commander
Headquartered at Pier 91 in Seattle, Washington
Part of Cruiser-Destroyer Force, Pacific Fleet,
under Rear Adm. Chester C. Wood, USN[6]

Escort Squadron 5 was commissioned at Seattle, Washington, on 30 July 1955. That same day, the squadron flagship USS *Haverfield*, the first DER on duty in the Pacific took up her station off Cape Flattery. The station was part of the "Pacific Contiguous Barrier" stretching along the U.S. West Coast from Washington to central California. Squadron mate *Savage* later relieved her of this duty, and was relieved in turn by *Wilhoite*. On 20 October 1955, these three ships were joined by the *Falgout*, and in mid-December by *Koiner* and *Lowe* as units of the squadron. Later to arrive were *Finch* in December 1956, and *Vance* and *Forster* in March 1957, filling out the squadron's allocation of nine radar picket ships.

Provided in the table are the ships' commissioning dates as DEs, years of service as DERs, and identities of their commanding officers when the ships were commissioned as radar picket ships (DERs).

Escort Squadron 5

Radar Picket Ship	DER Service Com. as DE	Commanding Officer when Ship Commissioned as DER
Falgout (DER-324)	1955-1969 15 Nov 43	Lt. Comdr. Walter Perry Smiley
Finch (DER-328)	1956-1969 13 Dec 43	Lt. Comdr. James Keith Athow
Forster (DER-334)	1956-1971 25 Jan 44	Lt. Comdr. Glenn Harold Brown Jr.
Haverfield (DER-393)	1955-1969 29 Nov 43	Lt. Comdr. B. G. Westerfield
Koiner (DER-331)	1955-1969 27 Dec 43	Lt. Comdr. V. W. Tracy
Lowe (DER-325)	1955-1968 22 Nov 43	Lt. Comdr. J. R. Bohlken
Savage (DER-386)	1955-1969 1 Nov 43	Lt. Comdr. Raymond E. Davis
Vance (DER-387)	1956-1969 1 Nov 43	Lt. Comdr. Albert M. Brouner
Wilhoite (DER-397)	1955-1969 16 Dec 43	Lt. Comdr. Lambert V. Forde

ESCORT SQUADRON 7, PEARL HARBOR, HAWAII

Motto: Guardians of the Pacific
Disestablished at Pearl Harbor in May 1960
Later reestablished at Guam, Mariana Islands

The first radar picket ship patrol on the Pacific extension of DEW line (termed the Pacific barrier) was made by the *Vance* in July 1958. Initially only three DERs were on station at a time, but by 1959 there were five of these type ships continually on patrol. The nine DERs of Escort Squadron 7 (CortRon 7) patrolled the barrier from 1958 to May 1960, when the squadron was disestablished. Between June 1958 and April 1959, CortRon 5 and seven of its DERs were transferred from Seattle to Pearl Harbor. This raised the number of DERs in Pearl Harbor to seventeen. In 1960, six Pearl Harbor DERs were decommissioned, *Haverfield* was transferred to Guam, and one was transferred to San Francisco to serve as a training ship. CortRon 7 was disestablished, and the remaining nine DERs went to CortRon 5.[7]

Before progressing to the involvement of destroyer escort radar picket ships in the Vietnam War, it's worthwhile to devote a few pages to particularly colorful DER activities. A discussion of the participation of *Wilhoite* in Operation DEEP FREEZE in the Antarctic, is followed by an overview of *Lansing*'s barrier patrol operations off the Aleutians, an area characterized by bitter cold, high winds, and rough seas.

OPERATION DEEP FREEZE 1961

Photo 2-2

Operation DEEP FREEZE, 1961.
From same-named cruise book

In autumn 1960 and winter 1960-61, the radar picket ship USS *Wilhoite* (DER-397) operated on the boundary of the Southern Ocean in support of Operation DEEP FREEZE. The Southern Ocean, also known as the Antarctic Ocean, is generally defined as south of 60° S latitude and encircling Antarctica. Deep Freeze is the codename for a series of U.S. missions to Antarctica, beginning with Operation Deep Freeze I in 1955–56, followed by Deep Freeze II, Deep Freeze III, and so on. Deep Freeze I created a permanent research station in preparation for more exhaustive research in later operations. Charged with supporting the U.S. scientists engaged in research, the U.S. Navy established Task Force 43 on 1 February 1955, under commander in chief, U.S. Atlantic Fleet, to carry out this work.[8]

The U.S. Navy's role in Antarctica during Deep Freeze in 1961 included continuing logistic support for the scientific undertakings. Primary missions included the supply and maintenance of the Naval Air Facility at McMurdo Sound, South Pole Station, Byrd Station, and the jointly operated U.S.-New Zealand Hallett Station as well as temporary facilities required by the scientists. An additional mission was to penetrate to the Bellingshausen Sea coast with the icebreakers USS *Glacier* (AGB-4) and *Burton Island* (AGB-1) in order to obtain oceanographic, cartographic, and geographical data, and to support the summer scientific program there.[9]

Photo 2-3

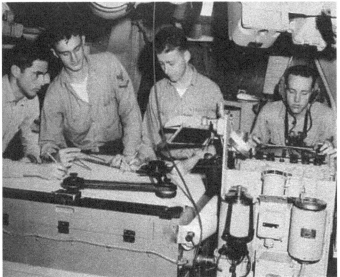

Watch team aboard USS *Wilhoite* track aircraft flying toward Antarctica. Operation Deep Freeze 1961 cruise book

The radar-equipped destroyer escort USS *Wilhoite* (DER-397) operating from Dunedin, New Zealand, patrolled an ocean station at 60°S, 170°E, in support of flights between Deep Freeze Headquarters at Christchurch and McMurdo Station. Christchurch was situated on New Zealand's east coast. Located 2,415 miles south of Christchurch on Ross Island (77°51"S, 166°40"E), McMurdo was the largest Antarctic station, and one located on the solid ground farthest south that was accessible by ship.[10]

After installing special electronic equipment, loading spare parts, and overhauling existing equipment, *Wilhoite* joined Task Force 43 on 8 September 1960. Her mission while on station was threefold:

- Provide logistics aircraft with navigation aid and weather information
- Act as a communications relay station when necessary
- Serve as a search and rescue ship in case of emergency[11]

On 23 September 1960, *Wilhoite* arrived in Dunedin, a city on New Zealand's southeast coast, to a heartwarming, waving, cheering welcome as the ship steamed up the fiord-like channel. This display of friendship was typical of the New Zealanders when the ship later made subsequent stops at Dunedin to replenish, refuel and relax. Four days later, *Wilhoite* departed for her first ocean station patrol. In the coming months, she completed six patrols—one predominately an oceanographic survey. In addition to her normal duties, *Wilhoite* was directed to collect oceanographic and hydrographic data whenever possible.[12]

Photo 2-4

USS *Wilhoite* (DER-397) steaming up Dunedin Harbor Channel.
Operation Deep Freeze 1961 cruise book

En route to her first patrol, *Wilhoite* encountered an iceberg 250 feet long and 150 feet high, before making the first of several stops at Campbell Island to off-load equipment and disembark personnel. Over the course of her six patrols, she visited the New Zealand sub-Antarctic Campbell and Auckland Islands, and Australia's MacQuarie Island, as well as Hobart, Tasmania, and Sydney, Australia. The radar picket ship returned to Pearl Harbor via Tahiti in March 1961.[13]

Later that year, sister ship *Vance* was designated an ocean station vessel with TF-43 in August 1961, for support of DEEP FREEZE 62. Temporarily based at Dunedin, she, like *Wilhoite* before her, served as a communication relay ship for aircraft bringing supplies to the Antarctic stations from New Zealand. She remained on station in the cold, bleak, southern waters into March 1962, before her return trek to Hawaii via Melbourne, Australia, and Papeete, Tahiti. *Vance* soon resumed barrier duties, mainly off the Aleutians, through February 1965.[14]

PICKET DUTY ON THE DEW LINE

Diagram 2-1

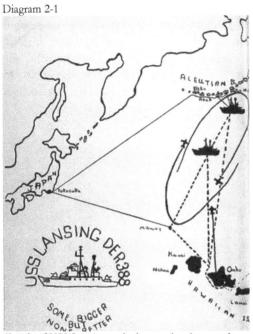

Sketch of USS *Lansing* track chart on barrier patrols
USS *Lansing* (DER-388) 1964-1965 cruise book

For *Lansing* (DER-388), one of the radar picket ships operating out of
Pearl Harbor, Barrier Patrols—or "Pickets," as they were called by
ships' crews—usually lasted about twenty-four days, port to port. Very
few other type naval vessels spent that long a time at sea without seeing
land. *Lansing*'s primary assignment was serving as a navigation, and air
search and rescue ship for naval aircraft patrolling the Pacific Radar
Early Warning Barrier. Her second mission was the detection and
reporting of air contacts gained by her radars. In performing these
functions, *Lansing* operated under the control of commander, Barrier
Force Pacific.[15]

Lt. Comdr. R. T. Shultz, USN, commanding officer of the *Lansing*,
describing the duties of his ship in the ship's 1964-1965 cruise book:

> Only those who have actually made DER pickets out of Pearl
> Harbor can fully appreciate what they were like. Our stations were
> off the Aleutians. Our fuel capacity was such that consistently bad
> weather on station, as was usually the case in the winter months, left
> us barely enough fuel to get back to port. Securing water for

washing and eating off paper plates to conserve water due to fuel shortages was often compulsory.

With the boiler secured during the night to save fuel there was no steam for heat to the berthing spaces or coffee for the mid and morning watches.   It was frequently necessary to lie to in disagreeable weather where continual rolls of 25-30 degrees were the accepted way of life. Salt water on the decks inside the ship due to cracks in the hull from rough weather was often encountered. The monotony of our long periods at sea had to be experienced to get the full impact of DER duty.[16]

The time between patrols—or "Inports" as *Lansing*'s crew called them—averaged about twenty-three days in length. Of this, five days were normally spent at sea off Pearl Harbor conducting exercises, such as gunnery shoots, tracking submarines, engineering drills, under way replenishments, or CIC exercises. The rest of the Inport was used to get the ship ready for the next Picket or cope with numerous inspections. Often, crew liberty had to be curtailed to meet the many demands. The Inport was invariably spent in Pearl Harbor. Lieutenant Commander Shultz wryly noted about this lack of diversity, "Although there is much to be said for Hawaii, our schedule didn't allow much opportunity to Join the Navy and See the World."[17]

ATLANTIC FLEET DERS ORDERED TO THE PACIFIC

Photo 2-5

Radar picket ships USS *Kretchmer*, *Camp*, and *Hissem*.
Courtesy of NavSource, photo by PH3 Robert L. Ziesler

On 7 July 1965, three Atlantic Fleet destroyer escort radar picket ships—*Camp*, *Hissem*, and *Kretchmer*—departed Newport, Rhode Island, bound for the Pacific and duty off Vietnam. The DERs reached Pearl Harbor on 28 July 1965; pictured above.

Radar Picket Ship	DER Service Com. as DE	Commanding Officer when DER joined the Pacific Fleet
Camp (DER-251)	1956-1971 16 Sep 43	Lt. Comdr. Frank N. Hannegan
Hissem (DER-400)	1955-1970 13 Jan 44	Lt. Comdr. Ronald I. Dean
Kretchmer (DER-329)	1956-1973 13 Dec 43	Lt. Comdr. Clarence E. Chinn

In addition to the three DERs from Newport, Rhode Island, two other DERs joined the force, bringing the total number of these ships to fourteen. *Brister* was ordered to duty from the Atlantic Fleet. *Newell* was taken out of "mothballs" on the U.S. West Coast, modified for her new duties, and dispatched to Hawaii for deployments to Vietnam.

Radar Picket Ship	DER Service Com. as DE	Commanding Officer when Ship Commissioned as DER
Brister (DER-327)	1956-1968 30 Nov 43	Ship transferred from Atlantic Fleet
Newell (DER-322)	1957-1968 30 Oct 43	Lt. Comdr. Ralph N. Sutton; ship recommissioned at Long Beach, Calif., and assigned to Pearl Harbor.

WARTIME DEMANDS EXTEND SERVICE OF DERS

In the mid-1960s, with the advent of improved radar and satellite early-warning capabilities, the radar picket escort ship was rapidly approaching obsolescence. However, with the United States stepping up its efforts to aid the South Vietnamese government in countering internal and external communist aggression, the ships received a new lease on life. In Vietnam, DERs could be invaluable for coastal patrol work. Accordingly, on 25 March 1965, *Vance*, *Brister*, and *Forster* sortied from Pearl Harbor, as Task Group 52.8, bound for the Philippines en route to the combat zone.[18]

3

Operation MARKET TIME

A place of streams and mangrove swamps, hard to get to, and even harder to get into.

—Vice Adm. Elmo R. Zumwalt Jr., USN, who succeeded Rear Adm. Norvell G. Ward, USN, as commander, Naval Forces Vietnam, describing the Ca Mau Peninsula on Vietnam's southern tip.

Photo 3-1

Operation Market Time, painting by Gene Klebe, 1965.
Naval History and Heritage Command #88-162-K

The destroyer escort USS *Vance* took up Operation MARKET TIME duties on 11 April 1965. From that day until the 24th, she operated near the 17th parallel as a part of Task Unit 71.1.1. During her assignment, she maintained communications between airborne Lockheed EC-121 early warning surveillance aircraft and the task unit commander aboard the destroyer USS *John W. Thomason* (DD-760). *Vance* returned to Market Time surface surveillance from 15 May to 4 June, this time in the Gulf of Thailand near the border between South Vietnam and Cambodia. She operated in company with wooden-hulled ocean minesweepers (MSOs) with a Vietnamese Navy liaison officer embarked to aid in the ship's "visit and search" activities. The DER continued these activities until sailing for Pearl Harbor early in September 1965.[5]

ESTABLISHMENT OF OPERATION MARKET TIME

Photo 3-2

Painting by Paul D. Ortlip, 1967, of an informal meeting between chief of Naval Operations, Adm. Thomas H. Moorer; Rear Adm. Kenneth L. Veth, commander U.S. Naval Forces, Vietnam; and Gen. William C. Westmoreland, USA.
Naval History and Heritage Command Accession #88-162-NO

In 1965, U.S. Navy ships were directed formally to assist the South Vietnamese Navy in its coastal surveillance and anti-infiltration patrol efforts. Operation MARKET TIME, a massive combined U.S. Navy and South Vietnamese Navy effort to stop Viet Cong infiltration of weapons and supplies into South Vietnam, was inaugurated on 11 March 1965. Gen. William C. Westmoreland, the U.S. commander of the Military Assistance Command in Vietnam, estimated that prior to 1965 Viet Cong forces in South Vietnam received about seventy percent of their supplies by sea, a percentage which by the end of 1966 had been reduced to less than ten percent. In *A Soldier Reports*, Westmoreland states: "I decided to institute MARKET TIME after South Vietnamese planes during the first two months of 1965 found two big trawlers unloading arms and ammunition along the coast, clear evidence that screening by a fleet of South Vietnamese junks was inadequate.[6]

Map 3-1

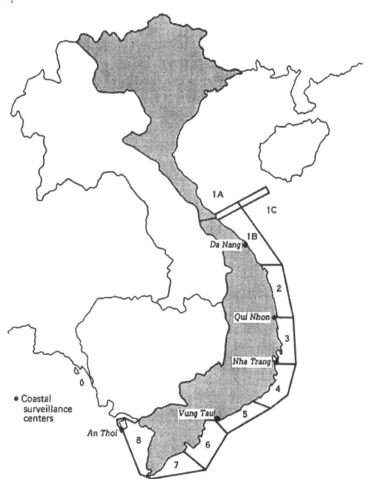

Original Market Time Barrier Areas with Coastal Surveillance Centers (CSCs)
Source: "Market Time"
(https://www.history.navy.mil/content/history/nhhc/research/library/online-reading-room/title-list-alphabetically/m/market-time-u-crc280.html: accessed 7 September 2018).

At the inception of MARKET TIME, the coast of South Vietnam was divided into eight patrol areas, with at least one ship assigned to each area. Five coastal surveillance centers were established at Da Nang, Qui Nhon, Nha Trang, Vung Tau, and An Thoi to coordinate the South Vietnamese Navy (VNN) and U.S. Navy units. A barrier forty miles long and ten miles wide was established at the 17th parallel, with at least three U.S. ships on station. Additionally, a P-3 Orion maritime patrol aircraft was continuously on station, and a Lockheed EC-121 early warning and radar surveillance aircraft flying at night to within fifty miles of the Chinese island of Hainan. The outer surface barrier was patrolled by deeper-draft vessels—DERs, MSOs, and MSCs and later, WHECs (Coast Guard high endurance cutters) and PGs (Navy patrol gunboats). The outer barrier was divided into nine large sectors in 1965, and no major change was made for the remainder of the operation.[7]

For the first three months of Market Time, the Seventh Fleet's Task Force 71 averaged fifteen ships (destroyers and minesweepers) on station. In June and July 1965, the destroyers were replaced by fourteen DERs, which were more efficient ships. They used less fuel, allowing them to remain on station longer, and had better electronics capabilities. The Navy's role in Market Time had expanded in April with a decision to purchase twenty "Swift boats" from Seward Seacraft. A Swift boat (PCF, Fast Patrol Craft) could handle up to 36 hours on patrol, although 24 hours was preferable. In addition to their own patrols, the radar-equipped boats were expected to be able to vector Vietnamese junks to suspicious contacts in the inshore areas and lead Coastal Force units otherwise unable to operate at night, to junk concentrations.[8]

In May 1965, U.S. Coast Guard Squadron 3, equipped with 82-foot cutters, arrived on station to patrol this barrier, and by February 1966, 26 cutters were in operation. Between 1967 and 1971, the force would be augmented by three Royal Australian Navy guided-missile destroyers. Nearest to shore was an inner or shallow water barrier. Here, in addition to the South Vietnamese Junk Force (later renamed the Coastal Force), the Navy deployed 84 Swift boats, 50-foot vessels armed with .50-caliber machine guns and mortars, which darted among the hundreds of shallow coves and inlets that dot South Vietnam's extensive coastline.[9]

EXPANSION OF THE NAVY'S ROLE IN VIETNAM

In early 1965, U.S. Navy activity in Vietnam was limited to support functions in the Saigon area, construction and medical activities, and advising the South Vietnamese Navy and Marine Corps. In March 1965, the first operational U.S. Navy units began counter-infiltration patrols. The Vietnam Coastal Patrol Force under commander, Task Force 71, was designated Operation MARKET TIME on 24 March. This command arrangement was short-lived. On 30 July, Task Force 71 was deactivated and operational control of MARKET TIME forces was shifted to commander, Task Force 115 in Saigon. These forces were comprised of surveillance aircraft, U.S. Coast Guard units, and U.S. Navy Swift boats.[10]

The second major influx of U.S. Navy operational units occurred in late 1965 with the inception of GAME WARDEN, designed to assist Vietnamese units in patrol of the Mekong Delta and Rung Sat Special Zone waterways, with river patrol boats (PBRs) as the principal patrol units. With these operations came the requirements for associated support facilities and new bases. U.S. Navy Harbor Defense and Harbor Clearance units were to be assigned to these areas, and mine countermeasures were to be employed on the main ship channels to Saigon, and in harbor and coastal areas. Additionally, the possibility of a U.S. River Assault Group was under consideration to supplement the Vietnamese River Assault Groups in operations in the Mekong Delta and the Rung Sat Special Zone.[11]

ESTABLISHMENT OF U.S. NAVAL FORCES VIETNAM

In recognition of its increasing commitments in Vietnam, the U.S. Navy decided to create a major Navy command with a flag officer to oversee and coordinate the efforts of the various naval organizations working in concert with one another. Commander, U.S. Navy Forces, Vietnam (ComNavForV), was established on 1 April 1966 in Saigon. Operating under commander in chief, U.S. Pacific Fleet, and commander, U.S. Military Assistance Command, Vietnam, ComNavForV was responsible for exercising operational control of the Coastal Surveillance Force, the River Patrol Force, and other Navy units as specifically assigned. It also served as the Navy area coordinator for South Vietnam.[12]

On 1 April in ceremonies aboard the destroyer escort USS *Lowe* (DER-325), Rear Adm. Norvell G. Ward, USN, assumed command of ComNavForV, while retaining the posts of chief, Naval Advisory Group, and, temporarily, commander, Task Forces 115 and 116. Capt. Clifford L. Stewart, USN, took over the Coastal Surveillance Force (CTF 115) on 16 April 1966, and the following month, Capt. Burton B. Witham Jr., USN, the River Patrol Force (CTF 116).[13]

OPERATION TEE SHOT V

The TEE SHOT concentrated patrol concept was employed in May 1966 in support of Operation DAVY CROCKETT II in the northern section of Binh Dinh Province. TEE SHOT was established in the coastal area from Dong Phu village south to Chanh Oai village to capture or destroy any hostile craft trying to flee the area. Participating units included the destroyer escort *Falgout* (DER-324), and two Swift boats—PCFs *42* and *48*—from Division 104 at Cam Ranh Bay. *Falgout* provided berthing for two spare crews for the boats, and other logistical support. Also participating were Coastal Groups 21 and 22, which maintained two junks on patrol at all times.[14]

Photo 3-3

A PCF ("Swift boat") made up alongside the destroyer escort USS *Newell*. Swift boats used DERs as remote bases, and rotated crews, enabling the patrol craft to remain on station for long periods at great distances from their parent bases.
Courtesy of NavSource (http://www.navsource.org/archives/06/322.htm)

In late morning on 7 May, *PCF-42* came under fire from the beach. The forward turret gunner was hit on the flak jacket by small arms fire, resulting in superficial wounds to his face and arms. The destroyer USS *Agerholm* (DD-826) was on a NGFS (naval gunfire support) station about 800 yards away, and the wounded man was transferred to her for treatment. TEE SHOT V concluded on 13 May. During the operation, 2,448 junks were detected, 1,210 inspected and 484 boarded. Twenty-three persons and six junks were apprehended and delivered to VNN authorities. No exfiltration (enemy soldiers trying to flee the shore in vessels) was detected or believed attempted.[15]

In addition to *Falgout*, seven other destroyer escorts identified below were assigned to MARKET TIME operations under CTF 115 control in May 1966. The DERS were in addition to twenty-six Coast Guard cutters, and six Navy MSOs (ocean minesweepers) and two smaller MSCs (coastal minesweepers) that were on patrol at various times during the month.

Radar Picket Ships Assigned to MARKET TIME in May 1966

- USS *Brister* (DER-327)
- USS *Falgout* (DER-324)
- USS *Finch* (DER-328)
- USS *Forster* (DER-334)

- USS *Koiner* (DER-331)
- USS *Kretchmer* (DER-329)
- USS *Lowe* (DER-325)
- USS *Vance* (DER-387)[16]

Map 3-2

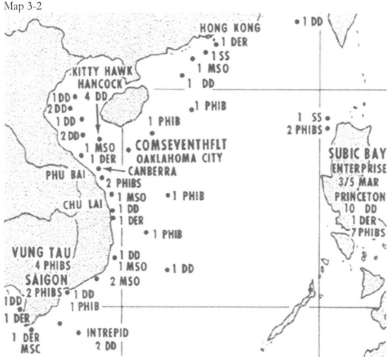

U.S. Navy Ship Locations on 16 May 1966 (*Oklahoma* is misspelled)
ComNavForV Monthly Summary, May 1966

The destroyer escorts, cutters, and minesweepers represented only a portion of the total U.S. Navy and Coast Guard ships present in the combat zone at any given time. As shown in the Ship Location Chart for 16 May 1966, there were on that day a variety of ships conducting flight operations, Market Time operations, and naval gunfire support missions. These included carriers, cruisers, amphibious ships (PHIB), destroyers (DD), destroyer escorts (DER), ocean minesweepers (MSO), and coastal minesweepers (MSC). A few ships were at U.S. Naval Base, Subic Bay, Philippine Islands, for crew liberty and maintenance, or en route or returning from liberty in Hong Kong. The Navy's capital ships—cruisers *Oklahoma City* and *Canberra*, carriers *Enterprise*, *Hancock*, *Intrepid*, and *Kitty Hawk*, and amphibious ship *Princeton*—are identified by name on the chart.

DESTRUCTION OF AN INFILTRATION TRAWLER

In late evening on 9 May 1966, while patrolling about four miles off the eastern coast of the Ca Mau Peninsula, the Coast Guard cutter *Point Grey* sighted two large bonfires on shore just to the north of the entrance to the Rach Gia River. The night was dark and overcast with passing rain squalls, typical of the early days of the southwest Monsoon season. Since this was an unusual activity, her commanding officer decided to monitor the area for the remainder of the night. Shortly after midnight, *Point Grey* sighted and challenged a steel-hulled trawler, but received no response. The trawler continued inbound for the beach area near the bonfires and grounded 400 yards from the shore.[17]

After daybreak, the *Point Grey* attempted to go alongside the trawler to board her, but encountered heavy fire from the shore. *Point Grey* then requested assistance from the Coastal Surveillance Center at An Thoi, which ordered the destroyer escort *Brister*, coastal minesweeper *Vireo*, cutter *Point Cypress*, and VNN and Navy aircraft to the scene. After *Brister* arrived, and as South Vietnamese A-1E Skyraider aircraft were bombing the beach, the *Point Grey* attempted another boarding. This second attempt was also unsuccessful. Receiving intense fire from Viet Cong positions in mangroves above the beach—which damaged her bridge and wounded three crewmen manning the mortar on the bow— the cutter moved farther to seaward.[18]

With evening approaching, the Coastal Surveillance Center directed the *Point Grey* and *Point Cypress*, to destroy the trawler with mortar fire in order to prevent the Viet Cong from taking off her cargo in darkness. During shelling, a violent explosion aboard the trawler caused it to break in two. Both sections heeled over and settled in the shallow water.[19]

Salvage operations begun the next morning recovered six crew-served weapons (operated by infantry) and nearly fifteen tons of 120mm mortar and 12.7mm ammunition of Chinese manufacture. Nameplates removed from the ship's machinery indicated that most of it was manufactured in East Germany in 1964; a few nameplates were in French and Chinese. Analysis of aerial photographs determined that the trawler was approximately 110 feet long, with two hatches, a blue-grey hull, and a white bridge superstructure. There were no flags or other identification markings on the hull.[20]

Following the removal of all salvageable material on 13 May, and the departure of the other units, *Brister* took the wreck under fire and completed its destruction, before resuming her patrol at 1900.[21]

In general, the features of this trawler—the first one captured by Market Time assets—were similar to those of a trawler intercepted by *Hissem* on 31 December 1965. That trawler had appeared to be preparing to infiltrate the southwestern tip of the Ca Mau Peninsula, but changed her plans when followed closely by *Hissem*. She was subsequently tracked into Chinese Communist waters. Both ships were similar to a camouflaged trawler discovered in Vung Ro Bay on 16 February 1965 by a helicopter on a medical rescue mission. The disguised ship was destroyed by air strikes. Diving operations on the wreck proved it to be a North Vietnamese infiltrator. Moreover, large arms caches found in the area suggested that other such trawlers had successfully infiltrated.[22]

It was believed that the route frequently followed by trawlers was east from Haiphong through the Hainan Strait, south through the South China Sea, and then west to the Ca Mau Peninsula. The southernmost region of South Vietnam, the peninsula was completely under Viet Cong dominance with the exception of a few population centers. The trawlers operated under the control of the North Vietnamese Naval Transportation Group 125. Infiltrating South Vietnamese waters, they offloaded their 100-400 tons of cargo directly over remote beaches or transferred the arms and munitions to sampans and junks several miles offshore. These small craft could mingle with thousands of similar boats used for fishing and transportation along the coast.[23]

CAPTURE OF AN INFILTRATION TRAWLER

Six weeks later, the *Point League* was on patrol in the early hours of 20 June, near the mouth of the Co Chien River. Investigating a large radar contact, she discovered a trawler running without navigation lights on a shoreward course. After informing the CSC of the situation, the cutter went to General Quarters and illuminated the ship with her searchlight. The unveiled trawler ignored a hail from the *Point League* and two bursts of machine gun fire across her bow, and returned fire. Heavy machine gun fire hit the cutter's bridge, wounding the executive officer and a crewman manning the mortar on the fo'c'sle.[24]

The trawler then cast adrift a junk she had in tow, and picked up speed. She grounded about 75 yards from shore near the river mouth. *Point League* stood off about 1,000 yards firing mortar rounds, and came under fire from Viet Cong positions behind the shoreline. *Point Slocum* arrived and the two cutters poured machine gun fire into the grounded trawler. Just after dawn, a scuttling charge exploded causing a large fire.[25]

Photo 3-4

North Vietnamese 99-foot trawler photographed by a SP-2H Neptune from Patrol Squadron Two on 19 June 1966, eighty miles east of the Con Son Islands. ComNavForV Monthly Summary, June 1966

Photo 3-5

USCG cutter *Point League* stands by after forcing a North Vietnamese trawler aground. National Archives photograph #USN 1116653

Arriving on scene at 0715, the destroyer escort USS *Haverfield* assumed control of the operation. With two U.S. Air Force F-100 Super Sabre aircraft providing close air support, resistance from the shoreline was finally controlled. It was decided that salvage of the trawler would be attempted in order to learn more about the vessel, its origins and the cargo on board. About 1000, a volunteer group from the cutters, *Haverfield* and the VNN units boarded the trawler, put out the fires and started to unload the 250 tons of cargo, of which about 100 tons were salvageable.[26]

The weapons were mainly of Chinese Communist origin, but there were some from the Soviet Union and a small number of North Korean rifles. Some boxes of Chinese ammunition were dated 1966, indicating a fairly rapid distributions system. Also recovered was a new 75mm spin-stabilized projectile believed compatible with Chinese smooth-bore weapons, which would have provided the Viet Cong a greater anti-tank and anti-patrol boat capability. Written instructions for weapons use were all in Chinese.[27]

CAPTURED TRAWLER TAKEN TO VUNG TAU

Photo 3-6

South Vietnamese Navy junk fighting fires aboard the North Vietnamese trawler. ComNavForV Monthly Summary, June 1966

After extinguishing the fires, patching the hull, and dewatering, the trawler was taken in tow to the South Vietnamese shipyard at Vung Tau for further examination. The 99-foot trawler had a 19-foot beam, and an estimated 7-foot draft, and 280-ton displacement. The vessel had a steel hull, painted green, with an ivory superstructure and two cargo holds. The only hull identification was the number 2135 on the bow. The basic hull configuration was similar to the *Hissem*-discovered trawler of 31 December 1965, the *Point Grey*-trawler of 10 May, and the trawler sunk in Vung Ro Bay in February 1965.[28]

The major difference was that the superstructure was farther aft. Armament consisted of .50-caliber machine gun mounts aft of the pilot house, on the forecastle, and amidships on both sides. These guns were covered by fishing nets when the trawler was first sighted. The trawler also carried fishing buoys and buoy marking poles in the waist as camouflage. The engine room was in excellent condition with propulsion provided by an East German, 225hp, four-cycle, solid injection and air-starting diesel. Crew complement was unknown, but there was berthing for fourteen aboard. A photograph taken by the SP-2H maritime patrol plane showed a total of eleven persons visible.[29]

Recovered documents yielded much information. Entries made in the navigator's workbook and on charts, suggested that the voyage had begun on 15 June about 100 nautical miles southwest of Hong Kong. Study of the ship's track indicated probable use of latitude sailing once in the area of the Con Son Islands, probably with the intention of using them as a landfall to fix the ship's position. An annotated chart suggested that the intended destination was possibly the Lang Nuoc River mouth in Vinh Binh province. An alternate track was plotted to the mouth of the Con Chung River.[30]

A review of known and suspected infiltration attempts by steel-hulled trawlers to date, revealed that each had been planned for high tide and first light. Lunar high tides averaged ten-to-twelve feet, enabling the shallow-draft trawlers to make the shore, or lay offshore to transfer their cargos of weapons and ammunition to smaller craft.[31]

4

Operation SEA MOUNT

The Fire-control men were buzzing around, setting parameters into the Ford Mark I Fire Control Computer, and turning switches on the Fire-Control panel, as the "Stable Element" came up to speed and rigidity providing a stable plane of reference for the guns.

Within minutes we could hear and feel the gun mounts rolling around to face the beach. FT3 Harry Jones stood at his station on the forward side of the Stable Element, with a trigger in each hand. Then came the first, Beep, Beep, Boom. Harry had pulled the trigger, warning the gun crews that we were firing, then fired the first salvo.

This went on for some time, continuous fire, then check fire, then fire for effect, then check fire; and so on. Finally, after what seemed like hours, General Quarters secure, and Condition Three was set, and mess gear was piped. By now it was time for the evening meal.

—Newt Robinson, former crewman aboard USS *DeHaven*, describing naval gunfire support conducted by his ship in support of Operation SEA MOUNT[1]

Market Time units—Swift boats and cutters armed with 81mm mortars, ocean minesweepers with rapid-fire 40mm guns, and DERs with 3-inch guns—were occasionally called upon to conduct naval gunfire support (NGFS) missions. Such action usually resulted from a requirement to provide urgent gunfire support to friendly units under attack. Infrequently, Market Time units were assigned pre-planned gunfire missions in support of ground operations near the coast.[2]

By virtue of their large-caliber, much longer-range guns, Seventh Fleet destroyers and cruisers, and for a period the battleship *New Jersey* as well, carried out nearly all the planned, and many of the urgent missions. The experiences of the destroyer USS *DeHaven* (DD-727) are representative of those of other ships performing such duties in South Vietnam. Shore bombardment of North Vietnam later in the war involved more risks to the firing ship(s).

Photo 4-1

Destroyer USS *DeHaven* (not shown, photo taken from on board) performing NGFS off the coast of South Vietnam, date and location unknown.
USS *DeHaven* (DD-727) Far East Tour 1966-1968 cruise book

Photo 4-2

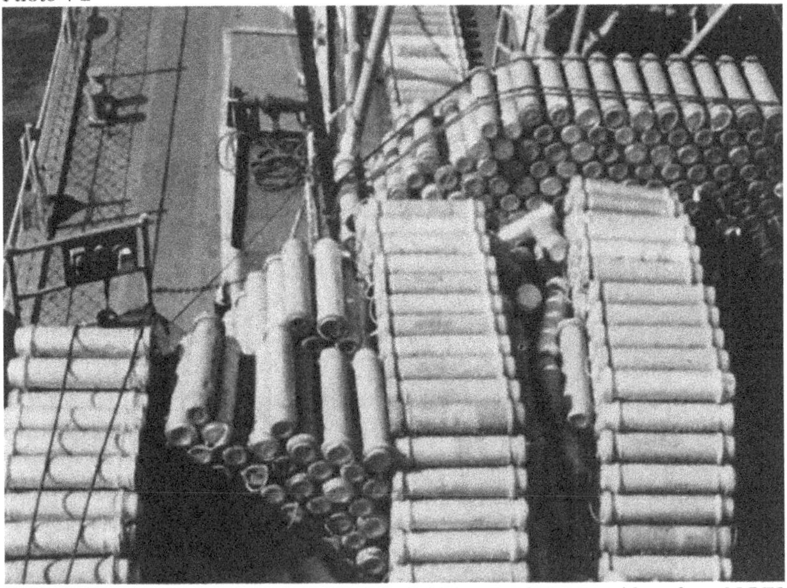

Stacked cases on *DeHaven*'s torpedo deck, in which spent brass cartridges from NGFS missions have been placed for shipment back to the United States.
USS *DeHaven* (DD-727) Far East Tour 1966-1968 cruise book

In early August 1966, *DeHaven* was operating off the east coast of South Vietnam, with her crew at General Quarters while conducting a naval gunfire support mission. Her crew was bewildered when, with very little notice, she broke away from her mission, and proceeded south around the southern tip of Vietnam and then north to Phu Quoc Island. The destroyer had received new orders, tasking her to perform shore bombardment in support of Operation SEA MOUNT. This code word referred to the first major military operation undertaken in an effort to clear the island of Viet Cong.[3]

During the operation from 4-30 August, *DeHaven* would be but one of a number of units—Seventh Fleet destroyers, Market Time Swift boats and cutters, and VNN Fleet command ships—providing gunfire support. Shortly after *DeHaven*'s arrival off the island, which lay off the south coast of Cambodia in the Gulf of Thailand, a Huey gunship landed with great skill on her tiny flight deck. *DeHaven*'s deck and those of sister *Allen M. Sumner*-class destroyers were intended for operation of small ship-based DASH drone helicopters. Before proceeding on, an overview of the capabilities of *DeHaven*, and the other twenty-four *Sumner*-class destroyers that served in Vietnam, is in order.[4]

PEDIGREE OF *DEHAVEN AND SISTER DESTROYERS*

USS *DeHaven* was commissioned on 31 March 1944, one of fifty-eight *Allen M. Sumner*-class destroyers built during World War II. These ships were characterized by their three twin 5-inch/38 caliber gun mounts, dual rudders, additional anti-aircraft weapons, and other advancements over the previous *Fletcher*-class. Naval architects extended the *Sumner* design fourteen feet amidships to create the *Gearing*-class destroyer, which was produced in larger numbers.[5]

By the late 1950s, the U.S. Navy's destroyer force was outdated in its ability to defend against modern aircraft and submarines. A FRAM (fleet rehabilitation and modernization) program was begun to upgrade and rebuild existing ships. FRAM I was intended to extend the useful life of ships by eight years. Restricted to *Gearing*-class ships, it included the removal of one 5-inch/38 mount and the addition of anti-submarine warfare weapons, sensors, and delivery systems:

- DASH (Drone Anti-Submarine Helicopter)
- ASROC (Anti-submarine Rocket)
- SQS-23 Sonar
- VDS (Variable depth sonar)
- Mark 32 torpedo tubes[6]

Photo 4-3

A Drone Anti-Submarine Helicopter belonging to the destroyer USS *Fechteler* (DD-870). Designed for the delivery of a torpedo to attack enemy submarines; at least one destroyer employed DASH for spotting naval gunfire.
USS *Fechteler* (DD-870) Southeast Asian 1967 cruise book

FRAM II, was planned to extend each ship's life by five years. It was a more modest upgrade, one received by thirty-three *Sumner*-class ships. The overhaul included the addition of the DASH system, Mark 32 torpedo tubes, and variable-depth sonar, but retained all three twin 5-inch/38 mounts. Twenty-five of the modernized *Sumner*s served in Vietnam. These destroyers are identified in the table by asterisks.[7]

Allen M. Sumner-class Destroyers - FRAM II

Ship	Date Completed	Ship	Date Completed
Boston, Massachusetts			
Ault (DD-698)*	12/62	*Hugh Purvis* (DD-709)	10/60
New York, New York			
Putnam (DD-757)	03/63		
Charleston, South Carolina			
Allen M. Sumner (DD-692)*	12/61	*Moale* (DD-693)	12/61
James C. Owens (DD-776)*	10/62	*Strong* (DD-758)*	11/62

Norfolk, Virginia

Borie (DD-704)	06/62	*Massey* (DD-778)*	07/60
Charles S. Sperry (DD-697)	06/60	*Robert K. Huntington* (DD-781)*	09/60
Douglas H. Fox (DD-779)	10/61	*Stormes* (DD-780)*	01/61
Ingraham (DD-694)*	12/61	*Waldron* (DD-699)*	12/62
Laffey (DD-724)	09/62	*Wallace L. Lind* (DD-703)*	07/62
Lowry (DD-770)*	12/60	*Zellars* (DD-777)	05/60

Mare Island, California

Lyman K. Swenson (DD-729)*	01/61	*Walke* (DD-723)*	10/61
O'Brien (DD-725)*	10/61		

San Francisco, California

Blue (DD-744)*	01/61	*John A. Bole* (DD-755)*	08/62
DeHaven (DD-727)*	08/60	*Lofberg* (DD-759)*	07/62

Long Beach, California

Alfred A. Cunningham (DD-752)*	09/61	*Mansfield* (DD-728)*	09/60
Buck (DD-761)*	07/62	*John W. Thomason* (DD-760)*	01/60
Collett (DD-730)*	08/60	*Taussig* (DD-746)*	09/62
Frank E. Evans (DD-754)*	10/61		

Following her modernization, the 376-foot *DeHaven* possessed in addition to her main battery of six 5-inch/38 guns, eight torpedo tubes and two drone anti-submarine helicopters. She could steam 8,000 miles without refueling, and was capable of a maximum speed of 33 knots.[8]

Photo 4-4

Destroyer USS *DeHaven* (DD-727), following modernization (FRAM II) in 1960.
USS *DeHaven* Far East Tour 1966-1968 cruise book

UH-1 HELICOPTER CARRYING ARMY LEADERSHIP

Aboard the helicopter on *DeHaven*'s flight deck were Lt. Col. Trevor W. Swett Jr., USA, and staff, who went to the wardroom to confer with Comdr. Donald A. Franz, USN, *DeHaven*'s commanding officer. Swett commanded the 5th Battalion, 7th Cavalry Division.[9]

Photo 4-5

UH-1 Iroquois helicopter ("Huey" gunship) aboard the USS *DeHaven*. USS *DeHaven* (DD-727) Far East Tour 1966-1968 cruise book

Map 4-1

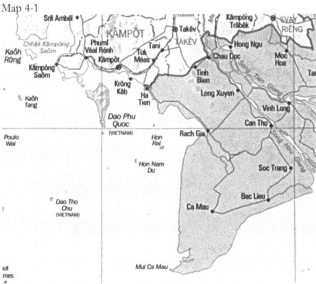

Phu Quoc is an island in the Gulf of Thailand. Sited on its southern tip was the An Thoi U.S.-Vietnamese Coastal Surveillance Center.

Operation SEA MOUNT was conducted by eight U.S. Special Forces personnel and a 220-man Mike Force. The latter unit of specially recruited indigenous personnel was periodically augmented by 10-30 Vietnamese National Policemen from Duong Dong Village on Phu Quoc. The operation consisted of three phases. The initial phase involved a sweep northward from An Thoi to Latitude 10°13' N. In the second phase, a series of amphibious raids were carried out on the east coast of the island, and against targets of opportunity.[10]

Supporting the raids were LCM landing craft and crews of USS *Tutuila* (ARG-4). Upon arriving at Phu Quoc on 19 July 1966, *Tutuila* (an internal combustion engine repair ship) had relieved the *Krishna* (ARL-38), taking over servicing the Swift boats of PCF Division 101. *Tutuila* also served as the base for WPBs of Coast Guard Division 11.[11]

A former *Tutuila* crewman described the Navy and Coast Guard forces based at An Thoi on Phu Quoc, and the mission of these forces:

> Arriving at An Thoi to relieve the USS *Krishna*, the *Tutuila* anchored just offshore, rafting with an APL ... which served as both headquarters and barracks for the Swift Boat crews. There the "Toot" served as principal repair facility, not just for PCF 101, and Coast Guard Division 11, but potentially for all US naval craft on the gulf side of South Viet Nam.

> The village of An Thoi was actually in Cambodian coastal water, but for some reason, the offshore border curved to the west, making all of Phu Quoc part of the Republic of Viet Nam. The patrol boat base at An Thoi was originally a US Coast Guard facility, with some South Vietnamese craft and a Thai gunboat for good measure. These were joined – almost a year prior to *Tutuila*'s arrival – by the boats of PCF 101.

> The facility at An Thoi was officially designated as a "Coastal Surveillance Force Combat and Logistical Base" where, in addition to our shipboard duties, we occasionally supplemented the five-man Swift Boat crews. An Thoi's boats – the 50-foot PCFs and the 82-foot Coast Guard Cutters, were responsible for stopping (or slowing) the waterborne supply of men and materials to the Viet Cong from nearby Cambodia. Also for patrol and interdiction along Viet Nam's Gulf (of Thailand) coast, from the Cambodian border, south past the city of Rach Gia and the U-Minh Forest, to Ca Mau Cape, the southernmost point of the country.[12]

Photo 4-6

The repair ship USS *Tutuila* (ARG-4) at anchor next to a berthing barge in the Gulf of Thailand off the coast of Vietnam. Fast Patrol Craft (Swift boats) of Coastal Division 11 are alongside the barge.
National Archives photograph #USN 1128006

In support of SEA MOUNT, *Tutuila* sailors served as coxswains, boat engineers, and bow hooks, operating the LCMs (landing craft, mechanized) used to land South Vietnamese troops at four places on the Phu Quoc coast. Separately, *Tutuila*'s boats carried supplies and ammunition to the Allied ground forces while helicopters evacuated casualties to the repair ship for medical attention.[13]

In the final phase of the operation, a base camp was established near Duong Dong and probes were made into areas of heaviest Viet Cong concentration. Sixteen Viet Cong were visually confirmed killed. Subsequent prisoner interrogation indicated another seventy-five enemy had been killed as well, and an indeterminate-number wounded. Two U.S. Special Forces personnel were killed and one wounded, and seven other friendly troops wounded. Spec/4 Jules T. Girtanner, from the 5th Special Forces Group, was one of the Green Berets lost.[14]

5th Special Forces Group beret flash 1964-1985 and 2016-present
Active: 21 September 1961-present
Nickname: The Legion
Motto: Strength and Honor

5

St. Paul Joins the Gunline

A gunfire mission begins with a call for fire from a Marine spotter in the mountainous coast of the Republic of Vietnam. He spots enemy movement, or a suspected bunker site, and begins a chain-reaction which leads to the mighty guns of SAINT PAUL.

This spotter, whether in a small plane circling overhead, or entrenched on a mountain top, calls a naval gunfire support group nearby. The target is cleared for fire, if there are no friendly troops in the area.

Within seconds after the call for fire comes in, the "Fighting Saint" is ready. Down in the gun turrets, a projectileman strains to load the breech of an eight-inch gun. In Combat the target is plotted and the brains of the ship, the walls of computers in Main Plot, set the guns at the precise bearing and range of the target.

Then comes the order - "Fire," Boom...Boom.

—USS *Saint Paul* CA-73 25th Anniversary Book

On 5 June 1966, the heavy cruiser USS *St. Paul* (CA-73) arrived off the coast of South Vietnam and took her station on the firing line. The "Fighting Saint" had earlier relieved USS *Canberra* (CAG-2) of her duties at Yokosuka as naval gunfire support ship. During her cruise, *St. Paul* would participate in Operations JOHN PAUL JONES, DECKHOUSE I, II, III, and IV, HASTINGS, EMERSON, AND COLORADO—firing in total almost 10,000 gun rounds at enemy targets.[1]

Such employment was not unique. But the *St. Paul* was unique, being the U.S. Navy's only surviving all-gun heavy cruiser. She had been commissioned on 17 February 1945—one of eighteen *Baltimore*-class heavy cruisers—and earned one battle star in World War II and eight battle stars during the Korean War. At 2159 on 27 July 1953, *St. Paul* had fired the last naval salvo of the Korean War, one minute before the armistice came into effect.[2]

Her main battery of 8-inch/55 guns, were carried in three triple turrets, two forward and one aft. She also bristled with twelve 5-inch guns in six mounts and, originally forty-eight 40mm guns (11x4, 2x2) and twenty-four 20mm guns. Post-war, her 20mm guns were removed and four 3-inch/50 twin mounts replaced her 40mm mounts.[3]

Photo 5-1

Heavy cruiser USS *St. Paul* (CA-73) under way, date and location unknown. Naval History and Heritage Command photograph #L45-248.07.01

BALTIMORE-CLASS HEAVY CRUISERS

Within the *Baltimore*-class of eighteen heavy cruisers was a subclass of three ships, termed the *Oregon City*-class, and one totally different ship completed after the war for special duties. *Oregon City*, *Albany*, and *Rochester* were completed with a redesigned bridge, shortened superstructure, and only one instead of two stacks. Their aircraft hangar was reduced in size and a centerline single crane replaced the two cranes fitted on the other *Baltimores*. USS *Northampton*'s design/employment was quite interesting (more about her follows).[4]

Three other *Baltimore*-class cruisers, in addition to *St. Paul*, would serve in Vietnam, but as guided missile cruisers, not gun cruisers. *Boston* and *Canberra* had their rear 8-inch turret and rear 5-inch turrets removed, replaced with Terrier missile launchers. *Chicago*'s entire superstructure was removed and a new aluminum-structure built, with 'Macks' (combined masts and stacks) replacing both her existing masts and two funnels. All of her 8-inch gun barrels were replaced and the ship was armed with four missile launchers. Two twin Talos surface-to-air missile launchers were carried, one fore and one aft.[5]

Summary information about all eighteen cruisers follow, including commissioning and final decommissioning dates:

Baltimore-class Heavy Cruisers

Ship/Disposition	Com./ Decom.	Ship/Disposition	Com./ Decom.
Baltimore (CA-68)	15 Apr 43/ 31 May 56	*Albany* (CA-123) Converted to a guided missile cruiser (CG-10)	15 Jun 46/ 29 Aug 80
Boston (CA-69) Converted to a guided missile cruiser (CAG-1), Vietnam service	30 Jun 43/ 5 May 70	*Rochester* (CA-124)	20 Dec 46/ 15 Aug 61
Canberra (CA-70) Converted to a guided missile cruiser (CAG-2), Vietnam service	14 Oct 43/ 2 Feb 70	*Northampton* (CA-125) Launched as (CLC-1) 27 Jan 1951, redesignated (CC-1) 15 Apr 1961	7 Mar 53/ 8 Apr 70
Quincy (CA-71)	15 Dec 43/ 2 Jul 54	*Bremerton* (CA-130)	29 Apr 45/ 29 Jul 60
Pittsburgh (CA-72)	10 Oct 44/ 28 Aug 56	*Fall River* (CA-131) Took part in two atomic bomb tests/Bikini Atoll	1 Jul 45/ 31 Oct 47
St. Paul (CA-73) Vietnam service	17 Feb 45/ 30 Apr 71	*Macon* (CA-132)	26 Aug 45/ 10 Mar 61
Columbus (CA-74) Converted to a guided missile cruiser (CG-12)	8 Jun 45/ 31 Jan 75	*Toledo* (CA-133)	27 Oct 46/ 21 May 60
Helena (CA-75)	4 Sep 45/ 29 Jun 63	*Los Angeles* (CA-135)	22 Jul 45/ 15 Nov 63
Oregon City (CA-122)	16 Feb 46/ 15 Dec 47	*Chicago* (CA-136) Converted to a guided missile cruiser (CG-11) Vietnam service	10 Jan 45/ 1 Mar 80

Before leaving the subject of these cruisers and returning to the *St. Paul* on the gunline, it's worth mentioning the service of *Fall River* and *Northampton*. *Fall River* served less than two-and-a-half years. She was decommissioned after taking part in Operation CROSSROADS, two atomic bomb tests carried out at Bikini Atoll in the Marshall Islands to investigate the effect of nuclear bombs on warships.

Photo 5-2

Atomic bomb-cloud as seen from the heavy cruiser USS *Fall River* (CA-131) off Bikini Atoll on 1 July 1946, as part of Operation CROSSROADS. Naval History and Heritage Command photograph #80-G-627452

Northampton was completed as a command and control ship and later reconfigured for use as a Presidential Command Post in the event of a nuclear war. In 1961 the *Northampton*'s mission was changed to National Emergency Command Post Afloat. She was redesignated as CC-1 on 15 April 1961, and carried out this role until decommissioned early in 1970. During these years, she didn't leave the western Atlantic, as she needed to be close enough for the president to reach her in an emergency. Although she was never required in this role, *Northampton* did host presidents John F. Kennedy and Lyndon B. Johnson from time to time. She was decommissioned after the U.S. military decided to employ aircraft for the emergency command post role.[6]

Photo 5-3

USS *Northampton* (CC-1) at sea, 26 June 1962.
Naval History and Heritage Command photograph #NH 106503

OPERATION DECKHOUSE

> *During the past six weeks the accomplishments of the SLF [Marine Corps Special Landing Force] have been impressive. It has been committed to combat 28 of those days, conducting two amphibious landings and subsequently joining sizeable forces ashore as a part of two larger operations.*
>
> —From an untitled document in a U.S. Marine Corps operational file related to Operation DECKHOUSE II[7]

St. Paul's first days on the gunline were busy. During the week of 5-11 June 1966, her nine 8-inch guns pounded Viet Cong gun positions, troop concentrations, tunnels, bunkers, and structures. Her secondary battery of 5-inch guns provided night illumination and destructive fire for smaller targets. During the cruiser's deployment in Vietnam, more than half of her targets would be bunkers and trench line. Destruction of such was important to deny the enemy shelter and hiding places, and storage of ammunition and supplies.[8]

Between 18-26 June, she and the other ships assigned to the Naval Gunfire Support Group—destroyers *John W. Thomason* (DD-760) and *Basilone* (DD-824), high-speed transport *Cook* (APD 130), and rocket ships *Clarion River* (LSMR-409) and *White River* (LSMR-536)—provided shore bombardment and rocket fire for Operation DECKHOUSE I. This was the first of several operations by the U.S. Marine Corps Special Landing Force (SLF), a mobile amphibious force employed in support of large unit operations throughout three of the four tactical zones.[9]

South Vietnam was divided into four Corps Tactical Zones, and the Special Capital Zone (Saigon area) for purposes of military operations. I-Corps was located in the region nearest North Vietnam and adjacent to the Demilitarized Zone (DMZ) between North and South Vietnam. The DMZ had been established in April 1954 as a result of the Geneva Conference ending the war between the Viet Minh and the French. Although nominally described as being at "the 17th parallel," the DMZ, extending from the Lao border east to the South China Sea, ran along the Ben Hai River for much of its length.

II-Corps encompassed the central-highlands region, north of the capital Saigon; III-Corps extended from the northern Mekong Delta to the southern central highlands; while IV-Corps was the southernmost of the four Tactical Zones.

DECKHOUSE I was conducted by the Special Landing Force near Song Cau, twenty-five miles south of Qui Nhon in II-Corps. The 1,500 Marines of Battalion Landing Team 3/5, HMM-364 and Detachment VMO-6 (armed helicopters) were carried to the assault area by the helicopter amphibious assault ship *Princeton* (LPH-5), dock landing ship *Alamo* (LSD-33) and the attack transport *Pickaway* (APA-222).[10]

Map 5-1

I, II, III, and IV-Corps Tactical Zones in South Vietnam

As U.S. Marines made the beach, guns and rockets from *Clarion River* pounded suspected Viet Cong posts ashore. At the same time, *Princeton* launched helicopters carrying other Marines farther inland to block enemy troops trying to escape those coming from the sea. "Huey" helicopters raked the area at the back of the beach, while Navy strike aircraft dropped bombs. Operations ashore included providing security to one flank of the Army's 1st Cavalry Division, seven miles to the south. Since Operation NATHAN HALE was not amphibious, the SPL, once established ashore came under the operational control of the 1st Cavalry. DECKHOUSE I ended on 27 June, and NATHAN HALE on the 30th.[11]

Photo 5-4

USS *LSM(R)-536* (landing ship medium, rocket) firing rockets at a Viet Cong infiltrated village in South Vietnam, June 1966.
US Navy photograph #USN 1137966, courtesy of USS LSM/LSMR Association

Earlier in the week of 12-18 June prior to DECK HOUSE, more than 150 targets were taken under fire by the destroyers *John W. Thomason* (DD-760), *Richard B. Anderson* (DD-786), *Morton* (DD-948), *Taussig* (DD-746), *John A. Bole* (DD-755), *Fiske* (DD-842), *Hopewell* (DD-681), *Chevalier* (DD-451), cruiser *St. Paul*, and rocket ships *White River* and *Clarion River*. Among the destroyer mix were four different variants. *Thomason*, *Taussig*, and *Bole* were of the *Allen M. Sumner*-class; *Anderson* and *Fiske*, *Gearing*-class destroyers; and *Hopewell* and *Chevalier*, *Fletcher*-class. The remaining "tin can," *Morton*, was of the newer *Forest Sherman*-class, which the following chapter introduces.[12]

6

Forrest Sherman-class Destroyers

The hours proved long, and the routine arduous with the ship running at flank speed 65 per cent of the time....   The carrier operations were demanding on destroyers, with launches and recoveries being conducted around the clock.

—USS *Davis* (DD-937) ship's history describing plane guard duty
while working with aircraft carriers in early 1966.

The start of this new year, nineteen sixty-nine, finds us hard at work, along the gunline. As a tribute at midnight in lieu of a toast, the Marines requested we shoot up the coast.

—Beginning of a mid-watch deck log entry on 1 January 1969,
by Ens. William S. Eggeling, USNR, Officer of the Deck,
as the destroyer USS *Davis* steamed off Da Nang.

Photo 6-1

Destroyer USS *Forrest Sherman* (DD-931) off Newport, Rhode Island, 7 October 1969.
National Archives photograph #K-77760

The first destroyer class designed after World War II was the *Forrest Sherman*-class. Conceived as an enlarged and improved *Gearing*, the 418-foot USS *Forest Sherman* boasted three 5-inch/54 caliber Mk42 rapid-fire guns, as well as two dual 3-inch/50 caliber guns, two dual Hedgehog depth-charge launchers, and four single 21-inch torpedo tubes amidships. These tubes were later replaced by Mk 32 torpedo tubes in two triple mounts. In addition to being well armed, she was also nimble and fast—as expected of a sleek destroyer. Powered by four 1,200 psi boilers, sending steam to two geared turbines driving two propeller shafts, she could make 32.5 knots.[1]

The eighteen ships of the class were the last all-gun destroyers when built. Superseded by the guided-missile-carrying *Charles F. Adams*-class when they were relatively new, it was not long before four of the *Forrest Sherman*s were modified. *Decatur* received a Tartar-missile launcher aft, replacing her after 5-inch guns, and was redesignated guided missile destroyer DDG 31 in 1966. *John Paul Jones*, *Parsons*, and *Somers* followed as DDGs 32, 33, and 34 a year later.[2]

Photo 6-2

Guided missile destroyer USS *John Paul Jones* under way in March 1979.
Naval History and Heritage Command photograph #NH 106788

Summary information about these ships is provided in the table. The commissioning and decommissioning dates refer to when the ships first entered service, and finally left service. The four DDs converted to DDGs were decommissioned during their overhaul and conversion. As indicated, all but two of the destroyers/guided missile destroyers (*Forrest Sherman*, and *Jonas Ingram*) served in Vietnam.

Forrest Sherman-class Destroyers

Ship/Disposition	Com./ Decom.	Ship/Disposition	Com./ Decom.
Barry (DD-933) Vietnam service	9 Jul 56/ 5 Nov 82	*John Paul Jones* (DD-932), converted to guided missile destroyer DDG-32, Vietnam service	5 Apr 56/ 15 Dec 82
Bigelow (DD-942) Vietnam service	8 Nov 57/ 5 Nov 83	*Jonas Ingram* (DD-938)	19 Jul 57/ 4 Mar 83
Blandy (DD-943) Vietnam service	26 Nov 57/ 30 Oct 82	*Manley* (DD-940) Vietnam service	1 Feb 57/ 4 Mar 83
Davis (DD-937) Vietnam service	28 Feb 57/ 20 Dec 82	*Morton* (DD-948) Vietnam service	26 May 59/ 22 Nov 82
Decatur (DD-936), converted to guided missile destroyer DDG-31, Vietnam service	7 Dec 56/ 30 Jun 83	*Mullinnix* (DD-944) Vietnam service	7 Mar 58/ 11 Aug 83
Du Pont (DD-941) Vietnam service	1 Jul 57/ 4 Mar 83	*Parsons* (DD-949), converted to guided missile destroyer DDG-33 Vietnam service	29 Oct 59/ 19 Nov 82
Edson (DD-946) Vietnam Service	3 Apr 59/ 15 Dec 88	*Richard S. Edwards* (DD-950) Vietnam service	5 Feb59/ 15 Dec 82
Forest Sherman (DD-931)	9 Nov 55/ 5 Nov 82	*Somers* (DD-947), converted to guided missile destroyer DDG-34 Vietnam service	9 Apr 59/ 19 Nov 82
Hull (DD-945) Vietnam service	3 Jul 58/ 11 Jul 83	*Turner Joy* (DD-951) Vietnam service	3 Aug 59/ 22 Nov 82

As indicated by the quoted material at chapter's head and by the following two photographs, the *Forest Sherman*s worked hard in Vietnam, on the gunline and in carrying out plane guard and other duties. *Edson* was decommissioned on 15 December 1988, the last of her class to leave service. Then based at Newport, Rhode Island, her last commanding officer was a "mustang" (a former enlisted man), Limited Duty Officer Comdr. Gideon Wilcox Almy III. He was justifiably very proud of his ship, and was quoted in the local newspaper in an article about the *Edson*, "I don't need missiles, I have three guns that always shoot." This was presumably in response to a question about the continued viability of the nearly 30-year old destroyer.

Photo 6-3

USS *Mullinnix* firing at enemy targets in South Vietnam, 30 October 1966. National Archives photograph USN 1118703

Photo 6-4

One of USS *Turner Joy*'s three 5-inch gun mounts, with blistered and charred paint on the barrel from day and night gunfire support operations south of the DMZ, April 1968. Naval History and Historical Center photograph #NH98261

Arnheiter and the *Vance*

The board having decided in your favor, albeit with reservations.

—Proviso by Adm. David L. McDonald, chief of Naval Operations,
on his endorsement of the Navy Ship Command Board's
selection of Lt. Comdr. Marcus A. Arnheiter, USN.[1]

Photo 7-1

Radar picket ship USS *Vance* (DER-387) off Oahu, Hawaii, 18 January 1968.
Naval History and Heritage Command photograph #NH 107602

Lt. Comdr. Marcus A. Arnheiter, USN, was relieved of his duties aboard
the USS *Vance* (DER-387) on 31 March 1966, only ninety-nine days
after taking command of the radar picket ship. The *Vance* was then, or

would likely soon be, as word spread about the reasons for his dismissal, the most infamous ship that served in Vietnam. When the facts came out, many in the press noted that there were striking similarities between the command climates under Arnheiter and the fictious Lt. Comdr. Queeg, as depicted in the 1951 Pulitzer Prize–winning novel *The Caine Munity* by Herman Wouk. That story, and the subsequent 1954 Oscar-nominated American film of the same name, took place in the Pacific Theater aboard a destroyer minesweeper in World War II.

As Queeg, who came to the *Caine* following arduous years of anti-submarine warfare in the Atlantic, became increasingly paranoid, he perceived problems that did not exist, and facilitated mistakes in ship operations because he was distracted by trivial matters such as shirts not being tucked in or hats unworn. He also was hard on his officers, refused to admit mistakes, and was seemingly unable to reach out to them for help. The protagonist in the story was the operations officer, Lt. Tom Keefer, who considered himself brilliant, disdained the Navy, and detested Queeg.

Keefer composed and sang a song depicting Queeg as a coward, turned the wardroom against Queeg, and ultimately convinced the reluctant executive officer, Lt. Steve Maryk, to relieve Queeg of command. This occurred on the bridge during a typhoon when the captain froze and failed to order the necessary engine and rudder commands to prevent the *Caine* from broaching and being lost.

Following the ship's safe return to port, Maryk, and Ensign Willie Keith who supported him in his action, faced court-martial. To save them, their defense lawyer had to, and did destroy Queeg's reputation. Queeg emerged from the proceedings a broken man, while Keefer, who lied under oath about his involvement in the affair, was unscathed.

EARLY NAVAL SERVICE

Born and raised in the New York area, Arnheiter entered the U.S. Military Academy in 1946, but flunked out the first year. Two years later he gained entrance to the U.S. Naval Academy, graduating in 1952 near the bottom of his class (628 out of 783 midshipmen). His initial sea duty was assistant navigator on the battleship *Iowa* (BB-61) from 1952 to 1954, during which he received an average evaluation (officer fitness report) from his commanding officer.[2]

After attending the Navy's electronics school and graduating last in a class of 39 students, he reported to the destroyer *Fiske* (DDR-842) as electronics officer. The commanding officer, greatly underwhelmed by Arnheiter's performance, wrote in a fitness report that he "will never make a naval officer" because of a variety of deficiencies, including "an inability to admit mistakes, lack of common sense, selfishness, poor judgment, and a compulsive tendency to concentrate his energies on minor details rather than his major duties." As a result of his poor performance, Arnheiter was passed over for promotion to lieutenant.[3]

Rather than resign from the service, he persevered, remaining at sea and serving as gunnery officer aboard the *Coolbaugh* (DE-217) and operations officer in the destroyer *Abbot* (DD-629).[4]

Photo 7-2

Officers comprising the wardroom of the USS *Abbot*, Lt. Arnheiter is seated in the front row, second from the right.
USS *Abbot* (DD-629) 1958 Mediterranean cruise book

Photo 7-3

Lt. Marcus Arnheiter, USN, receiving a $300 payout from the *Abbot*'s Navy-Marine Stadium Fund anchor pool.
USS *Abbot* (DD-629) 1958 Mediterranean cruise book

PENTAGON DUTY

Arnheiter's fitness reports improved; he was promoted to lieutenant in 1956, and was subsequently assigned to the Pentagon from 1960-1963. While working in the Navy's Briefing and Progress Analysis shop, he excelled in writing press releases about various Navy programs for popular newspapers and magazines. Arnheiter even authored a novel, *Shadow of Peril* (about the activities of a Soviet submarine off the U.S. East Coast), under the pseudonym Aleksandr I. Zhdanov, which was published by Doubleday in 1963.[5]

PRELUDE TO COMMAND

Arnheiter was promoted to lieutenant commander, and returned to sea. He served from May 1963 to March 1964, as operations officer aboard the guided missile destroyer *Worden* (DLG-18), and then as executive officer of the destroyer *Ingersoll* (DD-652) until May 1965. His fitness report for *Ingersoll* declared that he performed brilliantly, and was the "best DD XO [executive officer] in the fleet." This glowing report and a decent review in his next assignment on the staff of Cruiser Destroyer Flotilla Nine, resulted in Arnheiter successfully screening for command at sea, but only by the narrowest margin. Of the three members of the board, only Capt. Richard G. Alexander voted in his favor. (Apparently, one vote was enough.) Alexander also managed to have him placed on a list of officers who might be given command on an "emergency" basis. Hence, when *Vance*, a ship on an emergency wartime deployment, needed a new commanding officer in late 1965, Arnheiter received orders to assume command.[6]

ON THE GUNLINE

On 22 December 1965, Lt. Comdr. Marcus Aurelius Arnheiter, USN, assumed command of the *Vance* (DER-387) at Pearl Harbor. During his speech, he promised the crew action, excitement, and drama. Those who had served on Market Time patrols, knew they would be lucky to fire a shot in anger. The duties of DERs then assigned to such operations consisted mainly of screening sea traffic for Viet Cong infiltrators and material in the outer Market Time barrier. DERs also provided logistical support to Navy Swift boats (PCFs) and Coast Guard patrol boats (WPBs) working the inner barrier.[7]

As one of his first actions, Arnheiter ordered the ship's first lieutenant to purchase a speedboat in Hawaii for tactical as well as recreational purposes. Since he intended to use the 16-foot Fiberglas boat mainly for junk searches and for scouting out enemy positions on the shore, Arnheiter's use of $950 of recreational funds to acquire the craft was in violation of Navy policy. Subsequently, he had shark teeth painted on the bow, a machine gun mounted in the middle, and a proportionally very large 3- by 5-foot American flag affixed to a staff near the stern.[8]

Arnheiter later explained to the wardroom, using sketches and diagrams, how he intended to use the speedboat as bait to draw fire from the Viet Cong on the coast or in junks near the shore. A variation on this theme would be to send out the ship's larger, but slower motor whaleboat as a decoy to "incite the enemy." The ship's operations officer later remarked about the plan, "He had a three-wave invasion," describing how the captain sketched the speedboat dashing in close to the shore, with the motor whaleboat in between it and the *Vance*, which would be lurking just out of sight over the horizon.[9]

Vance left Pearl Harbor on 28 December, bound for Vietnam with stops at Guam and the Philippines en route. On 20 January 1966, *Vance* reported for duty to commander, Task Force 115, relieving sister ship *Finch* (DER-328) at Qui Nhon. *Vance* then took up patrol duties in her assigned sector in the outer barrier. On the morning of the 28th, *Leonard F. Mason* (DD-852), a destroyer with five-inch gun batteries instead of the twin three-inchers the *Vance* carried, came steaming past. Arnheiter queried her by flashing light where she was going, and was told she was heading north on an urgent mission. Arnheiter had previously learned from fleet radio messages that Operation MASHER, a major offensive involving the Army's First Cavalry Division (Air Mobile), was about to commence. Wanting to join the action, he set off after the *Mason* at his ship's near top speed of 17.5 knots.[10]

As *Vance* moved north, Market Time headquarters in Saigon radioed her and other patrol ships to stay out of the area off the coast where the operation was taking place so that the destroyers on gunfire missions would have full freedom of maneuver. *Vance*'s operations officer plotted the prohibited area on a chart, then took it and the message up to the captain on the bridge. Arnheiter read the message and looked at the chart and, the officer later recounted, "He just sort of grunted, and we kept on going right into that prohibited area."[11]

If fired upon, *Vance* had authority to return fire under the existing rules of engagement. However, she did not have authorization to move beyond her assigned patrol sector to the inshore barrier, to seek combat, nor was naval gunfire a part of the DE's regularly assigned duties in her sector. To conceal his action, Arnheiter directed that a false position report be sent to Coastal Surveillance Center Qui Nhon over the objections of the ship's executive officer. According to the operations officer, during this patrol period and in subsequent ones, Arnheiter also falsified reports on the number of junks and sampans inspected. One means of doing so, was to include in the total numbers, any junks or sampans sighted on the horizon—but not approached for examination or boarded for search.[12]

OPERATIONS MASHER AND DOUBLE EAGLE

Photo 7-4

Comdr. Otto D. Tiderman, USN, commanding officer of the destroyer USS *Barry* (DD-933), welcoming aboard representatives of the 1st Air Cavalry.
USS *Barry* 1965-1966 Around the World cruise book

Operation MASHER, which took place between 24 January and 6 March 1966, was the largest search and destroy operation to date in the war. During execution, its title was changed to WHITE WING, because President Lyndon Johnson desired a more benign name. The purpose of the operation was for the U.S. Army 1st Cavalry Division (Airmobile), South Vietnamese, and Korean forces to sweep through the central lowlands of the Binh Dinh Province, drive the North Vietnamese out, and destroy enemy supply areas. In coordination, 5,000

U.S. Marines made an amphibious landing (in an operation termed DOUBLE EAGLE) near Thach Tru in southern Quang Ngai Province, to block the northern escape route, as ground forces drove the enemy up the Bang Loa Valley. DOUBLE EAGLE was the largest amphibious landing since the Inchon landings in the Korean War. It is worth noting the services of one destroyer on the gunline in support of the landing.[13]

In the grey dawn on 28 January, the *Barry* (DD-933) stood offshore within 2,000 yards of the beachhead as wave after wave of Marines moved ashore from an amphibious task group. In ensuing days, *Barry* was called upon to provide naval gunfire support for Marine movements during daylight hours, and harassing fire at night. During the week of 28 January-4 February, in which she fired 700 rounds in combat support of the Marines, the destroyer had a coastal junk patrol under her command, manned by South Vietnamese sailors and American advisors. The junks were used as an infiltrate/exfiltrate patrol (as a deterrent to enemy forces trying to join or escape by sea) as an extension of friendly front lines.[14]

Barry detached from these duties on 5 February to support the 1st Air Cavalry's MASHER/WHITE WING in Binh Dinh Province, and remained on the gunline until 16 February.[15]

VANCE FIRES AT NON-EXISTENT ENEMY TARGETS

On 28 January 1966 and again the following day, Arnheiter took the *Vance* in close to Point Kim Bong, hoping to engage in a gunfire mission. To get a target, he badgered both the *Leonard F. Mason*, rightfully conducting shore bombardment in support of MASHER, and the aerial spotter directing her fire. On two occasions, *Vance* fouled the *Mason*'s gun range by getting between the destroyer and her target. On the afternoon of the 29th, Arnheiter, apparently growing impatient, radioed the spotter that he saw "some bunkers and trenches… on top of a sand dune." "It looks like a good mission for me" he said, and fired two rounds from his 3-inch guns without permission.[16]

The spotter ordered the *Vance*'s captain to "cease fire," telling him, "I am unable to see gun emplacement." Arnheiter replied that he could see it, and the spotter confirmed his request without air observation. Arnheiter immediately ordered his gunners to lay down rounds on the "emplacements"—a reckless move given the presence of American and South Vietnamese troops fighting 3,000 to 5,000 yards inland. The *Vance*'s operations officer observed, "there was nothing there but sand," and her gunnery officer christened the incident "the crab shoot."[17]

That night, using skills honed in the Pentagon, Arnheiter wrote and transmitted to his chain of command, a combined after-action report and press release touting the role that his ship had played to date in Operation MASHER:

> The *Vance* "directly supported the major push by the U. S. Army's First Cavalry Division" by responding to an "urgent fire request by the II Corps U.S. Navy gunfire support team. Proceeding at full speed to a position within 1,200 yards of the Vietcong-controlled coastline," the *Vance* delivered 17 rounds of "highly accurate bombardment against known Vietcong machine-gun bunkers and an entrenchment approximately 2.5 miles away. The very first round was observed to hit one of the bunkers."[18]

The message was also routed to other Navy headquarters and was, along with similar reports that followed, released to news media by the Navy information office in Saigon.[19]

On the afternoon of 30 January, Arnheiter took the *Vance* in to within 1,000 yards of the coast. After unsuccessfully enjoining the destroyer *Bache* (DD-470) to give him a target, he declared that he saw suspicious movement on the rock face of a mountain plunging sharply to the sea. (The executive officer later stated that the captain had told him earlier in the day that he was going to make believe the Viet Cong were shooting at the ship so he could fire the guns and give the crew the feeling they were "engaging the enemy.")[20]

Arnheiter fired at the spot with an M-1 rifle, shouted that he could see the muzzle flashes of Viet Cong guns and told the .50-caliber machine gunner to "neutralize" the enemy fire. When the machine gun opened up, bright flashes erupted on the rocks—which crewmen observing the action believed were ricochets of its own rounds. "They're shooting at us" Arnheiter yelled, and he ordered the *Vance*'s three-inch guns into action. The ship's chief corpsman upon going out on the main deck to see what was happening, observed the chief radioman looking through binoculars at the mountain. When asked, "what are we shooting at?" his response was, "two chickens." The fowl were running around the front yard of a Vietnamese peasant's hovel on a ledge off to the right of the target.[21]

RELIEF OF *VANCE*'S COMMANDING OFFICER FOLLOWS SHIPBOARD VISIT BY A CHAPLAIN

Arnheiter's eventual undoing was not spurred as a result of his flagrant disobedience of orders, falsifying of ship position reports, or reckless use of naval gunfire—although these actions, once known to seniors, obviously contributed to his relief for cause. Instead, a shipboard visit on 28 February 1966 by the chaplain of Escort Squadron 7 set in motion an abrupt end to his tenure as commanding officer. The two-week visit occurred following the Presbyterian minister learning that officers and men of the *Vance* had been writing letters to their wives about the commanding officer's unusual practices. Comdr. Donald F. Milligan, USN, the squadron commander and *Vance*'s operational commander, had also been receiving disturbing reports about Arnheiter from the captains of destroyers on shore bombardment duty.[22]

In the letters, Roman Catholics aboard *Vance* in particular, had complained about being forced to attend Protestant-style religious services. Once aboard, the chaplain listened to myriad complaints from the officers and men regarding Arnheiter's bizarre actions and behavior. A partial summary of these allegations follows, including some made during a subsequent investigation. Those previously discussed are not repeated:

- Encouragement by the captain for wardroom members to steal a silver coffee server and two large silver candelabras from the officer's club on Guam for use aboard the ship. The coffee server and one of the candelabras made it aboard *Vance*. He also encouraged them to siphon gasoline from vehicles on base for use in the speedboat.

- Fines levied by the captain on his officers for various minor infractions or deficiencies, the proceeds of which he used to buy cigars for his consumption.

- Practice of the captain in continuing his search for action (following the gunfire incidents described), of sending the speedboat and the motor whaleboat out as bait in the hope of drawing fire.

- Arnheither taking long showers, one lasting 27 minutes, while the crew was on strict water rations in the tropical heat. He also had fresh water poured every hour over blankets and an awning slung around his cabin to cool it.[23]

NAVY TAKES RAPID ACTION AGAINST ARNHEITER

As evidence mounted against Arnheiter's fitness for command, Milligan acted. On 29 March, he met with the Cruiser Destroyer Flotilla Three commander, Rear Adm. Donald Greer Irvine, and told him and Rear Adm. Thomas S. King Jr., who was replacing Irvine at the time, what he had learned. He recommended that Arnheiter be relieved, and an investigation be conducted. A request was made to the Bureau of Naval Personnel (BuPers) in Washington, and on the morning of 31 March

1966, *Vance*'s chief radioman handed his commanding officer a terse order from BuPers. It informed Arnheiter that he was relieved of command of the USS *Vance*, a radar picket destroyer escort on Vietnam patrol. He had been her commanding officer only ninety-nine days.[24]

Detached from *Vance*, Arnheiter was to "proceed immediately and report to the destroyer tender *Dixie* (AD-14) for temporary duty." The following day, Rear Admiral King ordered Capt. Ward W. Witter, commander, Destroyer Squadron 11, to conduct an informal JAG (Judge Advocate General) Manual Investigation into the affair. In all, thirty witnesses, including all of *Vance*'s officers testified under oath during the next three days. Arnheiter was present with counsel and exercised his right to confront witnesses and cross-examine them.[25]

When the investigation was completed, Arnheiter was assigned to the commander, Cruiser-Destroyer Force Pacific staff based in San Diego. While there he made a very favorable impression on Rear Adm. Walter H. Baumberger, who proposed that Arnheiter be given another command under close supervision "to provide an opportunity for reassessment of his abilities." King had recommended that Arnheiter be given a punitive letter of reprimand. Adm. Roy L. Johnson, commander in chief, Pacific Fleet, disagreed with both King and Baumberger. He recommended that Arnheiter not be penalized with a letter of reprimand, but that his relief be upheld "for cause" (for good reason) and that he never be given a command again.[26]

Vice Adm. Benedict Joseph Semmes Jr., chief of Naval Personnel, approved the detachment for cause on 9 September 1966, and directed that papers be filed in Arnheiter's personnel jacket. This action precluded him from ever receiving a Navy command, and a year later, he was passed over for promotion. Meanwhile, Baumberger had decided that he was wrong and that Arnheiter had learned nothing. The admiral said so in the last fitness report he gave Arnheiter before the *Vance*'s former captain was transferred to a graveyard job at Treasure Island, California, as communications officer on the staff of commander, Western Sea Frontier.[27]

Lt. Comdr. Marcus Aurelius Arnheiter, USN, did not go quietly into the night. His influence in derailing the career of a superlative officer selected as the pre-commissioning commanding officer of the battleship *New Jersey* (BB-62) follows later in the book. This occurred while *New Jersey* was being "brought out of mothballs" at the Philadelphia Navy Shipyard, to serve on the gunline in Vietnam.

8

Operation SEA DRAGON

Patrol the North Vietnam coastline from the demilitarized zone northward and destroy North Vietnamese waterborne logistics craft carrying arms and materials to enemy troops in the South.

—Orders received by the destroyers *Mansfield* (DD-728) and *Hanson* (DD-832) on the morning of 25 October 1966, which marked the beginning of Operation SEA DRAGON. Before the day was complete, they had destroyed several logistics craft and had been taken under fire by heavy shore batteries, returning the fire and destroying the batteries.[1]

Photo 8-1

Gunfire from USS *Mansfield* (DD-728) and USS *Hanson* (DD-832) striking targets along the coastline of North Vietnam between the Demilitarized Zone and Dong Hoi, on 25 November 1966.
National Archives photograph #K-35031

Working in all four corps areas of South Vietnam, U.S. Navy cruisers and destroyers, and Royal Australian Navy destroyers, continually supported friendly troops ashore with heavy gunfire. Daily, ships on the gunline were credited with destroying enemy staging areas, bunkers, supply and ammunition storage areas, and even entire companies of enemy troops. As the war began to grow more serious and the United States offered more assistance to the Republic of Vietnam, the tasks assigned to cruisers and destroyers grew—both in number and complexity—and additional U.S. Navy ships were sent to Vietnam, including ones from the Atlantic Fleet.[2]

On 25 October 1966, Operation SEA DRAGON was launched, expanding the area in which surface combatants operated to the coastal waters of North Vietnam. The operation was conceived to interdict seaborne supplies going from North to South Vietnam, destroy land targets with gunfire support, and destroy waterborne craft. Although the Ho Chi Minh trail (a logistical system that ran from North Vietnam to South Vietnam through Laos and Cambodia) was the prime enemy supply route until Sea Dragon began, the Tonkin Gulf was equally important to North Vietnam for moving supplies.[3]

Photo 8-2

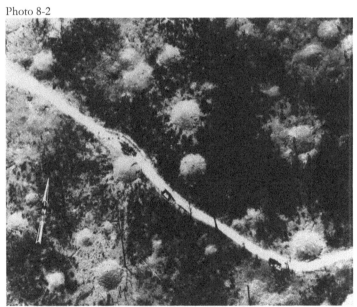

An aerial view of camouflaged trucks hauling supplies on a section of the Ho Chi Minh Trail in Laos, encircled by bomb craters, 16 January 1970. National Archives photograph #USN 1144308

Taking up their duties on the first day of SEA DRAGON were the destroyers *Mansfield* (DD-728) and *Hanson* (DD-832). *Mansfield*, one of the thirty-three *Allen M. Sumner*-class destroyers that would serve on the gunline off Vietnam during the war, had been commissioned on 14 April 1944. During Fleet Rehabilitation and Modernization (FRAM) in 1960, she'd retained all three of her 5-inch/38-gun mounts and gained Mark 32 torpedo tubes and VDS (variable depth sonar) to provide her greatly improved anti-submarine warfare capabilities.[4]

Spanning 390 feet in length and displacing 3,460 tons, *Hanson*—a *Gearing*-class destroyer—was a little larger. She had been commissioned on 11 May 1945, and completed her FRAM upgrade in December 1964. *Gearing* destroyers would be the workhorses in Vietnam, with eighty-seven serving on the gunline between 1965-1973. These type ships received extensive modernization and anti-submarine warfare capabilities. In addition to VDS and Mk 32 torpedo tubes, they were also fitted with an SQS-23 hull-mounted sonar, an anti-submarine rocket (ASROC) launcher, and a drone anti-submarine helicopter (DASH) capability. However, these improvements necessitated the removal of the destroyers' after 5-inch/38-gun mount.[5]

INCEPTION OF OPERATION SEA DRAGON

Photo 8-3

Signalmen aboard the destroyer USS *Mansfield* (DD-728) use a signal searchlight to communicate with USS *Hanson* (DD-832) during action against North Vietnamese shore batteries near Dong Hoi, Vietnam, 25 October 1966.
National Archives photograph #K-35012

At 0500 on 25 October 1966, *Mansfield* and *Hanson* entered North Vietnamese waters to open a new phase of the war by attacking waterborne logistics craft (whose acronym WBLC was pronounced WBLIC) and coastal lines of communications. Closing to within 14,000 yards of shore, the warships engaged coastal shipping with gunfire near Dong Hoi.[6]

At 0951, coastal defense batteries fired on the ships. The destroyers turned seaward to move away from the coast, and *Mansfield*'s aft 5-inch gun mount engaged the shore artillery with counterbattery fire. The ships escaped unscathed. Over the remainder of the day, they periodically closed the coast to fire on other targets, drawing additional, inaccurate fire twice that afternoon.[7]

A *Mansfield* crewmember, Tom Harper, later described the tactics his ship employed during SEA DRAGON operations. A dash by the destroyer shoreward, was followed by rapid movement along the North Vietnamese coast, with all three twin-mounts firing at targets, before swiftly opening the coast under the cover of smoke:

> "Normal" ops were to locate WBLCs near the shore, rush in at 25 kts perpendicular to the shore, go parallel to the coast, ... [with] all 6 guns [in] rapid continuous fire, turn stern to at the end of the run, light a smoke pot for cover, and leave as fast as we could! You could feel near misses [of enemy counterbattery fire] shake the ship a little, but with all the vibration we created from a 25kt dash and our guns firing, it was hard to tell some times.
>
> I really don't remember how many times we did this. The last time we went I was scared to death! We had survived all that time off 'nam and if we were going to get zapped, this was the time. I felt like a kid at Christmas when we left the last time! I mean, we survived a tour spanning 19 different months and we were ALIVE![8]

Rapid fire produced a lot of spent brass gun cartridges, with an associated requirement to retrieve and repackage them for eventual transfer to a supply ship or ashore, for return to an ammunition depot. This chore wasn't one that gunner's mates, and other sailors assigned to gun mounts, particularly enjoyed carrying out at the end of a long day. Harper explained:

> After every firing mission came the dreaded statement from the mount captain, 'Police brass.' So, we'd go out on deck, pick up all the empty powder casings and put them into a powder can, put a lid on it, and usually stack the cans along the life lines on the starboard side of the ship. This all took a long time and was not one of our

favorite tasks. If the mission was at night [when officers and senior enlisted could not see what was taking place], we'd often police [throw] the brass right over the side.

There was a trick here though, you had to throw the powder casing open end down, [in order that] it would turn over under the surface, "burp" out a large [air] bubble and slip into the depths. If you threw over open end up, it would pop back to the surface, and everyone knew you had not policed the brass properly, the empty brass was still floating and telling on you when daylight arrived! If you threw the powder can over, it was aluminum, it would float no matter how you threw it over, it was real light, so we'd take a fire axe and punch a hole in the closed end…and then it would sink.[9]

Daytime gunfire missions offered no chance to surreptitiously throw brass over the side, and stacks of cartridges would accumulate topside, until transferred to another Navy unit. Destroyers frequently refueled at sea from replenishment ships, which usually carried some ammunition, but were not ammunition ships. Thus, they had limited space for spent cartridges. Nevertheless, enterprising sailors found ways to get brass off their ship, and free up deck space. Harper recounted a practice used aboard *Mansfield*:

We often would put a small pile of empty brass in front of the #2 stack on the torpedo deck, and when we would go along another ship for unrep [underway replenishment], we would ask if they would take our empties. The only thing they could see was the small pile, we always went up portside to another ship, and they would always say OK. We of course would have the entire starboard side main deck lined with empties and we would pass those up to the pile to be shipped over to the unrep ship. Sometimes we were so good that we'd get hundreds of rounds off the ship before they would realize that they had been duped by a can [destroyer]![10]

By the end of October 1966, the destroyers assigned to Operation TRAFFIC COP (the initial phase of SEA DRAGON) had sunk 101 water craft and damaged another 94—expending 928 5-inch projectiles in doing so. Counterbattery fire against enemy shore batteries, accounted for another 426 rounds. Seventh Fleet achieved these impressive results without the loss or damage of a single ship or sailor. This changed in the last week of 1966.[11]

Photo 8-4

Crewmen aboard the *Allen M. Sumner*-class destroyer USS *O'Brien* (DD-725)
handle 5-inch/38 shell casings while in Vietnamese waters.
National Archives photograph #USN 1119671

DESTROYER *O'BRIEN* HIT BY NORTH VIETNAMESE SHORE BATTERY FIRE WITH MEN KILLED/INJURED

Since the rules require that the enemy gets the first shot, it is bad luck that he drew the first blood. Your counterfire and subsequent air strikes insured that he will not fire those guns again. Your determined action has my admiration. Your sorrow at the loss of two shipmates is fully shared.

O'Brien *has been hit at least once in each war since her commissioning, but never daunted. She has always fought back and taught the enemy never to tamper with the shamrock. Come back in fighting trim.*

—Rear Adm. Evan P. Aurand, USN, commander, Anti-submarine Warfare Group One, message 231138Z December 1966.

The rapid response of USS O'Brien *in engagement with North Vietnamese shore battery in Sea Dragon Ops was noted with pleasure. The effective counterbattery fire, timely reporting and overall control of the situation was characteristic of the professional performance traditionally associated with destroyer operations. Well done.*

—Adm. Roy L. Johnson, commander in chief, Pacific Fleet, message 280131Z December 1966.

Photo 8-5

USS *O'Brien* (DD-725) and sister units of Destroyer Division 232—*Eversole* (DD-789), *Alfred A. Cunningham* (DD-752), and *Benner* (DD-807)—steam in a line abreast, with two other destroyers, *Epperson* (DD-445) and *Bauer* (DE-1025), en route to join the 7th Fleet. USS *O'Brien* Western Pacific 1965-66 cruise book

In late morning on 23 December 1966, events took a grim turn when the destroyer *O'Brien* (DD-725) took a direct hit from a 75mm shore battery in the Dong Hoi area, while on patrol 7,800 yards off the coast. Three minutes later, while engaged in counterbattery fire, she received a second hit that caused moderate damage to her aft deckhouse. Damage Controlman Third Antone Perry Jr. and Fireman Thomas Lee Tiglas were killed by enemy fire.[12]

Photo 8-6

Destroyer USS *O'Brien* (DD-725) under way off Oahu, Hawaii, 15 May 1968. Naval History and Heritage Command photograph #NH 103027

O'Brien, the first U.S. Navy Seventh Fleet warship to be hit by an enemy shore battery in the Vietnam War, had been engaged in the interdiction of North Vietnamese shipping for the previous two days. The destroyer had damaged five coastal cargo ships with 5-inch fire, thirteen miles northwest of Dong Hoi the previous evening. Shortly after midnight, as she moved southward along the enemy coast, *O'Brien* had sighted other communist watercraft about eight miles northwest of Dong Hoi, and damaged five more. A short time later, four miles northwest of Dong Hoi, twenty other vessels came under her guns; at least ten of them were damaged by gunfire.[13]

Several hours later, shore battery fire opened up on *O'Brien*, then about four miles offshore. As the destroyer zigzagged seaward to make targeting more difficult for the North Vietnamese, her guns hammered out 130 rounds of counterbattery fire. U.S. Navy A-4 attack aircraft from the carrier *Kitty Hawk* (CVA-63) joined the attack on the enemy emplacement located about twenty-five miles northeast of Dong Ha. The destroyer *Maddox* (DD-731) raced to the scene, but the exchange of heavy gunfire was over by the time she arrived.[14]

S-2E Tracker anti-submarine aircraft from Squadron VS-38 aboard the carrier *Bennington* (CVA-20) were already on the scene, providing spotting for *O'Brien*'s guns and assisting jets, when two helicopters from the carrier (Squadron HS-8) arrived over the destroyer's deck. A doctor, Lt. Anthony D. Schilling, and Hospitalman Second A. J. Kacala were lowered to *O'Brien* and they immediately went to her wardroom and began treating the wounded. Four crewmen requiring more care were airlifted to the *Bennington* following initial first aid.[15]

That evening the *Gearing*-class destroyer *Benner* (DD-807) relieved *O'Brien* as she retired to Subic Bay for repairs. A Memorial Mass was held at the U.S. Naval Station Chapel on 31 December 1966 for Antone Perry Jr. and Thomas Lee Tiglas. In a separate awards ceremony, Rear Adm. Evan P. Aurand, USN, presented Boiler Technician First C. C. Olsen, Boiler Technician Second R. H. Scudder, Fireman H. D. Henson, and Fireman W. C. Wehunt with Purple Heart Medals.[16]

Photo 8-7

Damage to the destroyer USS *O'Brien* (DD-725) by enemy shore battery fire. USS *O'Brien* Western Pacific 1967 cruise book

DESTROYER *BENNER* JOINS THE GUNLINE

Photo 8-8

View of the North Vietnamese coast as the destroyer USS *Benner* (DD-807)
arrives offshore to take up Operation SEA DRAGON duties.
USS *Benner* Western Pacific 1966-1967 cruise book

Benner was assigned to Task Unit 77.1.1 on Christmas Eve as *O'Brien*'s
replacement, one of the destroyers interdicting waterborne logistic craft
along the coast of North Vietnam. That same day, commander,
Destroyer Division 232, Capt. Gilbert L. Clark, USN, broke (hoisted)
his flag in *Benner* and assumed command of the task unit. *Benner*'s patrol
area was a swath of water five miles off the coast, stretching northward
from 17°20'N to 17°56'N.[17]

     She spent Christmas Day patrolling along the coast and went to
General Quarters at 2300 when North Vietnamese batteries fired on
friendly reconnaissance aircraft. *Benner*, however, did not return fire,
there being a two-day truce in effect. During this period, from 0700 on
24 December to 0700 on 26 December, the enemy took advantage of
the cessation of hostilities and moved waterborne logistics craft
southward. The ship's surface search radar showed an unbroken line of
craft between the mouths of the Song Giang and Hun Giang Rivers at
midnight on 25 December. At the end of the truce, *Benner* was unable
to find any craft until 30 December when she took several beached craft
under fire. Enemy vessels earlier at risk had apparently disappeared into
the many small inlets along the coast.[18]

YEAR'S END, 1966

Destroyers are doing what destroyers do best, and their role hasn't changed since many of you were in them. Whatever the assignment, destroyers thrive on hard work and are continuing to perform in an outstanding manner. Something that may stir up a few memories for you, is the fact that some of our destroyers are now participating in their third shooting engagement. PRESTON *is one of them. Okinawa, Korea, and now Vietnam. Another,* O'BRIEN, *a triple veteran, last month conducted a successful 26-hour gunfire mission south of Da Nang which helped turn back a determined assault by hard core Viet Cong troops. She fired more than 48 tons of ammunition.*

—Paul H. Nitze, Secretary of the Navy, speaking at a Retired Flag and General Officers Symposium in January 1966. The year began with SecNav highlighting the actions of USS *O'Brien* coming to the aid of an Australian position under mortar attack on 22 November 1965 at Thach Ten, Quang Nagi province, and helping to turn back a North Vietnamese regiment. It ended with *O'Brien* being hit by enemy fire during Sea Dragon operations.[19]

On 31 December 1966, there were over 23,500 Navy and Coast Guard personnel in country, and 36,000 Navy aboard fifty-five Seventh Fleet ships off the Vietnamese coast. As part of expanding Navy operations, Sea Dragon destroyers amassed an impressive record by year's end. Aggressive operations resulted in 382 watercraft destroyed and 325 damaged; five coastal defense batteries destroyed and two damaged; and two radar sites destroyed with another two damaged. Just four days after the Sea Dragon operating area expanded northward to the 18th parallel, the Joint Chiefs of Staff (JCS) had authorized engaging shore batteries. This occurred when enemy shore-based search radars "painted" several destroyers with their radar waves, enabling more accurate targeting, and the ships received authorization to attack the sites.[20]

Because of concentrated coastal defense artillery in the limited Sea Dragon area, Adm. Ulysses S. Grant Sharp Jr., commander in chief, Pacific Command, asked the JCS to increase the number of destroyers assigned to the mission and to enlarge the Sea Dragon area to dilute enemy shore fire. In February 1967, Sea Dragon forces were authorized to operate as far north as the 20th parallel.[21]

SEA DRAGON CONVENTIONS AND PROCEDURES

Life aboard Sea Dragon destroyers was stressful and tiring, yet focus and morale remained high, owing to a combination of frequent action, immediate results from their efforts, and the possibility of being shot at. On patrol, typically one-third of the crew was at their battle stations, with at least one-gun mount fully manned, while the rest ate, slept and performed shipboard duties. In CIC, radarmen kept constant vigil over surface and air search radars, while receiving additional or collaborating contact reports from surveillance aircraft and other ships. When a target was identified, the ship's captain normally ordered General Quarters set and gave permission to fire. The gunfire direction officer, sometimes aided by spotter aircraft, would "walk" the initial rounds on to the target, then order, "All mounts, both guns, two salvos." The resultant "boom, boom, boom, boom ..." of rapid fire, signaled round after round of 5-inch, hurling toward an enemy vessel or shore target.[22]

Commanding officers might sometimes deviate from this pattern, particularly when engaging a single waterborne logistics craft, and if his ship was beyond coastal gun range. In these cases, he might engage the target with the ready mount and forgo the call to General Quarters to allow the remainder of the crew additional rest. If within the range of shore guns, the destroyer would turn seaward as soon as the action was completed, and move rapidly away from now, alerted enemy forces.[23]

Photo 8-9

Spent cartridges from *Benner*'s guns, and the destroyer opening the North Vietnamese coast at flank speed in 1967, following the completion of a SEA DRAGON mission. USS *Benner* Western Pacific 1966-1967 cruise book

9

Australian Destroyers Sent to Vietnam

From Vung Tau riding Chinooks to the dust at Nui Dat
I'd been in and out of choppers now for months
And we made our tents a home, V.B. and pinups on the lockers
And an Asian orange sunset through the scrub

And can you tell me, doctor, why I still can't get to sleep?
And night time's just a jungle dark and a barking M.16?
And what's this rash that comes and goes, can you tell me what it means?
God help me
I was only nineteen

—Lyrics from the song, I was only 19 by Redgum (1983),
unofficial 'anthem' of the Australian Vietnam Veterans

On 14 December 1966, following a request by the U.S. government for Australia to increase the resources it was committing to the Vietnam War, the Australian Cabinet approved the deployment of HMAS *Hobart* (D39). The 437-foot ship was one of three *Perth*-class guided missile destroyers built by Defoe Shipbuilding Company, Bay City, Michigan, for the Royal Australian Navy. Based on the U.S. Navy's *Charles F. Adams* design, *Hobart*, *Perth*, and *Brisbane* were armed with one Mk 13 Tartar missile launcher, two 5-inch/54 caliber Mark 42 guns, and two Mk 32 triple torpedo tube sets. (Two Ikara anti-submarine missile launchers were later installed.) Foster Wheeler D-type boilers sending steam to General Electric turbines, producing 70,000 shaft horsepower, propelled the 3,370-ton destroyers to a top speed of 35 knots. Ship's complement was 20 officers and 312 men.[1]

Between 1967 and 1971, all three destroyers deployed in support of the Vietnam War—*Perth* and *Hobart* three times, and *Brisbane* twice. During these deployments, the destroyers were integrated into the U.S. Seventh Fleet. The three ships operated primarily in the naval gunfire support role, but also performed screening duties for American aircraft carriers, and were involved in Market Time and Sea Dragon operations.[2]

Royal Australian Navy *Perth*-class Guided Missile Destroyers

Ship	Com./Decom.	Disposition
Perth (D38)	17 Jul 1965/ 15 Oct 1999	Sunk as dive wreck off Albany, Western Australia
Hobart (D39)	18 Dec 1965/ 12 May 2000	Sunk as dive wreck off Yankalilla, South Australia
Brisbane (D41)	16 Dec 1967/ 19 Oct 2001	Sunk as dive wreck off Mooloolaba, Queensland[3]

Photo 9-1

HMAS *Perth* (D38) at anchor with ship's officers and crew assembled on the fantail, missile deck, and gun deck of the missile destroyer; date and location unknown. http://www.seaforces.org/marint/Australian-Navy/Destroyer/Perth-class.htm

DESTROYER HMAS *HOBART* JOINS THE 7TH FLEET

Hobart arrived at Subic Bay on 15 March 1967 to join the Seventh Fleet. She replaced the USS *Fechteler* (DD-870) on 31 March, taking over the destroyer's gunfire support duties. By 0445 the following morning, she had already fired 100 rounds. *Hobart* remained on the gunline until 15 April, ending the period having fired a total of 1,651 5-inch rounds. She then rotated to Sea Dragon operations.[4]

United States and Royal Australian Navy destroyers deployed to Vietnam were then generally operating in one of four roles:

- Patrols along the coast of North Vietnam as part of Operation Sea Dragon to interdict coastal shipping, with secondary attacks on inland supply lines and military targets, along with coastal batteries that had fired on USN and RAN ships

- Naval gunfire support operations to assist ground forces, particularly U.S. Marine Corps units operating closest to the North Vietnam border
- Market Time operations, which aimed to stop the logistic supply and reinforcement of Viet Cong units operating in South Vietnam by intercepting and searching coastal shipping
- Escort and screening of U.S. Navy aircraft carriers involved in Operation Rolling Thunder airstrikes[5]

Destroyers assigned to Sea Dragon were normally split into northern and southern units (although during 1967 up to four units were operating at any given time), with each unit made up of two to three ships.[6]

Seven destroyers were usually stationed on the gunline off South Vietnam to conduct two types of missions: 'unspotted' shelling of areas where North Vietnamese or Viet Cong forces and facilities were known or believed to be, and 'spotted' fire missions in direct support of ground troops. For the latter mission, observers providing spotting were either airborne, or on the ground close enough to report the fall of gun rounds, and recommend corrections in firing bearing and range to the target.[7]

Photo 9-2

On 19 April 1967, four Marine gunfire support spotters landed aboard the destroyer USS *Fechteler* (DD-870) to observe a firing mission. The helicopter in which they arrived is shown above on the left, and the plane employed for spotting to the right. USS *Fechteler* (DD-870) Southeast Asian 1967 cruise book

Royal Australian Navy ships off Vietnam were expected to fulfill all duties of an equivalent American destroyer, but were prohibited by the Australian government from operating outside the theater on unrelated Seventh Fleet duties. Within the theater, they were never formally assigned to Market Time, but the overlap of the gunline and Market

Time operating areas resulted in RAN ships being called upon to assist in tracking suspicious ships or participating in raids.[8]

Operation ROLLING THUNDER was a bombing campaign begun in March 1965 and lasting through October 1968, in which U.S. air force and naval aircraft attacked targets throughout North Vietnam. The massive bombing was intended to put military pressure on North Vietnam's communist leaders and reduce their capacity to wage war against South Vietnam. The air strikes marked the first sustained American assault on North Vietnam and represented a major expansion of U.S. involvement in the war. Destroyer support for these operations entailed screening and escorting carriers conducting flight operations.[9]

Australia was the only allied nation to provide naval support to the United States during the Vietnam War. RAN destroyers in Vietnamese waters operated under the overall command of the U.S. Seventh Fleet but administratively they remained the responsibility of the Flag Officer Commanding Her Majesties Australian Fleet (FOCAF).[10]

HOBART JOINS SEA DRAGON NAVAL FORCES

After taking up Sea Dragon duty off North Vietnam, HMAS *Hobart* was fired on by shore batteries several times—on one occasion receiving minor shrapnel damage. Accidental explosions in the 5-inch/54-caliber mounts of *Manley* (DD-940) and *Bigelow* (DD-942) during the latter half of April 1967 resulted in the reassignment of all destroyers (including *Hobart*) fitted with these type guns to other duties while an investigation was carried out. The analysis concluded that a bad batch of ammunition was to blame. On 23 April, *Hobart* was attached to the carrier escort force for the *Kitty Hawk* (CVA-63). Six days later, the destroyer proceeded to Subic Bay for crew liberty and maintenance.[11]

HMAS *Hobart* returned to Sea Dragon operations from 8-18 May, as part of a task unit which also included the destroyers *Samuel N. Moore* (DD-747), *Collett* (DD-730), and *Allen M. Sumner* (DD-692). On 14 May, *Hobart* and *Sumner* destroyed two major concentrations of cargo barges and logistics craft in the vicinity of Cap Mui Lay—a perturbation in the coastline just north of the 17th parallel—following a report of their location by aircraft from the *Hancock* (CVA-19). The two destroyers took the position by surprise and destroyed 14 large cargo barges, six storage buildings, 2 loading platforms, and damaged 16 additional craft. Five coastal defense sites in the vicinity were taken under fire by Sea Dragon units, but no accurate estimate of damage could be made.[12]

The following day was nearly a repeat of the previous one, with *Hobart* and *Sumner* locating a concentration of twenty craft. The ships made quick use of their guns to destroy fifteen transport barges (ranging from 40-70 feet in length) and five storage buildings, and damage the remaining five craft. In later activity, the destroyers took a smaller group of waterborne logistics craft and four coastal defense sites under fire. Two craft were damaged, but no estimate of damage to the coastal sites could be immediately made.[13]

OPERATION BEAU CHARGER

The barrels are smooth, the barrels droop, we're out of powder, what's the scoop!!!!

—Message sent to the Seventh Fleet by Capt. Guy R. Griffiths, RAN, commanding officer, HMAS *Hobart*, at the end a long day spent with the crew at their battle stations, as her guns poured out rounds in support of Operation BEAU CHARGER.[14]

Just before and during the launching of the assault, a duel started between Navy fire support ships and NVA shore batteries. Although the NVA batteries hit no ships, 10 salvos bracketed the USS Point Defiance (LSD 31). After return fire silenced the shore batteries, the surface landing proceeded without further incident; there was no opposition.

—From *U.S. Marines in Vietnam: Fighting The North Vietnamese 1967* by Telfer, Rogers and Fleming (Washington, DC: History and Museums Division, Headquarters Marine Corps, 1984)

On 18 May 1967 in support of the Operation BEAU CHARGER, an amphibious and helicopter assault for a search and destroy mission, eleven Sea Dragon ships joined other vessels near the Demilitarized Zone (DMZ) dividing North and South Vietnam. The plan called for a search and destroy operation in the eastern area of the southern half of the DMZ in northern Quang Tri Province. The area selected was being utilized by the enemy as a base area for mounting attacks against Marine outposts along the southern boundary of the DMZ.[15]

The Amphibious Ready Group consisted of the amphibious assault ship *Okinawa* (LPH-3), attack transport *Bayfield* (APA-33), dock landing ship *Point Defiance* (LSD-31), and tank landing ship *Whitfield County* (LST-1169). The hospital ship *Sanctuary* (AH-17) had been provided for medial support as well as patrol craft *PCF-73* and Coast Guard cutter *Point Welcome* from in-country naval forces.[16]

Due to the proximity of enemy coastal defense batteries at Cap Mui Lay, assets from Task Unit 70.8.9 (the Naval Gunfire Support Force) were temporarily augmented by Sea Dragon forces. In direct support on D-Day were the heavy cruisers *St. Paul* (CA-73) and *Boston* (CAG-1), and destroyers *Fechteler* (DD-870), *Edson* (DD-946), *Joseph Strauss* (DDG-16), and HMAS *Hobart* (D 39).[17]

Enemy batteries on Cap Mui Lay announced their intention to oppose the operation by opening fire on *St. Paul* at 0400 as she was moving into position. *St. Paul*, *Fechteler*, *Sumner*, *Strauss*, and *Hobart* commenced prelanding fire at 0600. As rounds fell ten yards from the dock landing ship *Point Defiance* and fifty yards from her landing craft, the enemy gun position came under air and 8-inch gunfire attack. Enemy fire ceased at 0719 and *Point Defiance* resumed off-loading. Naval Gunfire Support continued against assigned targets as well as counterbattery fire, although handicapped by the loss of the Naval Gunfire Liaison Officer who was killed early in the assault.[18]

The collective gunfire support provided by the ships was the greatest concentration of naval gunfire since the Korean War. Although successful in knocking out enemy positions, the operation identified the need for naval gunfire to reach further inland. This realization launched the first steps that would result in recommissioning the battleship *New Jersey* (BB-62) on 6 April 1968.[19]

After counterbattery fire had silenced the enemy batteries, the amphibious landing proceeded without further incident—there was no opposition. The helicopter-borne assault forces experienced a different reception. The designated landing zone proved to be a "hot" zone, and only one platoon of Company A, the assault company, managed to land. Enemy forces closed in and the situation was very much in doubt. At 1100, elements of Company D and the rest of Company A, reinforced with tanks, joined up with the isolated assault platoon. The enemy withdrew only after air strikes began to hammer their positions.[20]

St. Paul and *Fechteler* were detached that day to return to Sea Dragon. *Boston* was directed to remain in general support of the Third Marine Amphibious Force unless highly lucrative targets requiring 8-inch gunfire developed in the Sea Dragon area. *Strauss*, *Sumner*, and *Hobart* were detached on 19 May. The Amphibious Ready Group, with *Boston* and *Edson* supporting it, remained as operations continued ashore.[21]

Two days later, *Mansfield* (DD-728) relieved *Edson* on 21 May as the NGFS ship directly supporting Beau Charger. *Ozbourn* relieved *Mansfield* the next day. Marine Corps search and destroy operations, sweeping to the south in order to clear the area, continued. Early on the morning of 23 May, *Ozbourn* (DD-846) came under fire from Tiger Island. The next day, with *Boston* again on the scene, *Boston* and *Ozbourn* were taken under fire by guns estimated to be 100mm-caliber. After return fire by the two ships, the target was believed destroyed. *Edson* joined the others for NGFS support.[22]

On 25 May, the missile cruiser *Providence* (CLG-6) participated in NGFS as Vice Adm. John J. Hyland, commander, Seventh Fleet, arrived aboard her to visit units of the Amphibious Readiness Group and Special Landing Force (ARG/SLF) for briefings. Early in the afternoon the flagship came under enemy fire. Approximately forty rounds were observed. One direct hit damaged her SPS-8B radar antenna, but no personnel casualties resulted. *Providence* commenced evasive maneuvers and counterbattery fire as *Edson* and *Ozbourn* joined in the action. The three ships saturated the area and enemy fire ceased. Following re-embarkation of the special landing force aboard the amphibious ships, Beau Charger was terminated in the early afternoon on 26 May.[23]

Photo 9-3

USS *Providence* (CLG-6) firing her guns, location and date unknown.
USS *Providence* Western Pacific 1966-1968 cruise book

On 27 May, while firing on enemy mortar positions at Cap Mui Lay, *Edson* came under heavy fire and received a direct hit on her forward mast. With the aid of the destroyers *Taylor* (DD-468) and *Bigelow* (DD-942), *Edson* saturated the enemy position with a hail of 5-inch fire, and maneuvered to seaward amid exploding rounds. Ten officers and men had been wounded, three serious enough to be evacuated by helicopter to Da Nang for treatment. *Edson*, having partially lost her radar and radio communications proceeded slowly to Subic Bay for three weeks of repairs. Like other ships on the gunline, she wore out her gun barrels performing NGFS. As noted in her 1967 cruise book:

> *EDSON* flew her battle ensign proudly and experienced some of her first hours [off Vietnam] accurately returning and suppressing frequent North Vietnamese counter battery. If success is to be determined in rounds fired at the enemy, we can look back on our 1967 cruise with much pride for *EDSON* literally wore her gun barrels smooth thus necessitating replacement in Subic.[24]

Photo 9-4

Splashes off the starboard side of USS *Edson* (DD-946) from enemy shore battery fire. USS *Edson*'s Western Pacific 1967 cruise book

HOBART RETURNS TO SEA DRAGON OPERATIONS

> *Departure of dragon from down under viewed with regret and sense of loss of long right arm. Hobart's aggressiveness and superb performance under fast moving, hot combat conditions left nothing to be desired. Proud to have you on this team and eagerly look forward to joining you in future shoot outs with the enemy.*

—Signal received by HMAS *Hobart* on 23 April 1967, from a senior U.S. naval officer praising the warship's actions in concert with those of American destroyers off Vietnam.[25]

Following her detachment from BEAU CHARGER, *Hobart* returned to Sea Dragon duties until 26 May, when she proceeded to Subic Bay for maintenance, and replacement of her 5-inch gun barrels. Returning to the gunline on 18 June, she was called upon to escort the amphibious ships involved in BEACON TORCH landings. This search and destroy operation from 18 June to 2 July, placed a U.S. Marine Special Landing Force south of Da Nang in the coastal region near the Quang Nam and Quang Tin provincial border. The objective was enemy-controlled area east of the Troung Giang River and southeast of the city of Hoi An.[26]

After mid-June, the number of fire missions conducted by *Hobart* decreased because of a need to conserve 5-inch/54 ammunition across the Seventh Fleet, and because the Marines in the area had established their own artillery units and were less reliant on naval gunfire. The destroyer rotated back to Sea Dragon duties on 23 June. Most gunfire missions were then against inland targets like truck convoys, owing to a reduction in the number of seaborne infiltration attempts, and the increasing availability of spotter aircraft to assist ships in taking targets beyond the visible horizon under fire.[27]

Photo 9-5

Billowing smoke from a catastrophic fire aboard the carrier USS *Forrestal* (CVA-59) as photographed from the flight deck of USS *Oriskany* (CVA-34) off Vietnam. National Archives photograph #USN 1125490

Hobart left the operational area on 10 July to undergo a period of maintenance at Subic via a port visit to Hong Kong for crew liberty. Returning to Vietnam, she was double-tasked to the USS *Forrestal* (CVA-69) escort group and Sea Dragon operations; three destroyers were required to escort the carrier at any time, with additional ships assigned to Sea Dragon duties. A catastrophic fire aboard the carrier on 29 July necessitated her removal from the operational area, and the Australian destroyer returned to Sea Dragon operations on 31 July.[28]

This tasking continued until 16 August. Following maintenance at Subic Bay, *Hobart* reported to the gunline on 6 September. Her time thus spend was short. On 14 September, *Hobart* arrived in Subic, handed off her duties to HMAS *Perth*, and sailed for home. During the deployment, *Hobart* fired over 10,000 rounds at 1,050 targets during 160 days at sea—and was fired on ten times, with no casualties. For her exemplary performance, the first Australian destroyer to serve on the gunline earned the U.S. Navy Unit Commendation. (See Appendix B for the associated citation for *Hobart*, and those of *Perth*, earned later.)[29]

BAPITISM BY ENEMY FIRE FOR *PERTH*

Photo 9-6

HMAS *Perth* under fire from North Vietnamese Coastal Defense sites; photograph taken by Master Chief Petty Officer Dexter Goad, USN, aboard the heavy cruiser USS *Newport News*, 18 October 1967.
Courtesy of Commodore Hector Donohue, AM RAN (Retired)

HMAS *Perth* arrived off Vietnam in late September 1967 and in October joined the heavy cruiser USS *Newport News* (CA-148) in the northern

SEA DRAGON task unit (TU 77.1.1). She fired her first mission against coastal defense sites near Sam Son. On the morning of the 18th, the two ships were searching for suspected WBLCs in the Song Yen River mouth, nine miles south of Sam Son, when they came under fire from twelve coastal batteries at a range of 16,500 yards. *Perth* sustained a direct hit on her after gun mount (Mount 52) from an 85 or 100mm round. Glancing off, it penetrated the upper deck and exploded in the confidential books vault, causing a fire which was quickly extinguished. Although the damage was minor, seven sailors were wounded, two seriously enough to be medevac'd to Subic.[30]

The ships turned away from the coast and, with engine order telegraphs set at Full Ahead, commenced evasive tactics by turning toward the enemy fall-of-shot. Both ships were targeted with some 200 rounds of enemy fire. *Perth*'s commanding officer, Capt. Peter H. Doyle later wryly observed, "It was a salutary lesson that by day, unless there were compelling circumstances to the contrary, the ship should not go within the range of North Vietnamese shore batteries unless preceded with heavy suppression fire."[31]

In mid-June of the following year, *Hobart* tragically suffered crew killed and wounded as a result of friendly fire. The following account jumps readers ahead of the chronological sequence of the book, but fits well with the subject of this chapter.

HOBART HIT BY FRIENDLY FIRE

In April 1968, *Hobart* rejoined the gunline on her second deployment. Returning to SEA DRAGON operations in June, Capt. Kenneth W. Shands took command of the southern task unit (TU 77.1.2). Initially comprised of *Hobart* and USS *Theodore E. Chandler*, they were joined by USS *Edson* on 15 June. The ships conducted shore bombardments of the North Vietnamese coast, and were fired upon unsuccessfully by enemy shore batteries before taking up surveillance operations the night of 16-17 June near Tiger Island for WBLC and to be alert for enemy helicopter activity, in view of the reports of North Vietnamese helicopter activity the night before.[32]

At 0309 on 17 June, *Hobart* detected an aircraft approaching from the vicinity of Cap Lay. Although evaluated as friendly it continued to close and at 0314 fired a missile that struck *Hobart* amidships, starboard side—killing Ordinary Seaman R. J. Butterworth and wounding two other crewmen. The warhead penetrated the main deck, damaging several compartments, while the body of the missile passed through the after funnel (stack) and into the forward funnel. As *Hobart*'s crew raced to their Action Stations, a second and a third missile hit the ship, fired by the same plane two minutes after the first.[33]

Although the second did not detonate, it breeched the transom, destroying the gunner's store and passed into the after seamen's mess decks. The third exploded in the same area where the first missile had hit with the expanding rod damaging the director equipment room, the Tartar checkout room, and the chief petty officer's mess killing Chief Electrician R. H. Hunt and injuring several other sailors who were closing up to their Action Stations.[34]

The aircraft then made a third pass. *Hobart* opened fire at 8,000 yards with her forward 5-inch gun mount in local control, firing five rounds that caused the plane to turn away before being lost on radar south of Tiger Island.[35]

As *Hobart*'s damage control parties assessed injury to the ship, the *Edson* reported she too had come under fire from air-launched missiles, suffering a narrow miss on her starboard quarter. Shands ordered the task unit to clear the area. The destroyers rendezvoused with the heavy cruiser USS *Boston* (which had been hit by a missile from another aircraft) and the destroyer USS *Blandy* before proceeding to Yankee Station. A helicopter from the USS *Enterprise* had evacuated *Hobart*'s two dead and three most seriously injured sailors to Da Nang, and she now departed for Subic Bay, to effect repairs. As her ship's company cleared away debris, they found and collected pieces of the missiles. *Hobart* arrived in Subic, on 19 June. Following repair of damage incurred, she returned to Vietnamese waters on 15 July, and resumed operations southeast of Da Nang.[36]

Commander, Seventh Fleet, Vice Adm. William F. Bringle, initiated an investigation of the attacks on *Hobart, Boston*, and *Edson*. Aided by missile debris that were definitely from U.S. air-to-air Sparrow missiles, the inquiry concluded that the ships had been mistakenly attacked by U.S. Air Force F-4 Phantoms. The inquiry also incorrectly concluded that Swift boat *PCF-19*, sunk shortly after midnight on 16 June, had also been hit by friendly fire from U.S. aircraft. The true cause of her loss, which prompted the actions by the USAF jets that damaged *Hobart* and *Boston*, apparently remained shrouded in secrecy for years.[37]

LOSS OF *PCF-19* TO ENEMY HELICOPTERS

I got a good look at one of the helos in the moonlight. It had a rounded front like an observation helo and it looked like two crewmen sitting side by side.... I could see the other helo. I watched as tracers began to come toward us as this helo opened fire. The guns were from the nose of the helo. Our guns opened up and I ran back to my position as the loader on the after gun. We heard a crash of glass and a splash as one of the helos hit the water, the other helo broke contact and left the area.

—Jim Steffes, ENC, USN (Retired), former crewman of *PCF-12*,
describing being attacked by what were believed to be North
Vietnamese Soviet-built MI-4 Hound helicopters.[38]

Throughout the spring of 1968, U.S. Marine Corps and other observers had reported hovering lights at night flying just north of the DMZ and out over water between North Vietnam and Tiger Island held by the enemy. Although the lights were presumed to be those of helicopters, daylight reconnaissance could find no trace of helicopters in the vicinity of the DMZ or on or near Tiger Island.[39]

The U.S. Coast Guard cutter *Point Dume* witnessed *PCF-19* being hit in early morning darkness on 16 June by two rockets from an unidentified source, and pulled two badly wounded survivors from the water. The skipper of *PCF-19*, Lt. (jg) John Davis, and two others topside had been propelled by the blast into the water. One of these men, Gunner's Mate Second John R. Anderegg, would later be awarded a Silver Star for saving Davis (who was blinded) and for trying to save Quarter Master Second Frank Bowman. Bowman apparently died in the water; his body was never found. *Point Dume* then proceeded to Cua Viet with the survivors. (She returned to the area several hours later, and also came under fire from an unidentified aircraft.)[40]

A second Swift boat, *PCF-12*, in responding to the attack on the *19* boat, reported being fired on by a helicopter—which was later identified as matching the characteristics of an MI-4 Hound, a Soviet helicopter fitted with machine guns and rocket pods. While searching for survivors, *PCF-12* was illuminated by four amber-colored illumination rounds directly overhead, making visible two aircraft hovering off her port and starboard beams. As the Swift boat turned to position the two helicopters off her bow and stern (minimizing her cross-section and thus her vulnerability, if attacked), one of the helicopters opened fire with machine gun tracer rounds.[41]

In the running gun battle that followed, *PCF-12* returned fire with her .50-cal. machine guns, and radioed that she was under attack by unidentified aircraft. Her gunners reported hitting one helicopter and hearing it splash in the water, at which point the other helicopter broke contact. *Point Dume* returned from Cua Viet, and *PCF-12* observed her firing tracer rounds at blinking lights in her vicinity.[42]

At daylight on 16 June, U.S. Navy divers from the ocean minesweeper USS *Acme* (MSO-508) began a survey on the wreck and recovered three bodies, two American and one South Vietnamese. Years later, in 2001, a third U.S. body was recovered on another dive. The five casualties were Bowman (still listed as an MIA), Boatswain's Mate Anthony Chandler, Engineman Second Edward Cruz, Gunner's Mate Third Billy Armstrong, and Bui Quang Thi (the South Vietnamese liaison). The sunken Swift boat had two entry holes in her forward berthing compartment and no exit holes—consistent with being hit by two rockets.[43]

The attacks on *Hobart* and the other ships were the capstone of a series of firing incidents between 15 and 17 June. F-4 Phantoms of the USAF Seventh Air Force, responding several hours after the attack on the Swift boats, were unable to distinguish between the radar signature of surface ships and airborne helicopters, and instead opened fire on *Hobart*, *Boston*, and *Edson*.[44]

AUSTRALIAN DESTROYERS' SERVICE IN VIETNAM

HMAS *Perth* would be awarded the U.S. Navy Unit Commendation for her first deployment, and the U.S. Navy Meritorious Unit Commendation for her second one. The service of HMAS *Brisbane* (D41), and HMAS *Vendetta* (D08)—the only *Daring*-class destroyer to go to war—will be taken up in a later chapter.[45]

HMAS *Hobart* (D39)

Dates of Service	Commanding Officer
7 Mar-27 Sep 1967	Capt. Guy Richmond Griffiths, DSO, DSC, RAN
22 Mar-11 Oct 1968	Capt. Kenneth William Shands, RAN
16 Mar-17 Oct 1970	Capt. Rothesay Cathcart Swan, RAN

HMAS *Perth* (D38)

Sep 1967-Apr 1968	Capt. Peter Hogarth Doyle, RAN
Sep 1968-Apr 1969	Capt. David Willoughby Leach, CBE, RAN
Sep 1970-Apr 1971	Capt. Ian Malcolm Burnside, RAN[46]

HMAS *Brisbane* (D41)

15 Apr-14 Sep 1969	Capt. Alan Antony Willis, RAN
5 Apr-5 Sep 1971	Capt. Robert Geoffrey Loosli, RAN

HMAS *Vendetta* (D08)

26 Sep 69-Mar 1970	Comdr. Eric Eugene Johnston, RAN[47]

10

Gunner's Mates, Fire Control Technicians and Gunfire Control

Light off, train out on the port beam and shift to automatic.

—This command, the standard verbal routine for conducting transmission checks in the dawning hours, marked the beginning of another day in the war zone for the gunner's mates and fire control technicians aboard the destroyer USS *Edson* (DD-946)[1]

Right, elevate, depress, MARK, MARK, MARK.

—Many tedious late hours were spent hearing those words during battery alignment aboard the *Edson*.[2]

Gunner's Mate
Petty Officer First
Class

Gunner's Mate was one of the original U.S. Navy ratings established in 1797. The others were: Quarter Gunner, Armorer, Yeoman of the Gunroom, Master's Mate, Midshipman, Cockswain, Boatswain's Mate, Ordinary Seaman, Seaman, Master-at-Arms, Sailmaker's Mate, Carpenter's Mate, Cooper, Cook, Steward, and Boy

The Fire Controlman rating was established in 1941, when it was split off from the Gunner's Mate rating[3]

Fire Control
Technician Petty
Officer First Class

On any given day off Vietnam, Second Division aboard the destroyer USS *Edson* (DD-946)—comprised of gunner's mates and fire control technicians—was a beehive of activity. The gunner's mates, occupied with pre-fire checks, bore erosion readings, magazine inspections, and overall maintenance and preservation of the ship's five guns, encompassed the larger portion of the division. The smaller portion of the division, the fire control technicians, occupied their working hours conducting computer checks, radar adjustments, and numerous daily tests necessary for proper positioning of the guns during firing. Working together, these two ratings ensured the destroyer's effective gunnery system.[4]

Photo 10-1

Gunner's Mate David W. Jutz greases the barrel chase of one of USS *Hull*'s (DD-945) after 5-inch/54 Mark 42-gun mounts, 1975.
Naval History and Heritage Command photograph USN 1166035

LINEAGE OF THE U.S NAVY'S GM AND FT RATINGS

Photo 10-2

USS *Constitution* berthed at the Boston Navy Yard, 28 August 1907.
Naval History and Heritage Command photograph #NH 55913

The Gunner's Mate rating was established in 1797, along with sixteen others, concurrent that same year, with launching of the 44-gun frigate USS *Constitution*. The United States Navy considers 13 October 1775, when the Second Continental Congress passed a resolution creating the Continental Navy, as the date of its official establishment. However, the Continental Navy was disbanded at the end of the American Revolutionary War. Two decades later, continued threats to American merchant shipping by Barbary pirates from four North African states led to the Naval Act of 1794, creating a permanent standing U.S. Navy.[5]

Following passage of the Act, work began on the construction of six frigates: *United States, President, Constellation, Chesapeake, Congress*, and *Constitution*. USS *Constitution*, the most famous, is still in existence. America's Ship of State and symbol of the country's fighting spirit is berthed in Boston Harbor. She earned her nickname "Old Ironsides" besting HMS *Guerriere* in a sea battle off Nova Scotia on 19 August 1812. In the course of the battle, an astonished British sailor observing 18-lb cannonballs bouncing harmlessly off the *Constitution*'s 25-inch oak hull, had cried out, "Huzzah! Her sides are made of iron!" The British were stunned by the loss of *Guerriere*, as observed by the *London Times*:

> It is not merely that an English frigate has been taken, after, what we are free to confess, may be called a brave resistance, but that it has been taken by a new enemy, an enemy unaccustomed to such triumphs, and likely to be rendered insolent and confident by them. …How important this triumph is in giving a tone and character to the war. Never before in the history of the world did an English frigate strike [surrender] to an American.[6]

From cannons to sophisticated weapons systems such as missiles and torpedoes, gunner's mates have long played an integral part in the success of the Navy. Weapons technology has changed much, but the nick name for the gunner's mate has held for centuries: "Guns."

The Fire Controlman (FC) rating was established in 1941, manned by sailors who had previously served in the gunner's mate (GM) rating. Before the advent of guided missiles and radar-controlled gunnery systems, fire controlmen directed the fire of ship's guns using range-finding equipment and performing ballistic calculations. These skills were most effectively employed when controlling fire support at land-based targets or during combat against surface vessels. Fire controlmen (FCs) were later redesignated Fire Control Technicians (FTs) due to the Navy's transitioning from guns to missiles for many of its ships' offensive and defensive weapons systems.

NAVAL GUNFIRE CONTROL

The accuracy of naval gunfire by ships on the gunline stemmed largely from a complex gunfire control system made up of a radar-equipped fire control director to locate and track targets and a fire control computer to compensate for variables. With the position of the ship and the relative position of the target known—the latter often provided by spotters—the fire control system aimed the ship's guns so that rounds were delivered on target.[7]

Photo 10-3

A seaman aboard the USS *Fechteler* (DD-870), positioned near a fire control director, wears sound-powered headphones, with binoculars at hand, to spot and report the fall of gun rounds fired by the destroyer.
USS *Fechteler* (DD-870) Southeast Asian 1967 cruise book

The first step in gunfire control was to accurately fix the firing ship's position, which could be done by taking visual bearings on geographical points or by taking ranges and bearings of the same points with the ship's navigational radar or fire control radar. Once the ship's position and target location had been plotted on a chart, the range and bearing from the ship to the target was determined.[8]

With the initial range and bearing from the ship to the target fed into the fire control computer, the computer compensated for the ship's course, speed, pitch, and roll, and for other variables such as the target's course and speed (if any), wind speed and direction, air temperature, and the initial velocity of the projectiles being fired. The computer's solution automatically aimed and elevated the gun barrels.[9]

U.S. Navy ships were capable of placing their first rounds within a few hundred feet of their target. Whenever possible, Navy, Air Force, or Army aircraft or ground spotters assisted the firing ship by spotting or locating the fall of shot in relation to the target. With spotters passing corrections to the firing ship, projectiles could literally be "talked" or "walked" to the center of a target in a matter of minutes.[10]

MOUNT DUTY ON THE GUNLINE

While ships' fire control computers could provide firing solutions, operation of naval guns was not automatic. Putting "lead on target" required actions by gunner's mates and other sailors assigned to the mount crews. In his book, *Navy Daze: Coming of Age in the 1960s Aboard a Navy Destroyer*, Michael R. Halldorson—a former crewman aboard the *Hopewell* (DD-681)—described such duties after returning to the gunline following a port visit to Yokosuka:

> It was hot and muggy and time spent inside gun mounts—where there was little air movement—was particularly toilsome. Hour after hour was spent at General Quarters either firing or waiting for the order to "commence fire" again. We were in battle dress—shirt collar turned up with top button buttoned, and pant legs tucked into socks—preventing our dungarees from breathing. Unlike during most shipboard activities, there was little idle chat and jokes; for the most part guys just endured the conditions. Then would come the firing order, and we would all come alert and resume our jobs: I trained the gun to the correct bearing as indicated by the main battery director; the pointer elevated or depressed the barrel; the powder man placed the powder in the tray; and the projectile man released the projectile from the hoist clamps, placed it in the tray ahead of the powder, then inserted the projectile and powder into the gun. We were then ready to fire.[11]

Halldorson emphasized that while he and shipmates knew little about the fire missions or their results, they were thoroughly aware of the sacrifices made by the ground troops they supported ashore:

> We were a finely-honed crew and we could perform this operation in a matter of seconds. We had reason to be proud. But, we had little knowledge of our overall mission. We were not told details about a particular target, such as where or what it was. We did not know the effectiveness of our fire, or results of any battle damage assessment. Our reality was the smell of gunpowder, the noise and violent shaking of the gunmount, and the acrid air inside the mount. Occasionally the executive officer would publish the results of our shore bombardment in the Plan of the Day. We did know that we were supporting our guys inland and that our job was necessary and much needed to save American lives. Thoughts of what our troops were going through inland were very sobering. We suffered mind-numbing hours on station, accompanied by thirst and hunger, but such inconveniences were nothing compared to the combat ashore.[12]

Du Pont and *Mansfield* Hit by
Enemy Fire with Men Killed

Our assignment in the U.S. Seventh Fleet to provide gunfire support for the THIRD Marine Division and the 12TH Marine Regiment at the DMZ was a challenging and rewarding experience. Challenging because of the long hours of firing day and night, and the constant threat of our being fired upon by North Vietnamese guns. Rewarding because we knew that our gunfire was helping the U.S. Marines and allied forces ashore.

As we look back in the years to come, I know that each of us will remember the continual team effort, the many records set and the jobs well done. Much of the drudgery, monotony, rough weather and the hard work that was necessary to fire more than 20,000 rounds of ammunition will be forgotten. What I am sure will remain with us is pride in the fact that we in DU PONT *were privileged to defend our way of life, support our nation's policies, and help another country in its struggle against oppression.*

—Excerpt from a memorandum by Comdr. Robert H. Small, USN,
to his crew, summarizing the performance of the destroyer USS
Du Pont, while operating with the Seventh Fleet off Vietnam.[1]

On 20 June 1967, the destroyer *Du Pont* (DD-941) stood out of Norfolk, Virginia, in company with the destroyers *New* (DD-818) and *Eaton* (DD-510), and guided missile destroyer *William V. Pratt* (DLG-13), bound for Southeast Asia. Commander, Destroyer Squadron 22 was embarked aboard the *Du Pont*. Upon arrival in the Western Pacific, and after a short period at Subic Bay, Capt. Ernest S. Cornwall Jr., USN, assumed his combat role as the commander of all the gunfire support ships in the South Vietnam area, designated Task Unit 70.8.9.[2]

The Seventh Fleet's gunfire support ships operating off South Vietnam collectively formed the Cruiser-Destroyer Group (Task Group 70.8). The subordinate Naval Gunfire Support Unit (Task Unit 70.8.9), in coordination with the U.S. Military Assistance Command, Vietnam, directed operations along the coast. Ships were assigned to the gunfire support unit from the cruiser-destroyer group and from the Royal Australian Navy, but some were also temporarily attached from carrier escort units, from the Sea Dragon force off North Vietnam, and from the amphibious force.[3]

Typically, one cruiser, four destroyers, one inshore fire support ship, and two medium rocket landing ships formed Task Unit 70.8.9. However, the number varied and dramatically increased in the first half of 1968, when the enemy's Tet Offensive engaged the naval gunfire support unit in its heaviest combat actions of the war. Drawing on resources from all areas and commands, but especially from Operation Sea Dragon, commander, Task Unit 70.8.9 concentrated during this period as many as twenty-two ships at one time on the gunline.[4]

During the period 7 August-1 December 1967, Cornwall and his staff aboard the *Du Pont* coordinated the actions of a then much smaller group of ships assigned to Task Unit 70.8.9, in providing support to allied forces ashore. Naval gunfire, in conjunction with aircraft strikes, was essential to knocking out the many enemy artillery batteries firing into South Vietnam from positions in the northern half of the DMZ and southern North Vietnam, and menacing allied ships and craft offshore. On 14 December, following the handoff of these duties to the next destroyer squadron or destroyer division commander thus assigned, Cornwall began the long return voyage to Norfolk with the Atlantic Fleet destroyers.[5]

DU PONT HIT COMING TO THE AID OF *ROBISON*

Photo 11-1

Destroyer USS *Du Pont* (DD-941) shelling enemy positions with her three 5-inch gun mounts while on the gunline in August 1967.
USS *Du Pont* 1967-1968 cruise book

Destroyer *Du Pont*'s duty on the gunline began in August in support of U.S. Marines fighting at the Demilitarized Zone. Under constant threat from Communist shore batteries, her gunners shelled enemy positions day and night. On 28 August, the enemy fired on the destroyer *Robison* (DDG-12), operating between *Du Pont* and the beach. As *Robison* maneuvered to seaward, *Du Pont* commenced counterbattery fire, immediately replacing the other destroyer as a target for some twenty 130mm rounds. One hit the barrel of Mount 52 (the forwardmost of her after gun mounts), exploded and sent shrapnel down into the mount and through it into the after deckhouse, killing Fireman Frank L. Ballant and wounding eight others. In addition to the mount being knocked out of commission, her deckhouse was essentially destroyed as well.[6]

Photo 11-2

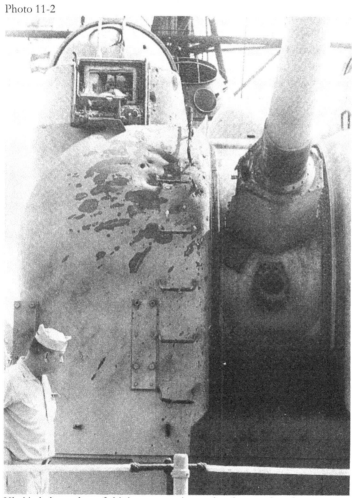

Khaki-clad member of ship's company inspecting damage done by enemy shore battery fire to Mt 52 aboard the destroyer USS *Du Pont* (DD-941). USS *Du Pont* 1967-1968 cruise book

Despite the casualties to crew and ship, *Du Pont* remained on station, supporting the Marines for another two weeks before heading for Subic Bay and repair of enemy-inflicted damage. She returned to the gunline on 10 October 1967. On 10 November, the eight men wounded on 28 August, listed below, received Purple Heart medals. At the end of seventy-five days in combat, *Du Pont*'s 5-inch guns had fired 20,000 rounds. Returning to Norfolk in January 1968, she went into drydock for remaining needed work.[7]

UNIT AND PERSONAL AWARDS

In addition to the eight Purple Hearts awarded to the men who had been wounded, Captain Cornwall, Commander Small, and Lt. Commander Young were awarded Bronze Star Medals for heroism. *Du Pont* received the Meritorious Unit Commendation, resulting in the associated pennant flying from the ship's mast, and every crewmember adding the MUC ribbon to others proudly worn on their uniform blouses.[8]

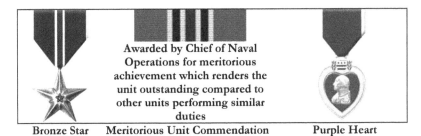

Awarded by Chief of Naval Operations for meritorious achievement which renders the unit outstanding compared to other units performing similar duties

Bronze Star   Meritorious Unit Commendation   Purple Heart

Bronze Star Recipients

Capt. Ernest S. Cornwall, USN	Commander, Destroyer Squadron 22
Comdr. Robert H. Small, USN	Commanding Officer, USS *Du Pont*
Lt. Comdr. James M. Young, USN	Operations Officer, USS *Du Pont*

Purple Heart Recipients

BM3 James P. Abrashiewsky	YN3 John R. Layne
RD3 James M. Doll	SN Wayne G. Miller
GMG2 Joseph A. Griffin Jr.	SN Russel P. Radar
SN Glen A. Hester	MM2 James C. Young

MANSFIELD HIT WITH CREWMEMBER KILLED

> Mansfield *was a good but tired ship. I remember all the problems with the Mark 1A fire control computer, the fluorescent light fixture mounts that would break when we fired all six guns, the gyro that used to periodically tumble, and how the water wash down system became so battered from the shock that we finally took it down. I also remember shooting gun barrels at over 100 percent wear until we finally figured out that it was causing all the premature bursts just beyond the end of the gun barrel.*

—Capt. Robert Kesteloot, USN (Ret.), who served as the executive officer aboard the destroyer USS *Mansfield* (DD-728) from May 1967 through October 1968.[9]

On 25 September 1967, while engaged in Sea Dragon operations off Dong Hoi, the *Mansfield* was hit by an 85mm round fired by a North Vietnamese coastal installation—killing Machinist's Mate Second Richard Archer, and wounding four other crewmembers, two seriously. The destroyer had just completed an initial run south at 25 knots with "guns free" (permission to fire) and were not fired upon. As *Mansfield* neared Point Bravo at the end of the firing run, the division commander signaled, 'Turn 18,' meaning, turn 180 degrees to starboard. The ship was about 14,000 yards offshore, and this maneuver brought her closer to shore on a reciprocal course.[10]

Decades later, *Mansfield*'s former executive officer and retired Navy captain, Robert Kesteloot, recalled that the officer in tactical command had just arrived in Vietnam, and was apparently unaware of conventions arrived at by hard-learned lessons. Moreover, it appeared that the situation was made worse by the enemy having monitored the destroyer on her first run, and thus roughly knew her course, speed, and range, when she retraced her path along the same track. He explained:

> First, we NEVER made turns towards the shore. A steering casualty could land you in the Hanoi Hilton [result in capture and becoming a prisoner of war]. Second, we NEVER retraced our original track. They had obviously been tracking us on the first run.[11]

When the round hit the ship, Machinist's Mate Second Richard Archer was standing in the open doorway to the wardroom looking aft down the passageway. A piece of shrapnel, struck him in the sternum and he died almost immediately, despite the doctor's best efforts. With wounded and dead, *Mansfield* proceeded to her homeport at Yokosuka for repairs, and then returned to Dong Hoi. Kesteloot later described destroying the gun emplacement, as subsequently verified by a BDA (bomb damage assessment) flight:

> Since I had previously been on the 7th Fleet staff, I went over to the schedulers and told them that we (the CO and I) wanted to return immediately to Sea Dragon and Dong Hoi. They obliged and, as I recall, that was our first target when we got back. We waited for the cover of friendly monsoon clouds and went in much closer than ever before and totally destroyed the gun site.[12]

PERSONAL AWARDS

In addition to the five Purple Hearts awarded to men killed or wounded aboard *Mansfield*, Commander Griffin was awarded the Bronze Star Medal for heroism.[13]

Bronze Star Recipients	
Comdr. Jack R. Griffin, USN	Commanding Officer, USS *Mansfield*

Purple Heart Recipients	
MM2 Richard C. Archer (KIA)	FN Thomas Fitzgerald
BT1 John W. Armstrong	BT2 Hildreth
BT2 Carper	

Although having suffered dead and wounded aboard the *Du Pont* and *Mansfield*, naval forces returned the enemy fire many-fold. By November, with six or seven destroyers continuously deployed offshore in I-Corps, enemy coastal gun emplacements and field artillery positions often were blanketed with gunfire. In fact, surface ships fired 500,000 rounds in 1967, approximately twice as many as the previous year, with the great majority of them falling on I-Corps targets.[14]

Carronade on the Gunline

We deployed most of the time in the coastal waters around the southern part of South Vietnam. We operated as a mobile artillery platform for units engaged south from Cam Ranh Bay to the Mekong Delta and around towards Cambodia. The ship was about half the size of a destroyer but had the firepower of 5 destroyers. With 8 rapid-fire rocket launchers we could put out a devastating rocket barrage with hundreds of rockets obliterating the equivalent of many city blocks.

—Capt. Ken Willcox, SC, USN (Retired), recounting his duty as the supply officer aboard the inshore fire support ship USS *Carronade* (LFR-1) in the late 1960s.[1]

Some readers may be disappointed that, while the name of the ship they served aboard in Vietnam may be found in a table in the book, there are scant or no details about its duties. Others may have served on the gunline aboard a vessel other than a battleship, cruiser, or destroyer, and wonder why its contributions are not recognized. While the scope of the book does not permit coverage of large numbers of the former, it does allow a brief glimpse into one very unique vessel amongst the latter, the inshore fire support ship USS *Carronade* (IFS-1/LFR-1).

Carronade was a one-of-a-kind ship designed and developed to fire rockets at close inshore targets. The idea for constructing a special rocket-launching ship originated during the closing of World War II. The 245-foot ship was commissioned at Puget Sound Bridge and Dredging Company, Seattle, Washington, on 25 May 1955 with Lt. Comdr. Daniel O'Connell Doran in command.[2]

Armed with one single 5-inch/38 dual-purpose gun mount, eight rocket launchers, and two 40mm AA gun mounts, *Carronade* was a vast improvement over the old LSMR (Medium Landing Ship, Rocket)— which had been employed during World War II to give close-in fire support to the troops ashore. Propelled by diesel engines, the small, sleek 1,500-ton vessel designed along cruiser lines could make a modest 15 knots, had a 10-foot draft—enabling her to operate in relatively shallow waters—and a ship's complement of 10 officers and 132 men.[3]

Photo 12-1

Inshore fire support ship USS *Carronade* (IFS-1) operating offshore, south of Da Nang, Vietnam, ready to provide fire support to U.S. Marines, 11 November 1967. National Archives photograph #USN 1127944

Carronade's eight dual launchers could fire her five-inch rockets at tremendous speed, which gave her fire power almost equivalent to that of a cruiser. A computer-aided fire control system made possible a shotgun barrage of rocket fire. When ready for a fire mission, her cleared decks presented a deceiving picture of serenity. In the decks below, handlers in the magazines loaded rockets into a hoist, and they were lifted into position in their launchers, ready for firing.

Simultaneously, the fire control computer was processing information such as speed, course, and roll of the ship, and distance and direction of the target. Seconds later, flaming rockets would roar upward, arch, and dive, with almost human-like control, exploding on the target.[4]

Photo 12-2

Members of USS *Carronade*'s Ordnance Division. Left to Right – Top Row: Ens. J. R. Salenjus, GMC Dry, GM1 Carey, Coupland, Harper, Deshotel, Hawk, Stevens, Wilson, Huguenin, Goff, FT1 Langer, Bowen, Szemly, Laub, FT1 Rose, Beal, Lt. (jg) M. R. Harvey. Front Row: Jentsch, Militello, Reeves, Tucker, Reed, Shinaberry, Corbett, Snell. USS *Carronade* 1959-1960 cruise book

Carronade made Western Pacific deployments in 1958 and 1959-1960, during which she participated in tests and exercises in the Pacific to demonstrate her effectiveness in operating with amphibious forces and conducting inshore fire. With the nation at peace, she was then decommissioned in February 1960 and laid up in the Pacific Reserve Fleet, San Diego Group. *Carronade* was recommissioned in October 1965 for service in the Vietnam War, as flagship of Inshore Fire Support Division 93 (IFDIV 93). She was redesignated LFR-1 in January 1969, and continued her Vietnam service until January 1970.[5]

During her war service, *Carronade* participated in numerous Vietnamese Counteroffensives and the Tet Counteroffensive in 1968. She was decommissioned in July 1970, struck from the Naval Register in May 1973, and finally sold for scrapping in September 1994. Her relatively short service resulted from a lack of repair parts support and, perhaps, because the Navy no longer needed her unique capabilities. Capt. Ken Willcox, SC, USN (Retired), her supply officer in the late 1960s, explained some of the challenges the crew of the inshore fire support ship faced in operating and carrying out combat missions:

> CARRONADE was the only ship of its kind in the Navy. So, repair could become a problem. When the rocket launchers needed repair, they had to be lifted out of the ship and air freighted back to the U.S. Most of our repairs were done at the Ship's Repair Facility (SRF) in Subic Bay, Philippines. We would go there every 6 weeks or so for refit and repairs.[6]

Willcox also described problems with the reliability of rockets, and the crew having to forsake showers and the use of air conditioning to support the rocket launchers. The wartime complement of the ship was then 180 sailors and 10 officers. During his service aboard her, *Carronade* was engaged most days in missions and at night, if there was not an operation ashore under way, she conducted harassment and interdiction fire at suspected Viet Cong areas of activity.

> The rockets were allegedly left over from World War II. They were not wholly reliable. Some would launch and splash down in the water. Others were duds that would not exit the launch tubes. The first time I saw one of the gunner's mates pounding on the nose of a rocket stuck in the launcher with a 2 x 4, I almost ducked for cover.

> The ship needed fresh water to cool the rocket launchers. But the ship could make only so much water. So, we had to take salt water showers…. Water was turned on in the sinks in the morning for 5 minutes so people could brush their teeth. We used paper plates and plastic forks/knives since we didn't have enough water to wash normal plates. We used our rocket reloading evolutions in Cam Ranh Bay to get showers and clean up. The ship was air conditioned, but the power had to be used for the rocket launchers, so the air conditioning was often turned off. There were many nights that were so hot that we slept on the deck.[7]

The rockets were 5-inch, spin stabilized, and of two types. One type had a range of one mile; the other, 5 miles. With eight rapid-fire rocket launchers, *Carronade* could put out a devastating rocket barrage. Her magazine carried 20,000 rockets. These were expended in about ten days, and the ship would then return to Cam Ranh Bay to reload. Each rocket, weighting about 75 pounds, was passed hand-to-hand by crewmembers down to the magazine.[8]

In addition to the challenges imposed by vintage rockets and the associated rocket launchers, *Carronade*'s propulsion system was also quirky. It relied on variable-pitch propellers to go ahead or astern vice stopping and reversing the direction of the shaft. But the ordered speed from the bridge did not always translate accurately to the screws, as Willcox described:

> "Ahead two-thirds" could find the ship going ahead one-third. Steering would occasionally fail as well. Most of the time in Vietnam we were cruising slowly at about 3 knots along a designated coastal stretch awaiting a call to fire from the Marine spotter planes, or Marines on the ground.[9]

CARRONADE GARNERS NUMEROUS UNIT AWARDS

Carronade's crew overcame the many challenges associated with service aboard a one-of-a-kind vessel, and faithfully carried out her inshore fire support mission. In the process, the ship earned numerous unit and service awards. Subsequent awards of a particular medal or ribbon were denoted by service stars affixed to it. A "V" device, when worn on certain decorations, distinguished an award for heroism or valor in combat instead of for meritorious service or achievement.

- Three Combat Action Ribbons (23 April 1966, 18 March 1968, 9 June 1968)
- Two Navy Unit Commendations
- Navy Meritorious Unit Commendation
- National Defense Service Medal
- Ten Vietnam Service Medals
- Thirteen Republic of Vietnam Gallantry Cross Unit Citations
- Republic of Vietnam Civil Actions Unit Citation
- Republic of Vietnam Campaign Medal[10]

OTHER INSHORE FIRE SUPPORT SHIPS IN VIETNAM

Photo 12-3

USS *St. Francis River* (LFR-525) en route to U.S. Naval Support Facility, Cam Ranh Bay, Republic of Vietnam, to load ammunition, July 1969.
National Archives photograph #USN 1140633

USS *Carronade* was the flagship of Inshore Fire Support Division 93, comprised of three former World War II vintage LSMRs (Medium Landing Ship, Rocket). These ships were decommissioned after World War II, laid up in reserve fleets, and brought out of "mothballs" for the Korean and Vietnam Wars. Redesignated inshore fire support ships (LFR) in 1969, they were placed out of service the following year, and sold for scrap. A summary of their naval service, and dates associated with combat action ribbons earned in the Vietnam War follow:

Ship	Comm./Decom.	Disposition
USS *Clarion River* (LFR-409)	16 May 45/6 Feb 47 5 Oct 50/26 Oct 55 18 Sep 65/8 May 70	Sold for scrapping in Nov 1970, to Nissho-Iwai American Corp., Sasebo, Japan
USS *St. Francis River* (LFR-525)	14 Aug 45/28 Mar 46 16 Sep 50/21 Nov 55 18 Sep 65/17 Apr 70	Sold for scrapping in November 1970, to Nissho-Iwai American Corp., Sasebo, Japan
USS *White River* (LFR-536)	28 Nov 45/31 Jul 46 16 Sep 50/7 Sep 56 2 Oct 65/22 May 70	Sold in November 1970 to Nissho-Iwai American Corp., New York, for scrapping[11]

Combat Actions Ribbons

USS *Clarion River* (LFR-409)	15-17 June 1967, 12 August 1968
USS *St. Francis River* (LFR-525)	5-6 January 1967, 30 October 1968
USS *White River* (LFR-536)	3 November 1967, 5 May 1969[12]

13

Battle of Khe Sanh

We always felt betrayed that so many guys died and then they just left it.

—Marine Cpl. Steve Wiese, surviving member of one of two squads
from 3rd platoon that was decimated while on patrol a short
distance from the base at Khe Sanh on 25 February 1968.
Bravo Company, 1st Battalion, 26th Marine Regiment,
would suffer that day 27 killed, one taken prisoner
and 19 wounded—only eight of the wounded,
including Wiese, were fit to return to duty.[1]

On 21 January 1968, a force of well over 20,000 North Vietnamese
Army (NVA) troops laid siege to a U.S. Marine combat base sited near
the village of Khe Sanh, in the far northwest corner of South Vietnam.
During the ensuing bloody battle of Khe Sanh (21 January-9 July), the
6,000 Marine defenders endured near-constant rocket and artillery
attacks, sometimes over 1,000 rounds per day, with a one-day peak of
1,307 on 23 February. Although the NVA never attempted an all-out
assault, smaller-scale ground attacks and infiltration attempts were
frequent. The only way to resupply the isolated base, located about
fifteen miles south of the DMZ, and seven miles from the Laotian
border, was by air-drop or high-risk landings by C-130 cargo planes and
helicopters at the airfield.[2]

Green Berets had erected the base in 1962, atop a plateau in the
shadow of Dong Tri mountain, overlooking a tributary of the Quang
Tri River. Surrounding it were piedmont hills, uninhabited jungle with
impenetrable undergrowth, mountain trails hidden from aircraft by tree
canopies high above the floor, tall elephant grass, and bamboo thickets.
As such, it was a natural infiltration route into South Vietnam and the
densely populated cities on the eastern coast of Quang Tri Province.[3]

Gen. William C. Westmoreland, USA (commander, U.S. Military
Assistance Command, Vietnam) considered Khe Sanh strategically
important. He also believed that drawing the NVA into a set-piece
battle in an isolated area, where the risk of civilian and collateral damage

was minimal, would enable the full application of U.S. power to pin down and destroy a mostly elusive enemy. The press, and some high-ranking U.S. military officers, drew comparisons between Khe Sanh and the 1954 siege of Dien Bien Phu in northwestern Vietnam, which ended badly for France. There, the Viet Minh surrounded and forced the surrender of a major French force. The shocking defeat resulted in Vietnam gaining its independence from France, and being split in two, creating North and South Vietnam.[4]

President Johnson decided that Khe Sanh must not be allowed to fall. So, the Marines were forced to defend an otherwise insignificant piece of ground against an enemy whose rockets outranged the Marines' artillery. Senior U.S. Marine commanders in Vietnam had, to no avail, pointed out that the NVA could easily bypass Khe Sanh if they chose, and questioned the wisdom of holding the base. Against overwhelming NVA ground forces, air power was the only viable means of defense. As a result, U.S. Air Force, Marine, and Navy aircraft dropped more bombs around Khe Sanh, over the next several months, than had been used in the entire Korean War.[5]

NAVY'S ROLE IN THE DEFENSE OF KHE SANH

The Navy made two significant contributions to the defense of the combat base. Use of carrier aircraft to conduct strikes, and dropping of acoustic/seismic sensors by Lockheed OP-2E "Neptune" aircraft of Special Observation Squadron 67 (VO-67). We will take up the much lesser known of these two activities first.

In November 1967, twelve old P2V-5F anti-submarine patrol planes arrived at the Nakhon Phanom Air Commando base in Thailand. Considerably modified into armed, jungle green gunships and designated OP-2E aircraft, they flew armed ground attack/reconnaissance and delivery of seismic and acoustic intrusion detectors to seed suspected communist infiltration routes.[6]

The detectors (which were based on sonobuoy technology, a listening device used to find enemy submarines) could identify troop and vehicle movement on the ground. Marine defenders at Khe Sanh credited the sensors for providing forty percent of the actionable intelligence, enabling artillery fire and air strikes against NVA movements around Khe Sanh.[7]

Special Observation Squadron 67 was disestablished on 1 July 1968. Its last combat mission implanting sensors was on 25 June 1968. During its existence, VO-67 lost one-quarter of its aircraft in combat and twenty crewmen, less than half of what the planners had envisioned.[8]

NAVAL AND MARINE CORPS AIR STRIKES

Photo 13-1

Marines watch from atop their bunkers at Khe Sanh as aircraft from the carrier USS *Enterprise* pummel the enemy just outside the base perimeter. USS *Enterprise* (CVN-65) Western Pacific 1968 cruise book

At the time of the NVA attack on Khe Sanh, aircraft launching from carriers on "Yankee Station" in the Gulf of Tonkin were flying daily strikes—weather permitting—on targets in North Vietnam as part of Operation ROLLING THUNDER, ongoing since 1965. Normally, three carriers were assigned to this mission: two on Yankee Station in the Tonkin Gulf, with a third undergoing replenishment and R&R, usually at Subic Bay in the Philippines. During the siege of Khe Sanh, and the Tet Offensive, begun on 30 January 1968, sometimes four and even five carriers operated from Yankee Station, including the *Ticonderoga, Ranger, Kitty Hawk, Coral Sea,* and later *Enterprise.* Requirements for additional cruisers and destroyers—on the gunline off South Vietnam, in association with the Tet Offensive, and to escort and provide plane guard duties for the added carriers—drew ships away from SEA DRAGON operations off North Vietnam.[9]

Enterprise joined Task Force 77, the aircraft carrier force operating in support of Rolling Thunder, after concluding tasking in response to the seizure of the intelligence collection ship USS *Pueblo* (AGER-2) by North Korea. *Ticonderoga* and *Ranger* were also drawn off Yankee Station briefly in reaction to capture of the lightly armed *Pueblo* by North Korean gunboats on 23 January 1968. At the time, she was operating in International waters, sixteen miles off the North Korean coast. This incident is taken up in the next chapter.[10]

SEIGE BROKEN, KHE SANH ABANDONED

In the end, the Marines at Khe Sanh held, at a cost of 274 killed. The U.S. Army also suffered casualties during Operation PEGASUS, a joint U.S. and South Vietnamese effort by 30,000 soldiers led by the 1st Air Cavalry Division to break the siege of Khe Sanh. While an armored column rumbled along a slender highway toward the combat base, helicopters lifted men and artillery into the hills above the remote plateau where 6,000 U.S. Marines had been cut off since January. The relief force found the surrounding area devastated by 110,000 tons of U.S. bombs, but they saw little of the two North Vietnamese divisions that had been besieging Khe Sanh.[11]

With the arrival of U.S. Army reinforcements in April 1968, the NVA temporarily withdrew, and the U.S. claimed victory. In July, the last Marines withdrew from Khe Sanh, destroying all the facilities, then the North Vietnamese claimed victory.[12]

Capture of the *Pueblo*

The last conversations we got over the radio were that help was on the way, and it obviously wasn't. I could not believe that we would be abandoned out there the way we were.

—Retired Marine staff sergeant Robert J. Chicca commenting on the failure of the U.S. government/Navy to come to the aid of, or mount a rescue operation following the capture of minimally armed USS *Pueblo* in international waters by overwhelming North Korean military forces.[1]

Photo 14-1

Brutal Ambush off Wonsan by Richard DeRosset depicts the savage attack on the USS *Pueblo* (AGER-2) by an overwhelming force of North Korean torpedo boats, MiG-21 fighter aircraft, and sub-chasers at 1343 on 23 January 1968. This action preceded the capture of the minimally-armed intelligence gathering ship in international waters northeast of Wonsan, off the North Korean coast. The accurate and dramatic painting was commissioned by Tom Massie, one of the eighty-two crewmembers that survived the attack and were held as prisoners of war by North Korea for eleven months.

In mid-afternoon on 23 January 1968, Comdr. Lloyd M. "Pete" Bucher, commanding officer of the intelligence-collection ship USS *Pueblo*, faced a no-win situation. Operating in international waters to the northeast of Wonsan, hundreds of miles from any possible help, his ship was surrounded by four North Korean *P-4* class motor torpedo boats, two modified *SO-1* class submarine chasers, and two MiG-21 fighters overhead, which had fired rockets into the sea nearby as an act of intimidation.[2]

Photo 14-2

Soviet *SO-1* class submarine chaser of the type used by North Korea to seize the USS *Pueblo* off North Korea on 22 January 1968.
National Archives photograph #USN 711530

Over the past two hours, Bucher had maneuvered, and ignored North Korean signals to heave to and other instructions, in an attempt to avoid being boarded, as more and more North Korean vessels arrived on the scene. He had thwarted the first boarding attempt while trying to clear the area, with no hope of outrunning the much faster North Korean units. From point-blank range, the North Koreans had fired bursts of 57mm gunfire, and well over a thousand rounds of machine-gun fire into *Pueblo*, destroying her radar and radio masts, and causing other damage. Fireman Duane Hodges was killed in action, and nine other members of *Pueblo*'s 83-man crew were wounded, including Bucher (leg injury). As a motor torpedo boat came alongside with a 10-man armed boarding party, Bucher was pretty much out of options.[3]

Pueblo was not a Navy warship, nor even a well-armed naval auxiliary. She was a small, "clapped out" former World War II Army cargo ship, hastily converted to serve as an intelligence collection ship, and armed with two .50-caliber machine guns. The prevailing view then in the U.S. Navy was that using combatant ships for intelligence-collection missions was a "waste." The Navy's destroyers and destroyer escorts were stretched thin serving on the gunline in Vietnam and fulfilling commitments in other areas of the world.[4]

Photo 14-3

Unnamed U.S. Army cargo vessel *FP-344* at the Kewaunee Shipbuilding &
Engineering Corp. shipyard, Kewaunee, Wisconsin, circa July 1944. She was
subsequently redesignated freight supply ship *FS-344*. Transferred to the Navy
in 1966, she became the USS *Pueblo* (AGER-2).
Naval History and Heritage Command photograph #NH 74690

Moreover, larger intelligence-collection ships (AGTRs) such as
USS *Liberty* (AGTR-5), were seen as being focused mainly on national-
level, rather than naval intelligence requirements. The result was a
hastily conceived plan to rapidly convert small, ex World War II Army
freight supply ships into intelligence-collection ships—and do it on the
cheap. As a result, *Pueblo* had a long list of material deficiencies, most of
which Bucher had tried to get corrected before her first mission, with
necessary repairs denied due to lack of funding.[5]

As the events unfolding would prove, of more significance than
problems associated with her age and poor material condition (including
unreliable engines that frequently broke down) were ill-conceived or
insufficient alterations and improvements made to prepare her for her
new mission. These shortcomings were further exacerbated by a lack
of foresight by Navy planners regarding the dangers she might face, and
problems associated with Bucher not having access to her intelligence
space, or knowing that large quantities of sensitive, classified materials
were contained within it.[6]

Pueblo's two .50-caliber machine guns were mounted in exposed, weather deck positions, one forward and one amidships, protected from the elements by canvas tarps. The covers were iced over, which would have required about ten minutes to chip away the ice, remove the tarps, and get the weapons loaded and operational. Any sailor attempting to do so would have been cut down by North Korean gunfire long before the weapons could be employed effectively. If unable to fight or flee, Bucher's next option was to scuttle the ship. However, no effective means to do so existed aboard *Pueblo*, and the shallow waters in which she was operating just outside North Korean territorial waters would allow easy salvage by the Communists.[7]

Photo 14-4

USS *Pueblo* (AGER-2) off San Diego, California, 19 October 1967. Naval History and Heritage Command photograph #USN 1129208

One of the most significant deficiencies of *Pueblo*—other than her paltry armament and lack of scuttling charges—was that she had no effective means to safely carry out rapid emergency destruction of classified material and equipment. Bucher had used ship's MWR (morale, welfare, and recreation) funds to buy and install an incinerator because the Navy would not pay for one. However, the incinerator was exposed to enemy fire and, in any case, could not rapidly consume bulk paper publications. Burning these materials in passageways and in the small unventilated "research" space, was tried, but proved untenable, as Robert J. Chicca, one of two Marines aboard *Pueblo*, later explained:

Burning in the passageway worked fine. I started it and for a while was fine, but then we found that we were burning up the oxygen and the paint off the bulkheads, and we started passing out in the passageway. I decided to move the fires to the fantail of the ship and use its hatch as cover for the Korean fire since it opened outward.... We stayed inside and had the fires outside. Worked fine until they started firing the larger rounds right through the side of the ship. Those rounds were what wounded many of us and killed Hodges.[8]

The use of sledgehammers and axes on the intelligence-collection equipment worked somewhat better, but not much. The ship had a surplus of classified publications on board, of which Bucher was unaware. The relationship between the ship CO and the OIC of the research detachment embarked aboard *Pueblo* had not been resolved before the mission. As a result of this ambiguity, Bucher did not have authority to enter the "research space" because he was deemed not to have a "need-to-know."[9]

Bucher ordered emergency destruction when the North Koreans opened fire, and received assurance that it was going well, but actually had no idea of how much classified material had yet to be destroyed when boarded. The result would be an intelligence collection bonanza for the North Koreans, and their overlords, the Russians and the Chinese. When the torpedo boat came alongside (with *Pueblo* under the guns of the other vessels, and with MiGs overhead), Bucher gave the order to accept a mooring line passed across. Bucher and some of the crew were prodded with bayonets, pistol-whipped, and beaten with rifle butts during the boarding. The beatings continued all the way into port, during the wait for a train, and on the train. Bucher did not technically surrender the *Pueblo*, nor did he strike her colors—the North Koreans hauled down the American flag at her mast top.[10]

No Navy ships were near at hand to provide assistance, nor were there aircraft anywhere on strip alert. The Air Force had offered to be at this condition prior to *Pueblo* getting under way, but the Navy had declined, since the mission was "routine." The reality was that no one in the U.S. chain of command had believed that *Pueblo* would actually have to defend herself, on this mission or any other, and had made no provisions to provide protection for her. The crew had been told that there were contingency plans in case something happened, but there were no such plans.[11]

ELEVEN MONTHS OF IMPRISONMENT, TORTURE

The *Pueblo* was taken to Wonsan Harbor, and her crew moved by train to Pyongyang and imprisoned in a building referred to by the men as "the barn." The commanding officer was isolated from the others, who were quartered three or four to a room. Members of the crew were interrogated, threatened with death, and many were severely beaten. "Confessions" to "criminal aggressive acts" were obtained from all as a result of these threats and ill-treatment. Propaganda photographs often showed smiling faces in association with obscene gestures, sailors extending their middle fingers to convey their true feelings about their captors, who did not then know the meaning of the hand gestures.[12]

After some forty days or more, the crew was transferred to other accommodations near military installations. The officers had individual rooms, the men were generally housed eight to a room. The food provided was deficient both in quality and quantity. Physical maltreatment continued throughout captivity, with the first and last period particularly brutal. The first was during the first three weeks of captivity, until all had "confessed." A final period of beatings occurred immediately prior to the release of the Americans, as part of a purge (effort) to identify those crewmembers who had earlier attempted to communicate their lack of sincerity to the western world.[13]

For some members of *Pueblo*'s crew, the physical abuse was almost continuous as described by Chicca:

> Some crew were not too badly treated, however, for many that was not the case. I was hit, kicked, beat, and harassed almost every day we were there. They did not like me at all and several others were in the same boat. The guards were on us all the time. My nose was broken twice and I was completely knocked out at least once and that was not during the beginning or the end. Sometimes they kicked me so much that I had to look at my feet when I walked to be sure they were moving.[14]

Physical abuse consisted of fist strikes and kicks to the head or groin, resulting in one of those beaten suffering a fractured jaw. Torture included crewmen being forced to squat for long periods with an inch square stick behind their knees, causing constriction of blood flow and for some, loss of consciousness. On 19 December 1968, the purge for "confessions" was abruptly discontinued, and four days later the *Pueblo* crew was released into South Korea at the DMZ.[15]

Photo 14-5

Rear Adm. Edwin M. Rosenberg, commander, Task Force 76 (center), and Comdr. Lloyd M. Bucher, commanding officer of USS *Pueblo*, enter an automobile as they leave the mess hall at the United Nations Advance Camp, Korean Demilitarized Zone, on 23 December 1968.
Naval History and Heritage command photograph #K-64726

ENTERPRISE SENT EARLIER TO SEA OF JAPAN

In late January 1968, the nuclear-powered carrier USS *Enterprise* (CVA-65) had been en route from Sasebo to Yankee Station, when her commanding officer, Capt. Kent L. Lee, USN, announced to the crew that North Korean patrol boats had intercepted and captured the *Pueblo* and taken it and her crew into Wonsan Harbor. While diplomatic negotiations for the return of *Pueblo*'s crew were begun, other Seventh Fleet ships joined the *Enterprise*, and she became the flagship of a special task force intended to maintain a strong military presence in case the crisis deepened. In Vietnam, at that time, the North Vietnamese and Viet Cong had launched the Tet Offensive, and some believed that seizure of the *Pueblo* was somehow related—a staged sideshow to distract the military attention focused on Vietnam.[16]

Photo 14-6

Vice Adm. Kim Yong-kwan, Korean chief of naval operations; Vice Adm. William F. Bringle, commander, Seventh Fleet; and Rear Adm. Donald G. Irvine, commander, U.S. Naval Forces in Korea, fly aboard the *Enterprise* for meetings with Capt. Kent L. Lee and Rear Adm. Horace H. Epes Jr., commander, Carrier Division One. USS *Enterprise* (CVAN-65) 1968 cruise book

The world's most powerful carrier on station in the Sea of Japan was reassuring to the American people, but irritating to the North Koreans. In the first week in February, as talks at Panmunjom continued without encouraging results, *Enterprise* drew back to the East China Sea, but no changes developed in the North Korean attitude. Ultimately, following twenty-eight meetings held in Panmunjom, an agreement was reached for the release of the eighty-two survivors and the body of the crewmember killed in action.[17]

To obtain it, the United States signed a document containing an apology and an admission of espionage and violation of North Korean territory. The chief U.S. negotiator made it clear that his signature did not signify acceptance by the United States of the numerous false statements in the document.[18]

Photo 14-7

Representatives of the U.S. and North Korean governments meet on 22 December
1968 at Panmunjom, Korea, to sign the agreement for the release of *Pueblo*'s crew.
Maj. Gen. Gilbert H. Woodward, U.S. Army, Senior Member, UN Command Military
Armistice Commission, is in the left foreground, with his back to the camera.
Naval History and Heritage Command photograph #K-64733

REPATRIATION OF CREW AND AFTERMATH

Photo 14-8

Sergeant Robert J. Chicca, U.S. Marine Corps, greets his wife, Ann Marie, on his
arrival at Naval Air Station Miramar, California, 24 December 1968. Their infant
son James is held by Chicca's mother, Mary Chicca (left in the photograph).
Official U.S. Navy photograph held by the Naval History and Heritage Command

Pueblo's crew was released from captivity on 23 December, and arrived in San Diego on Christmas Eve, 1968. Soon, a Navy court of inquiry recommended that Comdr. Lloyd M. Bucher be brought to trial by general court-martial for:

> permitting his ship to be seized while he had the power to resist, failing to take immediate and aggressive protective measures, complying with the orders of the North Koreans to follow in to port, failing to complete destruction of classified material, and permitting material to fall into the hands of the North Koreans, and for failing to ensure, before departure for sea, that his officers and crew were properly organized, stationed and trained in preparation for emergency destruction of classified material.[19]

The board, comprised of five flag officers, also recommended:
- trial by courts-martial of Lt. Steve Harris, officer in charge of the research detachment
- that *Pueblo*'s executive officer receive a letter of admonition
- a letter of reprimand for Rear Adm. Frank Johnson, commander, Naval Forces Japan
- a letter of reprimand for Capt. Everett B. Gladding, head of the Naval Security Group Activity in Japan[20]

Many senior naval officers concurred with commander in chief, U.S. Pacific Fleet, Adm. John J. Hyland's endorsement letter, which used adjectives like "incredible, shocking, and unforgivable" to describe Bucher's decision not to fight. American public opinion, however, supported Bucher's decision not to sacrifice his crew in a hopeless battle. Disillusioned by the high casualties in Vietnam, particularly after the Tet Offensive, most American public opinion tended toward Bucher being made a scapegoat for failures much higher in the chain of command. Bucher's incredible personal story, as an orphan of famed Boys Town in Omaha, Nebraska, who overcame great odds to become a naval officer, also captured the public's favor.[21]

Ultimately, Secretary of the Navy, John H. Chafee, determined that there would be no disciplinary action for any of the crew of *Pueblo*, because the torture and deprivation they had endured at the hands of the North Koreans was suffering enough. Chafee also dismissed the proposed disciplinary actions against Johnson and Gladding as there was more than enough blame to go around for many others involved in the planning for the whole affair.[22]

WELL DESERVED AND OVERDUE RECOGNITION

Bucher and his crew were vilified in some Navy circles, and by many senior personnel for decades—making one wonder whether they were aware that he had faced an overwhelming force of Communist armed vessels and jets overhead with two machine guns. This same pervasive attitude also delayed approval of some unit and personal awards ultimately received by deserving *Pueblo* crewmembers. A summary of these awards follows; the rank or rate of recipients reflect that when they were released, and not necessarily when eventually awarded medals.

Navy Cross Medal
Sergeant Robert J. Hammond, U.S. Marine Corps

Silver Star Medal
Lieutenant (junior grade) Frederic Carl Schumacher, U.S. Navy,
Fireman Duane Hodges, U.S. Navy (posthumously)

Bronze Star Medal (Combat V)
Ron K. Berens, U.S. Navy
Robert J. Chicca, U.S. Marine Corps
Timothy L. Harris, U.S. Navy
Peter M. Langenberg, U.S. Navy
Wendell G. Leach, U.S. Navy
Lieutenant (junior grade) Frederic Carl Schumacher, U.S. Navy

All *Pueblo* military crewmembers were authorized the:

- Navy & Marine Corps Commendation Medal (Combat V)
- Navy & Marine Corps Combat Action Ribbon
- Prisoner of War Medal
- Armed Forces Expeditionary Medal

The Naval & Marine Corps Achievement Medal (Combat V) was awarded to Rushel J. Blansett, Monroe O. Goldman, Charles B. Law Jr., Lawrence W. Mack, Donald R. McClarren, John Mitchell, Clifford C. Nolte, Ralph E. Reed, and Angelo S. Strano.

The two civilian oceanographers aboard the *Pueblo*, Dunnie R. Tuck Jr. and Harry Iredale, received the U.S. Navy Distinguished Civilian Service medal, and U.S. Navy Superior Civilian Service medal, respectively, and also POW medals.[23]

LEST WE FORGET

Photo 14-9

A Navy Yeoman Second Class holds a U.S. flag, to be used to drape the coffin of Seaman Duane Hodges, who was killed on 23 January 1968. Hodges' body was returned to American custody with the ship's other crewmen, at the Korean Demilitarized Zone, 23 December 1968.
Naval History and Heritage Command photograph #K-64690

15

1968 Tet Offensive

The Tet Offensive commenced on the night of 30–31 January 1968 with attacks by about 84,000 NVA [North Vietnamese Army] and VC [Viet Cong] troops against about 155 South Vietnamese cities, government, and military targets, including some U.S. targets such as the U.S. embassy in Saigon. Communist forces attacked 36 of the 44 provincial capitals in South Vietnam, and almost every military installation came under some form of mortar, rocket attack, or infantry assault.

—Excerpt from U.S. Naval History and Heritage Command article
U.S. Navy Operations in Vietnam, January-March 1968.[1]

Photo 15-1

Destroyer USS *Cone* (DD-866) on the gunline during the Tet Offensive.
USS *Cone* 1967-1968 Western Pacific cruise book

On 29 January 1968 the Allies began the Tet-lunar new year expecting the customary 36-hour peaceful holiday truce. Such was not to be. Capitalizing on the lull in war posture, the North Vietnamese and Viet Cong launched a large-scale offensive on targets across South Vietnam.

Assaults began in the northern and central provinces prior to dawn on 30 January, followed by ones that night in Saigon and the Mekong Delta regions. Enemy forces attacked or fired upon scores of provincial capitals, autonomous cities, district capitals, and hamlets, and raided a number of military installations including almost every airfield. The coordinated effort lasted three days. However, Saigon and Hue came under more intense and sustained attack.[2]

The Tet Offensive engaged the U.S./Australian naval gunfire ships in Vietnamese waters in the first half of 1968 in the heaviest combat actions of the war. Drawing on resources from all areas and commands, but especially from Sea Dragon forces, commander, Task Unit 70.8.9 (Naval Gunfire Support Unit) concentrated as many as twenty-two ships at one time on the gunline. As the tempo of naval gunfire support increased from February through June, the majority was in support of American and allied forces in the I-Corps Tactical Zone, located to the immediate south of the DMZ.[3]

In February, Navy ships off South Vietnam fired more than 94,000 rounds. Of this total, Air Naval Gunfire Liaison Company (ANGLICO) teams in I-Corps controlled missions for nearly 18,000 of those rounds, which did not include the missions in support of the Third Marine Division along the DMZ to the north. This trend continued, slightly reduced by June, but over the first half of 1968, Navy gunfire support exceeded that of the entire previous year.[4]

Map 15-1

Abbreviated map of South Vietnam, showing only I-Corps, and part of II-Corps of the five total Corps Tactical Zones

Collectively, four U.S. Navy cruisers, thirty-five destroyers, and the battleship *New Jersey* earned seventy-six combat action ribbons in 1968. The dates of these actions are listed chronologically in the table to associate ships operating together when taking enemy shore battery fire, or engaged separately, but on the same, or nearly the same date(s). The cruiser *Newport News*, and destroyers *Hamner* and *Richard S. Edwards* were the first naval gunfire ships to earn combat action ribbons—following commencement of the Tet Offensive—and the destroyer *Arnold J. Isbell* the last to qualify for one in 1968, for action on 1 November.

There were other USN ships which served on the gunline, or took part in Sea Dragon operations in 1968. Only those which earned combat action ribbons are included in the table. One omission is the guided missile destroyer HMAS *Perth*, which was not eligible for the award, being a unit of the Royal Australian Navy. *Perth* saw much action during her deployment to Vietnam from 2 September 1967 to 10 April 1968, including being hit by enemy fire.[5]

Combat Action Ribbons Earned by Ships in 1968 on the Gunline, or for Sea Dragon Operations (following the Tet Offensive)

Ship	Date(s)	Ship	Date (s)
Hamner (DD-718)	3 Feb 68	*St. Paul* (CA-73)	27 May 68
Richard S. Edwards (DD-950)	3 Feb 68	*Hull* (DD-945)	28 May 68
Newport News (CA-148)	3 Feb 68	*Harwood* (DD-961)	28-29 May 68
Hoel (DDG-13)	4 Feb 68	*Buchanan* (DDG-14)	29 May 68
Hoel (DDG-13)	8 Feb 68	*Turner Joy* (DD-951)	29 May 68
Loftbert (DD-759)	8 Feb 68	*Henry B. Wilson* (DDG-7)	3 Jun 68
Cone (DD-866)	9 Feb 68	*St. Paul* (CA-73)	6 Jun 68
Johnston (DD-821)	9 Feb 68	*Blandy* (DD-943)	10 Jun 68
Johnston (DD-821)	12 Feb 68	*Theodore E. Chandler* (DD-717)	14 Jun 68
Bordelon (DD-881)	16 Feb 68	*Boston* (CAG-1)	17 Jun 68
Hull (DD-945)	21 Feb 68	*Cochrane* (DDG-21)	28 Jun 68
Canberra (CAG-2)	27 Feb 68	*Steinaker* (DD-863)	6 Jul 68
Bordelon (DD-881)	28 Feb 68	*Blue* (DD-744)	16 Jul 68
Newport News (CA-148)	29 Feb 68	*St. Paul* (CA-73)	16 Jul 68
Hull (DD-945)	1 Mar 68	*Blandy* (DD-943)	29 Jul 68
Blue (DD-744)	3 Mar 68	*George K. Mackenzie* (DD-836)	29 Jul 68
Buchanan (DDG-14)	3 Mar 68	*Hollister* (DD-788)	31 Jul-1 Aug 68

Newport News (CA-148)	3 Mar 68	Edson (DD-946)	3 Aug 68
Newport News (CA-148)	6 Mar 68	Boston (CAG-1)	8 Aug 68
Hollister (DD-788)	14 Mar 68	Maddox (DD-731)	8 Aug 68
Hollister (DD-788)	20 Mar 68	Du Pont (DD-941)	9 Aug 68
Epperson (DD-719)	27 Mar 68	Boston (CAG-1)	25 Aug 68
Mansfield (DD-728)	11 Apr 68	Du Pont (DD-941)	28 Aug 68
Newport News (CA-148)	16 Apr 68	Rupertus (DD-851)	30 Aug-2 Sep 68
Collett (DD-730)	22-23 Apr 68	Joseph Strauss (DDG-16)	30-31 Aug 68
Epperson (DD-719)	1 May 68	Joseph Strauss (DDG-16)	1-2 Sep 68
Hull (DD-945)	1 May 68	Blandy (DD-943)	2 Sep 68
Boston (CA-69)	3 May 68	Furse (DD-882)	7 Oct 68
John R. Craig (DD-885)	3 May 68	Towers (DDG-9)	7 Oct 68
Boston (CA-69)	5 May 68	Canberra (CAG-2)	19 Oct 68
Epperson (DD-719)	5 May 68	Leonard F. Mason (DD-852)	19 Oct 68
Theodore E. Chandler (DD-717)	6 May 68	Davis (DD-937)	26 Oct 68
Turner Joy (DD-951)	6 May 68	New Jersey (BB-62)	26 Oct 68
John R. Craig (DD-885)	7 May 68	Berkeley (DDG-15)	27 Oct 68
Theodore E. Chandler (DD-717)	8 May 68	Davis (DD-937)	28-29 Oct 68
St. Paul (CA-73)	8 May 68	New Jersey (BB-62)	31 Oct 68
Collett (DD-730)	16 May 68	Hugh Purvis (DD-709)	31 Oct-1 Nov 68
Henry B. Wilson (DDG-7)	16 May 68	Arnold J. Isbell (DD-869)	1 Nov 68[6]

GUNFIRE SUPPORT FOR THE BATTLE FOR HUE

Fighting house-to-house is the dirtiest of all fighting.... Just as a rat must be drawn from his burrow to be eradicated, an enemy soldier, burrowed in a building, must also be pulled from his hiding place to be eliminated. Normally, he will not come out without a fight. The attacker must go in and dig him out.

—Maj. Ron Christmas, USMC, company commander in Hue[7]

The ships on the gunline maintained high rates of fire during this crisis period, with the heavy cruisers firing an average of eight hundred rounds each day. In February, the guided-missile heavy cruiser *Canberra*, guided-missile light cruiser *Providence*, and seven other ships poured fire into enemy targets in Hue, including the fortified Citadel.[8]

Located approximately sixty miles south of the Demilitarized Zone, Hue consisted of two distinct towns separated by the Perfume River. The Citadel, built on the northern bank, had once served as the residence for Annamese emperors. The southern side, about half the size of the Citadel, consisted primarily of French style residential areas along with the city's university and the French provincial capital. Hue, the predominant cultural, spiritual, and educational center of Vietnam, was also the site of the headquarters of the 1st Infantry Division of the Army of the Republic of Vietnam and a compound for I-Corps' Military Assistance Command, Vietnam, advisors.[9]

At Hue, two combined North Vietnamese Army and Viet Cong regiments (the 4th and the 6th) infiltrated the city and fought the three U.S. Marine Corps, three U.S. Army, and eleven South Vietnamese battalions defending it. The battle for Hue began on 31 January, and officially ended at midnight on 27 February. Lasting twenty-six days, it was the longest and bloodiest of the Tet Offensive. Americans lost 216 killed and 1,364 wounded in action, while the South Vietnamese lost 384 killed and 1,830 wounded. Some 5,800 civilians died, at least 2,800 of which were killed by the VC, who sought out and executed local and national government officials, intellectuals, soldiers and their families, and others with pro-U.S. sentiments, or who could identify them and compromise their efforts. The United States' estimate of VC and North Vietnamese casualties was 5,000 with 1,042 killed.[10]

EFFORTS BY THE CRUISER *CANBERRA*

The guided-missile heavy cruiser USS *Canberra* was well into her fourth deployment to Vietnam, when the Tet Offensive broke out. Three months earlier, she had rendezvoused at dusk on 26 October 1967 with USS *Newport News*, the big triple-turret gun cruiser she was to relieve, and be relieved by, many times during her tour of duty in the combat zone off Vietnam. The clamor of the ship's General Quarters alarm the following day, calling the crew to their battle stations, signaled the first full day of wartime steaming during her latest combat tour.[11]

Off the DMZ and in support of the battle for Hue, *Canberra* fired around the clock with her crew at Condition III (wartime steaming), utilizing her 8-inch turrets and 5-inch mounts. The pace of the heavy cruiser's firing increased as the deployment progressed. During her last twenty-six days, she fired an average of 644.7 rounds per day, or one round every two minutes and 10 seconds. Backbreaking work, and sometimes sleepless nights were required to keep up this pace on the gunline. There was nothing easy about rearming in the late evening, and then moving back to the firing line, only to empty the magazines in the next 12-hours, necessitating another rearming the following evening.[12]

Photo 15-2

Nighttime gunfire mission being carried out by the cruiser USS *Canberra* (CAG-2). USS *Canberra* Western Pacific 1967-1968 cruise book

While carrying out Sea Dragon operations off North Vietnam, *Canberra* patrolled the coastal waters of the Tonkin Gulf in search of waterborne logistics craft (WBLC), and used her 8-inch guns to destroy military and supply targets far inland.   Cruisers and destroyers thus employed were operating as far north as the Bay of Brandon (Baie du Brandon on the map).   (*Canberra* also spent eighteen days in the frigid cold of the Sea of Japan, as part of the Naval force assembled there to demonstrate American resolve, following the capture of *Pueblo* and the imprisonment of her crew by North Korean forces.)[13]

Map 15-2

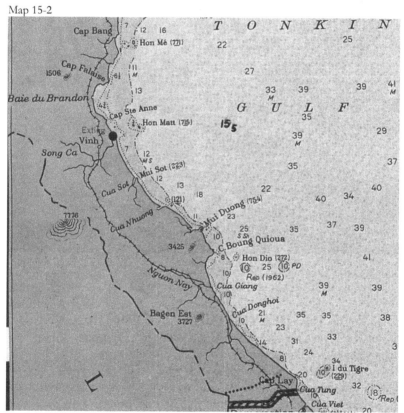

Section of North Vietnamese coastline above the Demilitarized Zone (DMZ)
USS *Canberra* (CAG-2) Western Pacific 1967-1968 cruise book

During Sea Dragon operations, *Canberra* used her gunfire control computers to assist with targeting, moving swiftly in and out of coastal areas on firing runs.   As a result of her exclusive gunnery use, and in part due to her outdated "Terrier" guided missile system, she was reclassified back to heavy cruiser in May 1968.   By this action, *Canberra* regained her original hull number, CA-70, in use from commissioning on 14 October 1943 until it was changed to CAG-2 on 4 January 1952. *Canberra*'s missile launchers and guidance radars were removed in 1969, following her last Vietnam cruise. Decommissioned in February 1970, she was stricken in July 1978 and sold for scrapping two years later.[14]

Photo 15-3

Crewmen in USS *Canberra*'s (CAG-2) Main Battery Plot work to obtain firing solutions, aided by fire control computer, during shore bombardment off Vietnam, March 1967. Navy History and Heritage Command photograph #USN 1142153

DUTY OF THE DESTROYER *CONE* ON THE GUNLINE

While the bigger guns of the cruisers could pour out high volumes of large-caliber rounds at more distant targets, the dozens of destroyers that served on the gunline proved their value again and again. *Cone* was a long way from Charleston, South Carolina (which she had left on 15 November 1967), when her first taste of combat came in early February, while assigned to duty in an area fronting the Demilitarized Zone. As Marine spotters, positioned to detect enemy troop movement, called for fire, her guns hammered at their assigned targets inland.[15]

Firing night and day for nearly six weeks in February through April, *Cone* expended 12,861 rounds of her 5"/38 ammunition. Dusk curtailed the destroyer's activities and limited her gunfire support missions at night to an occasional round or two for harassment, interdiction, or illumination. Subsequent gunline assignments took her south to Xa Phan Thiet, Tuy Hoa, Da Nang, the Bay of Van Fong, Nha Trang, and positions along the Qui Nhon Peninsula. Duty with the Sea Dragon forces for several days sent her well north of the DMZ.[16]

BOMBARDMENT INFLICTS LOSSES ON THE ENEMY

Naval gunfire support was critical to the recapture of Hue, and during the first eight months of 1968, inflicted over two thousand casualties on the reeling Communist forces. In March, the heavy cruiser *Newport News* reduced the flow of ammunition to enemy units when it destroyed a North Vietnamese Army logistics complex north of the Cua Viet River. In May, the guided missile destroyer *Henry B. Wilson* decimated a North Vietnamese battalion, killing eighty-two of the unit's troops.[17]

OPERATION THOR, 1-7 JULY 1968

...to get us as near to his weapons and to his forces as possible, drench us with high angle fire weapons, engage us in close and violent combat, accept willingly a substantial loss of life for the opportunity to kill a lesser number of our men, and to withdraw into his North Vietnam sanctuary to refurbish.

—Lt. Gen. Victor H. Krulak, commanding general, Fleet Marine Force, Pacific, warning American commanders in July 1967 about the disadvantages of waging war in the DMZ sector, telling them they had to face "the brutal facts" that the Marines were "under the enemy's guns."[18]

In the summer of 1968, the North Vietnamese Army (NVA) dominated the DMZ with its long-range, flat-trajectory 122mm and 130mm guns and 152mm howitzers. With more than one hundred artillery pieces that could outrange all U.S. artillery, except for a few Marine (8-inch) and Army (175mm) gun batteries, the NVA was able to curb operations of the Marine logistical base at Dong Ha and interdict supply routes along the Cua Viet River and Route 9—the northernmost west-east road in South Vietnam, which ran roughly parallel to the DMZ.[19]

Maj. Gen. Rathvon M. Tompkins, commander of the Third Marine Division, had proposed, in March, a combined arms operation around Mui Lay to reduce NVA infiltration and destroy artillery that had been targeting the Cua Viet and Dong Ha bases, and neutralize supporting enemy infantry operations south of the Demilitarized Zone.   The operational area would extend from the southern edge of the DMZ about eight-and-a-half miles north to Mui Lay, and fifteen-and-a-half miles inland from the coast.[20]

The approved operation was conducted from 1 to 7 July. Code named THOR, it involved combined aerial, ground, and ship bombardment of the North Vietnamese batteries in the Cap Mui Lay sector of the DMZ. In perhaps the largest demonstration of joint supporting arms of the war, carrier aircraft flew 512 sorties and dropped 812 tons of ordnance upon the NVA positions, and three cruisers and six destroyers fired over 19,000 rounds of 5-inch, 6-inch, and 8-inch ammunition against enemy gun positions.[21]

Photo 15-4

Briefing by *Cochrane*'s assigned Naval Gunfire Liaison Officer aboard the guided missile destroyer during a visit to Da Nang in March 1968.
USS *Cochrane* (DDG-21) Western Pacific 1968 cruise book

U.S. Navy Aircraft Carrier, Cruiser and Destroyer
Participants in Operation THOR

Carriers	Cruisers	Destroyers
America (CVA-66)	*Boston* (CAG-1)	*Benner* (DD-807)
Bon Homme Richard (CVA-31)	*Providence* (CLG-6)	*Boyd* (DD-544)
Constellation (CVA-64)	*St. Paul* (CA-73)	*Cochrane* (DDG-21)
Ticonderoga (CVA 14)		*Henry B. Wilson* (DDG-7)
		O'Brien (DD-725)
		Turner Joy (DD-951)

Based on aerial photography and observation, the bombardment by Naval aircraft and ships caused extensive damage, hampering NVA artillery support and coastal defense ability in the Cap Mui Lay area.[22]

About this time, the Navy was preparing to add a powerful new arsenal to its naval gunfire capability, the recently refurbished battleship *New Jersey* (BB-62) with her 16-inch guns. On 16 July, Marine Corps ANGLICO liaison teams participated in a targeting planning conference for the ship, which was to arrive in the waters off Vietnam at the end of September. Her duty in Vietnam is taken up in a subsequent chapter.[23]

The heavy cruiser *St. Paul*—a participant in Operation THOR and previously, the most powerful naval gunfire ship in the fleet—would meet up with the *New Jersey* at sea in late September 1968.

Photo 15-5

St. Paul with the *New Jersey*, the day before she left the gunline, 30 September 1968. USS *St. Paul* (CA-73) 1968 cruise book

After firing more than 52,000 rounds—wearing out the rifling in her barrels—the *St. Paul* regunned in Subic Bay. Navy's Ship Repair Facility personnel, with the help of her gunner's mates, replaced her nine eight-inch barrels and ten five-inch barrels.[24]

Photo 15-6

Three eight-inch, 16-ton barrels await their new turrets.
USS *St. Paul* (CA-73) 1968 cruise book

TET PROVES TO BE TURNING POINT IN THE WAR

[I]t seems now more certain than ever that the bloody experience of Vietnam is to end in stalemate... [I]t is increasingly clear to this reporter that the only rational way out then will be to negotiate, not as victors, but as an honorable people who lived up to their pledge to defend democracy, and did the best they could.

—News anchorman Walter Cronkite in CBS (Columbia Broadcasting System) "Report from Vietnam: Who, What, When, Where, Why," which aired on 27 February 1968. The excerpt came at the end of the hour-long special, which Cronkite acknowledged was subjective, his opinion.[25]

Although U.S. and South Vietnamese forces managed to hold off the attacks on more than 100 cities and outposts in South Vietnam, news coverage of the massive Tet Offensive shocked the American public and eroded support for the war effort. Despite heavy casualties, North Vietnam achieved a strategic victory, as the attacks marked a turning point in the Vietnam War and the beginning of the slow, painful American withdrawal from the region.[26]

16

Termination of SEA DRAGON Operations in 1968

What was Sea Dragon? It was: "five rounds, rapid continuous, fire when loaded;" it was the jet like whine of the forced draft blowers responding to the command, "Right full rudder, all ahead flank;" it was, "Believe we hold a WBLIC bearing … ;" it was the shudder and crash of the guns; it was ammunition dumps, truck parks, bridges, general impairment of enemy logistics; most of all it was little sleep and lots of "General Quarters, General Quarters …."

—USS *Cochrane* (DDG-21) Western Pacific 1968 cruise book

Photo 16-1

Members of USS *Bordelon*'s (DD-881) bridge watch team during Sea Dragon operations. USS *Bordelon* Western Pacific 1967-1968 cruise book

Sea Dragon operations began off North Vietnam on 25 October 1966 to interdict enemy sea lines of communication and the movement of supplies south, and to destroy with naval gunfire land targets and waterborne craft. They were discontinued on 1 November 1968 in concert with the initiation of peace talks in Paris between the United States and North Vietnam. The operations had been reduced in number earlier in the year as a result of the 1968 Tet Offensive in late January.[1]

Navy warships were needed desperately to defend besieged allied forces south of the DMZ, and almost all the available destroyers joined the Naval Gunfire Support Unit (Task Unit 70.8.9), which, at one time, amassed twenty-two warships on the gunline. As urgent need for these ships lessened, those no longer needed returned to Sea Dragon operations.[2]

The destroyer *Bordelon* (DD-881) participated in Sea Dragon from 20 January to 11 February, both before and after commencement of the Tet Offensive. First, with the Australian guided missile destroyer HMAS *Perth* (DDG-38), whose commanding officer served as the task unit commander, and then with *Hoel* (DDG-13), with her embarked commander, Destroyer Division 152, as unit commander. For twenty-three days, *Bordelon* cruised along the North Vietnamese coastline, always on the alert for illusive waterborne logistics craft, blasting shore targets once or twice a day, halting the southward flow of material and supplies. Targets included logistics craft, truck convoys, storage areas, highway choke points, and coastal defense sites. A description of SEA DRAGON practices and tactics then in effect, follows.[3]

SELECTION/CATEGORIES OF ENEMY TARGETS

The targets assigned to ships conducting Sea Dragon operations were selected by commander, Seventh Fleet Cruiser-Destroyer Force, following the evaluation of aerial reconnaissance photographs and other intelligence information. These targets fell into three categories:

- Military targets near populated areas. These were fired on only when spotting aircraft was available, and strict control was maintained on bombardment of these targets to ensure accurate firings on military areas only.

- Military targets encountered on coastal logistic routes from North to South Vietnam, away from civilian areas. Waterborne logistics craft and truck convoys were in this category, and could be engaged without spotting aircraft.

- Coastal defense sites were attacked when specifically designated as targets, or received suppressive fire during engagement of other targets, or counterbattery fire after taking Sea Dragon ships under fire.[4]

TACTICS EMPLOYED AGAINST SHORE TARGETS

Task unit ships normally operated in pairs, with one of the ships (usually the destroyer whose guns had the longest range) designated the primary firing ship. On the run in toward the target area, both the command ship and second destroyer—the "shotgun"—concentrated their fire on coastal defense sites. When the position for opening fire against the shore target was reached, the "shotgun" (whose primary duty was to provide defensive/covering fire) continued with suppressive fire against the defense sites while the command ship engaged the target. At completion of the mission, the ships retired at high speed, while continuing to fire on the coastal defense sites until out of range.[5]

This procedure was employed even if it was believed that the coastal defense sites in the area were not active, because artillery batteries were often moved from one site to another. After a rapid shift of guns and ammunition, a defense site classified unoccupied by naval intelligence could be active a day later. Accordingly, all sites were treated as active, and fire from them was always expected. Sea Dragon ships were not permitted to remain within range of an active coastal defense site. Upon coming under fire, they were required to move away, engaging the enemy with counterbattery fire as they retired.[6]

Once the ships were outside the range of the coastal artillery, they were able to shell the defense sites at maximum range, using spotting aircraft to pinpoint the targets. As with NGFS (naval gunfire support) for friendly ground troops, an airborne spotter flew near shore targets to give corrections. For Sea Dragon operations, the spotting aircraft were generally from aircraft carriers. Damage to inland targets beyond visual range was confirmed by aerial reconnaissance. WBLCs were detected and tracked by aircraft, by ship radar and, sometimes, visually.[7]

EXCHANGE OF SEA DRAGON SHIPS

Cruisers and destroyers moved in and out of Sea Dragon duties, as requirements for them to refuel, rearm, or other taskings took them away from the North Vietnamese coastline. HMAS *Perth* returned to Sea Dragon on 14 February 1968, relieving the *Hoel*, and her commanding officer, Capt. Peter Hogarth Doyle, assumed the dual role of commander, Task Unit 77.1.0 and commander, Task Unit 77.1.2. The former involved his functioning as the surface action group commander, responsible to commander, Seventh Fleet Cruiser Destroyer Force (Task Group 77.1) for the planning and conduct of all Sea Dragon operations. The latter was operational command of *Perth* and *Mansfield* (DD 728) during Task Unit 77.1.2 operations in the southern Sea Dragon area.[8]

1968 OPERATIONS PRIOR TO THE TET OFFENSIVE

Perth had earlier joined the heavy cruiser *Newport News* (CA-148) on 9 January for the northern Sea Dragon patrol. On that day, she fired at coastal defense sites while the cruiser bombarded bridges, railway crossings, truck convoys, and two missile sites north of Cap St. Anne in the southern part of the Bay of Brandon (which lay just to the north of Vinh). Four days later, *Perth* fired a spotted mission of sixty rounds on a highway choke point and associated coastal defense sites south of Mui Ron. On 16 January, the two-ship task unit (77.1.1) destroyed seven WBLCs and damaged two others north of the Bay of Brandon, as well as firing on coastal defense sites.[9]

Photo 16-2

HMAS *Perth* fires on North Vietnamese coastal defense sites from her station aft of the cruiser USS *Newport News* (CA-148), 23 February 1968. National Archives photograph #USN 1130076

The following day, *Newport News* attacked WBLCs in the Cua Bang immediately south of Cap Bang, while *Perth* fired on the numerous coastal defense sites which ringed the Bay of Brandon. Additional suspected missile sites were attacked on the 19th, *Perth*'s last day in the northern Sea Dragon area. *Perth* left *Newport News* on 20 January to relieve the guided missile destroyer *Goldsborough* (DDG-20) as command ship of Task Unit 77.1.2, now comprised of *Perth* and *Bordelon*.[10]

The task unit fired on a river crossing south of Mui Ron three times on 22 January as truck convoys reached it. This effort appeared to stop truck movement south of the river. However, increased traffic south to the DMZ soon became noticeable. Choke points, highways, and storage areas received high priority as targets, and the northern task unit (*Newport News* and *Blue*) was assigned to assist *Perth* and *Bordelon*.[11]

Perth and *Bordelon* were firing at a highway bridge near Cap St. Anne on the afternoon of 25 January, when they were tracked by enemy radar and received about thirty rounds from coastal defense artillery sited just north of the cape. As the ships withdrew, several rounds fell between them. Although task units had received enemy fire about seven times per month for the previous six months, this was the single attack on a task unit in January. At *Perth*'s request, attack aircraft from the *Coral Sea* (CVA-43) soon arrived to carry out a strike on the coastal defense site. An A-4 Skyhawk was hit by a surface-to-air missile (SAM) and the pilot, Comdr. Thomas E. Woolcock, ejected ten miles from the task unit. His rescue was coordinated by the *Perth*. One of the several SAMs fired was seen to pass over *Perth* and explode a mile distant.[12]

SEA DRAGON OPERATIONS IN FEBRUARY-MARCH

Early in February, with heavy fighting continuing around the DMZ, Task Unit 77.1.2 continued to operate as far north as the Bay of Brandon, and also covered southern Sea Dragon responsibilities, while Task Unit 77.1.1 was providing naval gunfire support for military operations in the DMZ.[13]

Perth was relieved by *Hoel* on 2 February, so that she might proceed to Subic Bay to re-gun (replace worn-out barrels) and carry out routine maintenance. As previously mentioned, the Australian missile destroyer returned to Sea Dragon operations on 14 February, relieving *Hoel* and joining *Mansfield*. *Perth* and *Mansfield* took advantage of a spell of bad weather on 23 February to fire at targets near Vinh, unhampered by enemy radar or coastal defense fire. Vinh (twelve miles inland from the mouth of the Song Ca River, south of Cap St. Anne) and its associated river port Ben Thuy, was a major logistic staging point with many military storage areas. That same day, *Perth* relieved *Hoel* as command ship of Task Unit 77.1.2, with the *Blue* assigned as support ship.[14]

Perth and *Blue* relieved *Buchanan* (DDG-14) and *Hollister* (DD-788) in Task Unit 70.8.9 on 12 March for a short assignment. In support of U.S. Marine forces near the DMZ, *Perth* was assigned twenty-three H&I (harassment and interdiction) targets to be fired on twice during the night. In doing so, she delivered more than 400 rounds onto trenches, bunkers, artillery sites, troop positions and a sampan concentration. The two ships returned to the southern Sea Dragon area on the 14th. The following day, *Perth* scored direct hits on three bridges on the Song Giang River and started fires in the area. On 22 March, the Australian destroyer fired on bridges and artillery sites in the Bay of Brandon in a 'farewell visit' and, in the final action of Sea Dragon operations, sank a ferry in the Cua Ron south of Mui Ong. *Perth* was relieved by *Epperson* (DD-719) the next day.[15]

EPPERSON AND *MANSFIELD* TAKE HEAVY SHORE BATTERY FIRE, LUCKILY RECEIVE LITTLE DAMAGE

> *The* Mansfield *was out there about 400 yards away and firing like hell, we were both cranking every knot out of the old girls and the shell splashes were all around us. There were EASILY 30 or 40 splashes visible at the SAME time. How we never got more damage than punctures in the aluminum superstructure I will never know. Afterwards, we were told to pick up the shell fragments "for analysis" but there was so much that the guys just threw it over board.*

> —Former Naval officer Jerome D. Williams, describing the scene from the bridge wing of the destroyer *Epperson* (DD-719), as she and the *Mansfield* (DD-728) began receiving enemy shore battery fire while proceeding seaward after completing a SEA DRAGON mission, targeting bridges and buildings near Vinh, North Vietnam.[16]

On 27 March 1968, the *Epperson* came under a barrage of shore battery fire while she and *Mansfield* were conducting a SEA DRAGON operation. Ens. Jerry Williams, who had recently reported aboard the "Eppie," was on the bridge at the time. He was assigned as junior officer of the deck for General Quarters, and remembers not being particularly vital to the combat action that day:

> I really couldn't DO anything constructive and with the CO [commanding officer] and Officer of the Deck on the bridge, I was told to just stay out of the way and learn....[17]

Photo 16-3

Ens. Jerry Williams standing next to a telescopic alidade (mounted on a gyro compass repeater) on the *Epperson*'s bridge wing during a more tranquil time than this operation. Courtesy of Jerome Williams

Williams described an Australian correspondent and *Epperson*'s signalmen topside frantically seeking shelter as the first indication that she was being shelled by shore battery fire:

> An Aussie reporter came in from the bridge wing like he's an Olympic sprinter and got the CO's temper up for such a brazen display of self-preservation. The skivvy wavers [signalmen] dove head first into nonexistent foxholes on the bridge wings and that's when the Captain told me to go out and see if we were being fired on.[18]

SEA DRAGON operations, at that time, involved two to three ships patrolling fifteen miles up and down the coast of North Vietnam. The ships had a list of choke points where the roads came down to the coastline because of mountainous terrain, and they could attack any of the chokepoints. *Epperson*, with commander, Destroyer Squadron 25 embarked, was the firing ship for this operation, and *Mansfield* "rode shotgun." As *Epperson* fired at buildings and bridges near Vinh, *Mansfield* took known gun emplacements under fire. A spotter aircraft assisted by providing damage reports.[19]

Photo 16-4

Destroyer USS *Epperson* (DD-719) off the coast of Oahu, Hawaii, 29 August 1968.
Naval History and Heritage Command photograph #NH 98875

On the run in, *Mansfield* was positioned on the *Epperson*'s port
quarter until five miles from shore. On command, both ships made a
flank turn to starboard, in order to parallel the coast and bring all
mounts on each ship to bear. During the firing run, *Mansfield* was astern
of *Epperson*. At completion, after making another right turn, *Mansfield*
was then on *Epperson*'s starboard quarter as they headed seaward. Both
ships were making flank speed and zigzagging, in an effort to avoid
enemy shore battery fire. Lt. (jg) Jim West, who was the officer of the
deck aboard *Epperson*, later described the operation:

> From 15 miles out, we came to course 270 or so at flank speed,
> headed straight toward the beach with *Mansfield* on our port side.
> The NVA guns had a range of 12 miles and ours only 9 miles. The
> sea was like glass and the sky clear blue. As we approached the
> beach, I was concentrating on giving my commands in a clear calm
> voice so the kids (I was 24) didn't get antsy.
>
> Relatively soon CIC announced a search radar bearing [the ship's
> combat information center detected enemy radar emissions] so they
> knew we were coming. CIC also announced the range to the beach
> every thousand yards. It seemed to take forever. Next CIC
> announced a "firecan radar" bearing so now they were working on

a fire control solution [use of fire control radar to target the ships] and we weren't even at 9 miles yet.

We both opened up with mount 51 around 8 miles in and continued with "rapid continuous fire." At 5 miles in we turned starboard to bring all mounts to bear with the *Mansfield* behind us. A few minutes later the signal came to head seaward. We zigzagged out and I had the discretion as to when to zig and zag. I had just ordered left full rudder, and as the bow began to slowly move to the left, a shell hit the water right off the starboard bow and it was game on. Both ships were under fire and later on the *Mansfield* sent us some pictures of the shells landing behind us. There was some shrapnel found on the signal bridge.[20]

Photo 16-5

Painting *Sea Dragon Operation off Vinh* by Richard DeRosset.

The artillery fire was originating from a position off the ships' starboard quarter, about 140 degrees relative to the headings they were steering. Ensign Williams, attired in khakis with flak jacket and helmet, was on the starboard bridge wing. (Inside the bridge were the commanding officer, officer of the deck, helmsman, lee helmsman, and quartermaster. The commodore, Capt. Alfred G. Russillo, was in the combat information center.) Following the first splash, the after-gun mounts of both destroyers began pouring rounds back down the enemy's firing bearing. *Mansfield* and *Epperson* emerged from the volley unharmed, with no casualties, but a defensive measure by *Epperson* inadvertently facilitated some consternation back home among family members of her crew.[21]

Epperson had lit off a smoke pot after she began taking fire, to veil her movements from the enemy gunlayers. Upon sighting the resultant smoke screen, the North Vietnamese believed their guns had caused her grave harm. Radio Hanoi later claimed that the destroyer had received several direct hits and burst into flames. A spokesman for the Navy explained that *Epperson* had been shelling a main bridge on Highway 1A, a major enemy infiltration and supply route. "After firing her rounds at the target, and scoring 12 direct hits with several secondary explosions, the *Epperson* turned seaward. She was immediately bracketed by enemy fire.... The *Epperson*'s guns countered with heavy fire which landed on the enemy firing site."[22]

ACTIVITY INSIDE THE MOUNT 52 HANDLING ROOM

Photo 16-6

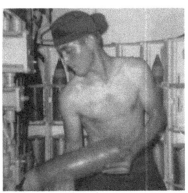

Seamen Mike Mestas and Vince Volk loading 5" gun rounds and powder charges into *Epperson*'s after gun mount as rapidly as possible.
Courtesy of Vince Volk

Much labor was required of *Epperson*'s gun crews to unremittingly load 5-inch projectiles and powders as her guns kept pouring out rounds during SEA DRAGON operations. Requirements for continuous rapid fire, particularly when under enemy fire, demanded herculean efforts. Seaman Vince Volk later described the actions occurring when the above photographs were taken:

> My friend, Seaman Mike Mestas and myself were in the upper handling room of Mount 52 loading as fast as we would. You can see by the sweat on my hat and the dirt on my hands that we were

doing this for a long period. We would go to rapid continuous fire on command and I really didn't think I could keep up.

The *Epperson* would charge in firing with Mount 51 [forward mount] and as soon as we (Mount 52) [after mount] were out of lock [free to fire] we would open up and give those bastards a broadside. Then when Mount 51 went into lock we would continue our rapid continuous fire as long as we were in range, all the while taking evasive action.

What was rather difficult was loading the hoists as the ship was at flank speed and taking hard turns. It was a real balancing act. When we received a cease fire [command], I had this overwhelming feeling of accomplishment as did all of my shipmates.

We were all proud and all gung ho. I venture to say that given the order to sail into Haiphong Harbor with our 5" 38's blazing away that not a man would have questioned the order and would be ready to go. That order never came, but I can tell you this, I served with a great crew! Something I will never forget.[23]

Seaman Fire Controlman Gregory Roberts, in fire control plot, was in communication via sound-powered phones with the gun mounts. He later recalled that the "gun mount captains were very excited to say the least [while receiving enemy fire]. We set the guns to "auto" and fired as soon as the shells were rammed for our counter fire. I had a tough time relaying bore condition to CIC as the captains were too busy." Upon firing, gun crews were required to report the condition of the bore, whether "fouled" or "clear." Fouling occurred if a brass powder casing became stuck after firing.[24]

VIEW FROM THE STARBOARD BRIDGE WING

From the bridge wing, Williams had begun counting all the splashes around *Epperson*, but lost track after 40-50, because they were coming in so fast. In describing the scene, he recalled that every radio circuit patched to the bridge lit up, there was mass confusion everywhere, and "I never heard a twin 5-inch mount fire as fast as those guys did then." He also put that day in perspective to subsequent ones in Vietnam:

Later on, we were fired at several more times but never was there more than one or two guns and they were just hoping for a lucky hit, like when we got too close in on the DMZ. There was never anything in the Eppy's career during the two years that I was on board that matched that Sea Dragon firing run.[25]

SEA DRAGON MISSIONS REDUCED, THEN HALTED

In April 1968, the stretch of North Vietnam's coastline, off which Sea Dragon ships were allowed to carry out offensive operations, was reduced by one-third to below the 19th parallel. This decision by higher authority was based on fewer WBLC sightings and requirements for employment of ships elsewhere, further south. Nonetheless, the smaller interdiction campaign continued through the summer with shore bombardment around Ha Tinh, Vinh, and Phu Dien Chau. In August and September, the heavy cruiser *Newport News* and three destroyers struck numerous shore targets and sank or damaged nearly 1,000 waterborne logistics craft. On 29 September, the battleship *New Jersey* arrived on station with 16-inch guns that could reach eighty-five percent of the military targets in the North.[26]

The battleship spent a month with Sea Dragon forces wreaking havoc along the North Vietnamese coast. Logistic complexes, troop concentrations, fortified caves, watercraft, the Thanh Hoa Bridge, and Hon Matt Island's coastal artillery all fell victim to her 1,900-pound rounds. When President Johnson enacted a moratorium on 1 November, on attacks in the North, *New Jersey* moved south to provide heavy naval gunfire support until she left Vietnam in April 1969.[27]

The same order that sent the *New Jersey* southward also brought Operation SEA DRAGON to a close after two years. While carrying out their duties, 68 Sea Dragon ships were fired upon in 169 separate incidents, with 38 receiving enemy fire on three or more occasions. Of these 68 warships, 29 were hit, with three ships hit twice. Despite improved accuracy of shore-based artillery, North Vietnamese gunners failed to put any ship out of commission, although nineteen withdrew to Japan or the Philippines for repairs.[28]

Epperson's commanding officer, Comdr. Cedric Sterling Wallace, USN, was awarded the Bronze Star Medal with Combat "V" for heroic achievement and leadership, and saving his ship from combat damage received during a battle in the Vietnam War.[29]

17

New Jersey Joins the Gunline

VIETNAM
Communist supply routes and storage dumps protected by heavy concentrations of anti-aircraft guns and missiles. Invaders and extortionists hidden by jungle foliage and impassible terrain. Allied troops menaced by artillery and rocket positions. Coastal targets far beyond the range of cruiser and destroyer guns.

They were calling it a different kind of war. They asked for a different kind of weapon. They got it. A battleship? Not quite. That era is history. Instead, a long-range gun battery, more powerful than any other afloat. Or on wheels. Or locked in concrete. A mobile artillery piece that thumbs its nose at roadmaps and rain and mud and enemy forces.

Firepower – Twelve tons at a time where it's needed and when. A cough of flame from a throat of steel. Thunder rolling across a humid sea. The unearthly whistling roar of shells. The earth-shaking payoff—On Target!

Call it a floating artillery. Call it a Battleship. We call it NEW JERSEY.

—From Dreadnought 68-69 (USS *New Jersey*'s 1968-1969 cruise book)

Photo 17-1

Battleship USS *New Jersey* (BB-62) bombarding enemy targets near Tuyho,
on South Vietnam's central coast, during her last period on the gunline in March 1969.
U.S. Navy photograph, from collections of the Naval History and Heritage Command

A single battleship, the USS *New Jersey* (BB-62), served on the gunline during the Vietnam War. The 45,000-ton behemoth, a product of the Philadelphia Naval Shipyard, was commissioned on 23 May 1943 and saw combat duty in World War II. She was decommissioned on 30 June 1948, and laid up in "red lead row" in a reserve fleet. A little over two years later, she was recommissioned on 21 November 1950, for the Korean War. Decommissioned a second time on 21 August 1957, she was once again forgotten, until yet another war prompted her return to service a second time on 6 April 1968.

In late 1964, the growing U.S. involvement in Southeast Asia prompted consideration of the possible reactivation of one or more of the four *Iowa*-class battleships to support U.S. ground forces in Vietnam. Ultimately, only *New Jersey*—in better material condition than her three sisters—was brought out of "mothballs." The process was lengthy because Adm. David L. McDonald, the chief of Naval Operations, was opposed to returning her or any other battleship to service. Upon his retirement on 1 August 1967, the Navy announced that it was going to reactivate the *New Jersey* for Vietnam duty.[1]

Photo 17-2

Floodlights illuminate the USS *New Jersey* (BB-62) as she rests on blocks in Drydock No. 3 at the Philadelphia Naval Shipyard in November 1967. National Archives photograph K-42810

PROSPECTIVE COMMANDING OFFICER ARRIVES

That thing was the biggest shambles inside when I arrived six weeks after it had been first opened that I ever saw any ship in, in a shipyard, other than new construction.

—Observation by Capt. Richard G. Alexander, USN, prospective
commanding officer of the *New Jersey*, regarding the condition
of the battleship early in her reactivation at the
Philadelphia Naval Shipyard.[2]

You're dealing with an individual who had been wrong very few times in his life, and he's not going to let go of this dying cat yet.

—Naval officer commenting on why he believed Captain Alexander
supported Lieutenant Commander Arnheiter to the point of
committing professional suicide. He elaborated that
throughout his unusually fine career, Alexander had
always been outspoken on controversial subjects
and had usually been proved correct.[3]

On 22 August 1967, Capt. Richard G. Alexander, USN, was ordered to the Philadelphia Naval Shipyard for duty as prospective commanding officer in connection with the recommissioning of the *New Jersey*. He had been assigned to the Bureau of Naval Personnel since July 1964— first serving as Head of the Cruiser Destroyers Maincraft Placement Section, Officer Distribution Division, and later as Director of the Plans Division. During this duty, he had recommended Lt. Comdr. Marcus Arnheiter for command, and helped to facilitate his receipt of orders to the radar picket ship USS *Vance*.[4]

Upon his arrival in Philadelphia, Alexander was disappointed to learn that the *New Jersey* was not expected to arrive in Vietnam until some fourteen months after the start of the yard period. He believed that the need for her shore bombardment was so urgent that she should be hurried out as quickly as possible. While Alexander was trying to get the ship and her crew ready for duty overseas, his mind was also on the "Arnheiter Affair," involving the former commanding officer of the *Vance*, who had been summarily relieved of his duties.[5]

Alexander, who had known Arnheiter for a number of years, took up his cause. He argued that the deposed skipper had been removed from his ship without due process and had been undermined by a disloyal group of junior officers. Alexander later explained that he decided to intervene only after commander, Cruiser-Destroyer Force, Pacific Fleet, following a thorough review of the case, recommended that Arnheiter be restored to command. Alexander met with the Secretary of the Navy (SecNav) on 7 November 1967, and soon after, released a 27-page statement to the press, which he had prepared on Arnheiter's behalf (and presented earlier to SecNav).[6]

Adm. Thomas H. Moorer, who had succeeded McDonald as chief of Naval Operations, considered Alexander's statement "somewhat intemperate" and faulted his judgement in releasing it, rather than pursuing the matter through regular Navy channels. In late December, Alexander was asked to request a transfer from the *New Jersey* to shore duty. He did so, and was ordered to a dead-end posting as assistant chief of staff for Operations in the Boston Naval District. Alexander retired less than two years later—having never been selected for the admiral's stars, which earlier had seemed so likely.[7]

Alexander's replacement aboard *New Jersey* was Capt. J. Edward Snyder Jr., a classmate in the Naval Academy class of 1945, which had graduated a year early in an effort to get officers out to the fleet in World War II. Snyder had been about to drive cross country from Washington, DC, to California to take command of the heavy cruiser *St. Paul*, when he received orders to take Alexander's place in Philadelphia.[8]

Photo 17-3

Capt. J. Edward Snyder Jr., USN,
commanding officer, USS *New Jersey* (BB-62).
Dreadnought 68-69 (USS *New Jersey*'s 1968-1969 cruise book)

NEW JERSEY REJOINS THE FLEET

Following much renovation, fitted with improved electronics and a helicopter landing pad, and with her World War II 40mm anti-aircraft battery removed, the *New Jersey* was recommissioned on 6 April 1968. With Captain Snyder in command, she departed Philadelphia on 16 May. After calling at Norfolk, Virginia, and transiting the Panama Canal, the battleship arrived at her new home port of Long Beach, California, on 11 June. The next several weeks were occupied with intense pre-deployment training off San Diego, interspersed with maintenance and upkeep periods in port.[9]

One can well imagine the quantity of maintenance and preservation required aboard a ship the size of the *New Jersey*. Fortunately, she had a large crew of some 2,000 men to meet these requirements.

Photo 17-4

Sailors cleaning *New Jersey*'s wooden decks with "holystones," blocks of sandstone about the size of bibles, in which push sticks were fitted. Dreadnought 68-69 (USS *New Jersey*'s 1968-1969 cruise book)

Photo 17-5

Sailors wire brushing *New Jersey*'s anchors, as part of ground tackle
painting and preservation.
Dreadnought 68-69 (USS *New Jersey*'s 1968-1969 cruise book)

Finally, deployment to the Western Pacific was at hand. *New Jersey* stood out of Long Beach on 3 September 1968, making stops at Pearl Harbor and Subic Bay before sailing 25 September for her first tour of gunfire support duty along the Vietnamese coast. She arrived off Da Nang on the morning of the 29th, where nearly three dozen news media personnel came aboard to observe and report on the world's only active battleship. The following morning dawned grey and choppy, bringing with it her first bombardment mission in Vietnam.[10]

Photo 17-6

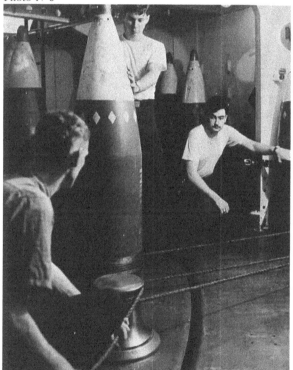

1,900-pound projectiles for the *New Jersey*'s 16-inch gun turrets. Dreadnought 68-69 (USS *New Jersey*'s 1968-1969 cruise book)

Shortly after 0700, the crew was called to General Quarters. The initial target was a supply dump a few miles north of the Benhai River, the border between North and South Vietnam along the 17th parallel, termed the Demilitarized Zone (DMZ). With assistance from a Marine Corps TA-4 Skyhawk spotter plane, the target was soon eliminated by 1,900-pound projectiles blasted from turret barrels amidst a wreath of bright orange flame. On 1 October, the battleship fired at targets 7 to

12 miles north of the DMZ. A TA-4 jet en route to the battleship to spot for her was hit by North Vietnamese anti-aircraft fire. The pilot and rear seat observer ejected near the *New Jersey*, and were plucked from the sea by the guided missile destroyer *Towers* (DDG-9), serving as the battleship's "shotgun" escort.[11]

Photo 17-7

Sailors aboard *New Jersey* receiving powder cases for her 16-inch guns. Dreadnought 68-69 (USS New Jersey's 1968-1969 cruise book)

On 2 October, *New Jersey* went alongside the ammunition ship *Haleakala* (AE-25) for her first replenishment at sea. During the four-hour evolution, she received ninety-six 16-inch projectiles, 644 5-inch projectiles, and associated powder. In the coming days, the battleship often fired both day and night missions off North Vietnam. At night, her guns provided H&I (harassment and interdiction) fire. Since no visible spotting was available, there were no corrections to ensure that rounds were falling on prearranged targets. But, at minimum, the H&I missions forced the enemy to back off and "keep their heads down."[12]

During the daytime, jet aircraft were used for spotting because their greater speed made them less vulnerable to anti-aircraft fire and surface-to-air missiles than propeller-driven aircraft. The 16-inch rounds fired by the *New Jersey* frequently had a flight time as long as seventy-five or eighty seconds, depending on the range from the ship to the target. Communications with the aircraft provided the pilot a count-down of time elapsed during projectile flight. Just before impact, the pilot would dive down to see where the rounds landed, then immediately regain altitude to reduce exposure to enemy fire.[13]

New Jersey continued to move up the coast of North Vietnam. On 12 October, she used A-7 attack aircraft from the carrier *America* (CVA-66) to spot her fire against heavily fortified caves at Vinh. The battleship fired at the caves on the following two days as well, and during the afternoon of 14 October, at coastal artillery pieces on the island of Hon Matt. During the latter mission, the airborne spotter reported a secondary explosion and the destruction of an artillery piece, and then exclaimed—You've blown away a large slice of the island, it's down in the ocean.[14]

POLITICAL CONSIDERATIONS BRING A HALT TO BOMBARDMENT OF TARGETS IN NORTH VIETNAM

During the remainder of the month, *New Jersey* fired at targets in both North and South Vietnam; providing preparatory fire from 23-27 October for a battle involving U.S. troops in the II-Corps area. On 1 November, the battleship received messages from the Joint Chiefs of Staff indicating that all of North Vietnam was now off limits to U.S. bombing and shore bombardment. Within a few days Vice President Hubert Humphrey was to face Republican challenger Richard Nixon in the presidential election. Humphrey had been hampered by his support of the war (Nixon pledged to get the U.S. out of Vietnam), and now President Lyndon Johnson was making a conciliatory gesture which might aid in bargaining for peace.[15]

As a result of this direction, *New Jersey* thereafter fired her guns in support of allied ground troops in South Vietnam, instead of being employed to interdict the supply train in the north. On 8 November, she was detached from the gunline and proceeded to Subic Bay, to give the crew their first liberty ashore in a month and a half. Returning to the gunline, *New Jersey* racked up her biggest one-day score on 25 November, when she was credited with destroying 117 structures and thirty-two bunkers.   She made another trip to Subic in December, arriving there on the 10th, followed by a port visit to Singapore.[16]

New Jersey returned to her station off the DMZ on 22 December. After two days of shooting, ship's company was treated to a USO show from atop turret one, in which Bob Hope, Les Brown's band, former football player Roosevelt Grier, and Ann-Margret and other gorgeous girls entertained the officers and men.[17]

Photo 17-8

Bob Hope, Ann-Margret, and Les Brown's band aboard *New Jersey*, as part of Hope's Christmas USO Show in 1968.
Dreadnought 68-69 (USS New Jersey's 1968-1969 cruise book)

FIRST QUARTER 1969, FINAL GUN DUTY IN VIETNAM

> *In the tunnels beneath a bunker there can be as many as 30 men hiding... that's why we want to use the 16-inch projectile. It penetrates and obliterates a bunker. It's the most effective weapon for this type of target.*

—Explanation by Lt. Comdr. Norman Corlett, Navy Liaison Officer with the First Marine Division, as to the importance of *New Jersey* big guns to an impending operation. He explained that the targets were bunker and tunnel complexes, part of a staging area for a suspected Viet Cong regiment.[18]

Christmas came and went quickly, and the ship resumed her firing missions through year's end. The first day of 1969 found the *New Jersey* on the gunline off South Vietnam operating in support of the Third Marine Division just south of the DMZ. She fired at targets in and south of the buffer zone, destroying nine bunkers and four structures near Con Thien, and continued to support the Third Marines until 3 January, when she moved down the coast. From off Da Nang, *New Jersey* provided gunfire support to the First Marines over the next several days. On the 11th, she steamed farther down the coast to the Mo Duc area of the Quang Ngai Province. Her tasking was to conduct diversionary bombardment on 12 January, to mask amphibious landings on the Batangan Peninsula the following morning.[19]

OPERATION BOLD MARINER

The *New Jersey* fired four prearranged unobserved missions on Sunday and that night her secondary battery continued to put rounds into the Mo Duc area. At 0400 on 13 January, she moved north to take up her fire support station off Batangan for the actual landings by two Marine Corps battalion landing teams. The objective of BOLD MARINER was to cordon off the peninsula, where the entire population was considered hostile, and trap the 300 or so guerillas operating there. The landings—purported to be the largest of the war to that date—were carried out as scheduled, the helicopter troops landed at 0700 and the first boat wave an hour later. Fire support was not requested, and the *New Jersey* left at noon to proceed to Subic for upkeep and rearming.[20]

Photo 17-9

U.S. Marines land on the Batangan Peninsula in Quang Ngai Province,
South Vietnam, on 13 January 1969, by amphibious tractors from ships
of the Seventh Fleet, to commence Operation BOLD MARINER.
NARA photograph A800449 (Reference Number: 127-GVB-60-A800449)

New Jersey returned to the gunline off Da Nang on 10 February. She
destroyed twenty bunkers and sixteen military structures in Communist
strongholds south of Da Nang on the 12th, in the operation referred to
in the preceding quoted material.   The battleship remained near Da
Nang until the night of 13 February supporting the Korean Marines and
elements of the U.S. First Marine Division.   On Valentine's Day, the
14th, she moved north to a position just below the DMZ to provide
support for the Third Marines.[21]

New Jersey's busiest night during the preceding and remaining fire
missions in 1969 (and of the entire deployment), came on 22 February.

Date/Period	Employment
1-11 Jan 69	Naval gunfire support, South Vietnam
11-13 Jan 69	Naval gunfire support, Operation Bold Mariner, South Vietnam
10-22 Feb 69	Naval gunfire support, South Vietnam
23 Feb 69	Massive main and secondary battery support by *New Jersey* credited with saving Marine outpost Oceanview, from being overrun by large contingent of North Vietnamese regulars
24 Feb-12 Mar 69	Naval gunfire support, South Vietnam
21 Mar-1 Apr 69	Naval gunfire support, South Vietnam[22]

DEFENSE OF U.S. MARINE OUTPOST OCEANVIEW

Oceanview had its own devils for those that were up there. You knew you were the closest thing to the DMZ, and if the NVA wanted to pick a serious fight, they could overrun the place in a heartbeat.

—Observation by Richard Lennon, a retired Marine captain who served at Outpost Oceanview during the Vietnam War.[23]

At a little past 0100 on 22 February, as *New Jersey* was engaged in conducting prearranged unobserved fire, she received an urgent call for fire from a Marine outpost under attack. The outpost, named Oceanview, was located in a very isolated spot on the coast north of the Cua Viet River, and just south of the DMZ. Manned by about twenty Marines and a three-man Naval Gunfire Liaison team, it had sprung up in sand dunes to serve as a forward observation post. The post lay as far north as any American was stationed during the war, and could be reached only by Amtrac (amphibious tractor) or helicopter.[24]

Oceanview was attacked by a force later estimated to be about 130 North Vietnamese regulars, as part of the second Tet Offensive. In spite of a conditional Tet truce unilaterally declared by the Communists, many American and South Vietnamese military leaders thought there would be a reprise of the attacks that had occurred all over South Vietnam in 1968, but the 1969 Tet passed with little additional activity.[25]

The Communists struck during the week after Tet, launching attacks against 115 cities and military bases. Most of the attacks by the People's Army of Vietnam (PAVN) and Viet Cong (VC) centered on military targets near Saigon and Da Nang and were quickly beaten off. Some speculate they were mounted to test the will of new U.S. President Richard Nixon, who retaliated the following month by secretly bombing North Vietnamese Army/Viet Cong sanctuaries in Cambodia.[26]

A chronological record of the night's action from the *New Jersey's* operation report follows:

0106: Emergency call for fire from forward observation post, Third Marine Division. Unknown number of enemy troops attacking. Commenced secondary battery fire, two mounts, increasing to four mounts and adding main battery as attack intensified.
0400: Continued high explosive fire multiple targets main and secondary batteries while providing spotter illumination.

0530: Attack intensity diminishing, continued responding to calls for fire, spotter reports enemy withdrawing carrying casualties.
0633: Ceased all fire, attack repulsed.[27]

A total of 1,710 five-inch rounds was fired that night in nearly six hours of continuous fire. At various times throughout the night the *New Jersey* was teamed with the Coast Guard cutter *Owasco* (WHEC-39) and two artillery batteries. One spotter, Lance Corporal Roger Clouse, controlled all fire that night; at one point, he was directing six batteries simultaneously.[28]

NEW JERSEY DECOMMISSIONED

> *War is hell, and it is also expensive, and the American people have tired of the expense of defending freedom.*
>
> —Comment by Capt. J. Edward Snyder Jr., USN, during the ceremony where he relinquished command of the battleship USS *New Jersey* to his successor, Capt. Robert C. Peniston, USN.[29]

Her first Vietnam deployment completed, *New Jersey* departed Subic Bay on 3 April 1969 for Japan. She arrived at Yokosuka for a two-day visit, sailing for the United States on 9 April. She arrived at Long Beach on 5 May 1969, her first visit to her home port in eight months. Through the summer months, *New Jersey*'s crew toiled to prepare the mighty warship for another deployment. Deficiencies discovered on the gunline were remedied, and all hands looked forward to another opportunity to prove her worth in combat. Reasons of economy soon dictated otherwise. On 22 August 1969, the Secretary of Defense approved a list of ships to be inactivated; at the top was *New Jersey*.[30]

Five days later, Capt. Robert C. Peniston assumed command of a ship already earmarked for the "mothball fleet." *New Jersey* departed Long Beach on 6 September for the Puget Sound Naval Shipyard in Washington. She arrived on the 8th, and began the necessary pre-inactivation overhaul to ready herself for decommissioning. On 17 December 1969, *New Jersey*'s colors were hauled down and she entered the inactive fleet, echoing the words of her last commanding officer: "Rest well, yet sleep lightly; and hear the call, if again sounded, to provide fire power for freedom."[31]

18

Frank E. Evans Cut in Half in Collision with *Melbourne*

The facts show that no collision alarm or any other alarm was sounded in EVANS prior to the collision. As a consequence, only those personnel on watch topside were aware a collision was imminent and all others suffered the collision without any prior warning. The testimony of the survivors describes the disorientation and confusion of personnel awakened while the ship was being rolled 90 degrees by MELBOURNE.

—Commander in Chief, U.S. Pacific Fleet's endorsement on
Rear Admiral J [remainder of name redacted]
investigation report of 18 July 1969.[1]

Photo 18-1

Destroyer USS *Frank E. Evans* in drydock at Subic Bay, 6 June 1969, after she was involved in a collision with the Australian aircraft carrier HMAS *Melbourne*. Naval History and Heritage Command photograph #NHF-124

USS *Frank E. Evans* (DD-754) was serving in her third conflict, on the gunline off the coast of South Vietnam, when she was ordered out of the combat zone to participate in the SEATO exercise Sea Spirit. (The Southeast Asia Treaty Organization is an international organization for collective defense in Southeast Asia, established on 19 February 1955.) The *Allen M. Sumner*-class destroyer had been commissioned on 3 February 1945, early enough to participate in the closing stages of World War II, and saw much action during the Korean War—receiving one battle star for WWII and five stars for Korean war service.[2]

Photo 18-2

Destroyer USS *Frank E. Evans* (DD-754) under way in January 1969.
Naval History and Heritage Command photograph #NH 107148

In early morning darkness on 3 June 1969, *Evans* was one of five escorts operating with the Australian aircraft carrier HMAS *Melbourne* about 650 miles southwest of Manila, during conduct of the exercise. The other four ships were the American destroyers USS *James E. Kyes* (DD-787) and USS *Everett F. Larson* (DD-830), and New Zealand and British frigates HMNZS *Blackpool* (F77) and HMS *Cleopatra* (F28). At around 0300, *Evans* was ordered to change station from her position in the screen, 3,500 yards ahead of the carrier and to her port side, to one 1,000 yards astern for "plane guard" duty. This assignment involved following close behind a carrier to be in position to rescue the pilots of any planes that ended up in the sea during flight operations.[3]

While changing station, instead of turning to port to maneuver to her new position behind the *Melbourne*, the destroyer turned to starboard instead, passed under the carrier's bow, and was cut in two. The *Evans* had been 3,500 yards in front of *Melbourne* on her port side, steaming a parallel course to *Melbourne*'s. When the *Evans* turned to starboard to cross in front of *Melbourne*, the latter ship's commanding officer, Capt. John Phillip Stevenson, sent a message over voice radio from bridge to bridge warning *Evans* that she was on a collision course. *Melbourne* radioed to the *Evans* that she was turning to port and sounded two short blasts on her siren. *Evans* then spun hard right under *Melbourne*'s bows, resulting in her being struck port side.[4]

Petty Officer Ron Baker, who was in *Melbourne*'s radio room, later described the sensation felt aboard the carrier:

> It was like riding over a piece of corrugated iron on a bicycle. There was a shuddering as we went over something and the initial reaction was, 'We've run aground!' Of course, this was all split-second thinking, and then we realized we were in 1,100 fathoms of water so the chances of running aground were pretty slim. Another thought that went through our heads was that we'd hit a submarine, because we knew there was a Russian submarine in the area monitoring the exercise.[5]

Photo 18-3

HMAS *Melbourne* after the collision with the destroyer USS *Frank E. Evans*.
Courtesy of Commodore Hector Donohue, AM RAN (Retired)

One of *Evans'* lookouts, Seaman Marcus Rodriguez, was thrown into the air by the force of the collision, landed on the flight deck of the carrier and suffered grave injuries. The forward motion of the carrier rolled the *Evans* deeply and violently to starboard, dividing her into two sections in the vicinity of frame 92. The bow section rolled to starboard to an angle approaching 90 degrees, and began to settle with a marked stern-down trim. As it floated down the port side of *Melbourne*, its list increased to about 150 degrees. The bow section continued to rotate further to starboard, inverted, rose up in the air by the head, and disappeared into the deep, after end first.[6]

Of the 10 officers and 101 enlisted men in the forward section of the ship, 4 officers and 33 men survived. Those who were awakened by being thrown from their bunks, found themselves standing or lying on the starboard sides of their compartments, and had great difficulty in selecting escape routes. Seventy-four perished.[7]

As the *Evans* rolled over to starboard and broke in two, the after section righted itself and then drifted slowly down the starboard side of *Melbourne*. It came abreast of the carrier's starboard quarter, and was secured alongside her at approximately 0325. The other four escort ships (*Blackpool*, *Larson*, *Cleopatra*, and *Kyes*) were then ordered to close *Melbourne* to pick up survivors.[8]

RESCUE EFFORTS

Aircrew and aircraft handlers aboard the carrier had been preparing to launch S-2E Tracker anti-submarine aircraft before the collision. Their engines were shut down immediately, and the crews rushed to help; some dangling fire hoses over the carrier's side as makeshift ladders, while others secured *Evans'* after section alongside *Melbourne* with wire cable. Airmen and seamen then dropped over the flight deck down onto the *Evans* to help survivors climb up onto the carrier.[9]

A number of *Melbourne*'s crew were decorated or commended for their actions that night including Lt. Comdr. Colin Patterson, the flight deck officer, who became a Member of the British Empire for his courage in the rescue operations which included boarding the *Evans'* aft section and searching it for survivors. Lt. Robert Burns, a Clearance Diving Officer, was awarded the George Medal "for exceptionally brave conduct and gallantry in saving life at sea following the collision between HMAS *Melbourne* and the American destroyer *Frank E. Evans* on 3rd June, 1969." The text for his medal citation reads:

After the call to emergency stations at 0315 following the collision, Lieutenant Burns proceeded to the quarterdeck and on arrival sighted an American sailor struggling in the water and calling for help. At this time, *Melbourne* was still moving through the water and without knowledge of the rescue organisation which later came into being, he immediately and without hesitation dived some 20 feet into the water to render assistance. After supporting the man, who was both injured and exhausted, he towed him to one of the life rafts launched by *Melbourne*. He lifted the sailor onto the raft, tended to his injuries and then returned once more to the water to swim some 200 yards to a second survivor who was calling for assistance. He towed him to another life raft, some distance away and rendered first aid. Hearing further cries in the distance he left the raft and carried out a further search in the sea endeavouring to ensure no one had been overlooked, but could find no one. Lieutenant Burns acted with great courage in diving from a moving ship at night and without any regard to his personal safety or own recovery. The brave conduct and gallant actions undoubtedly saved the lives of two American sailors and served as an outstanding example to others in *Melbourne* carrying out rescue operations.[10]

Photo 18-4

Lt. Robert James Burns, RAN
Courtesy of Commodore Hector Donohue, AM RAN (Retired)

When the life raft was brought alongside *Melbourne*, Captain Stevenson was in the boat bay and, on looking down exclaimed, "What the hell are you doing there Burns?" This was how he first learnt of Burns' bravery.[11]

Wessex helicopters of No. 817 Squadron (a Royal Australian Navy Fleet Air Arm squadron aboard *Melbourne*) were also busy locating and retrieving survivors from the sea. It was a bright, moonlit night, but the water's surface near *Evans* (in shadows alongside *Melbourne*'s starboard side) was blackness. Aircrewman Jock Donnelly used a 10-inch signal lamp as a spotlight, calling out to the rescuers, 'There's another one!' His helicopter, not having a winch, employed its landing light to locate survivors, while the other Wessexes hauled them up into the aircraft.[12]

Lt. Comdr. Desmond Rogers, No. 817 Squadron's commanding officer, received the Air Force Cross for his efforts and the performance of his squadron. The 817 also received a Meritorious Unit Commendation from the U.S. Secretary of the Navy, for the exemplanary efforts of its aircraft and crews, as delineated in the citation:

> Thirty-eight of the 111 men in the forward section of USS *Frank E. Evans* were able to escape or were thrown into the water. Within 25 minutes of the collision all these men had been returned to the *Melbourne*. The helicopters and men of 817 Squadron were called upon for maximum effort, not only during these first critical minutes when survivors were being illuminated in the water, but also during the more than 15 hours during which search operations continued.[13]

Aboard *Melbourne*, Captain Stevenson ordered the band onto the deck, and the beer vault was opened for the American survivors. Australian sailors later recalled their mates giving away the clothes from their backs, while the clothing store was opened and blankets were passed out. The survivors were later transferred to the carrier USS *Kearsarge* (CVS-33). (The remainder of Task Force 472 had earlier received orders to close *Melbourne* for rescue operations.) Before they were flown off, the Americans stood on the quarterdeck and gave the Australians three cheers.[14]

FRANK E. EVANS HULK TOWED TO SUBIC BAY

Melbourne had been badly holed forward of her collision bulkhead and her trim tanks were flooded. Immediate action was taken to shore up damaged hull plating, and it was estimated that she would be ready to proceed at slow speed in approximately six hours. After all the survivors were removed from the after section of *Evans*, *Melbourne* released what remained of the destroyer and it moved approximately 1,000 yards clear. Every piece of floating debris in the area was recovered, the search was called off at 1830, and *Melbourne* then proceeded slowly to Singapore.[15]

At 0500 on 3 June, a damage control team from the *Everett F. Larson* boarded the slowly sinking after half of the *Evans*. Their orders were to survey the damage and if able, to prevent her from sinking to allow for recovery of valuable equipment and records. The officer in charge of the team realized that removal of flooding water low in the ship was causing the *Evans* to become top-heavy with an associated risk of capsizing. Part of the team began removing topside weight. Within a matter of minutes, about 5 tons were jettisoned by cutting loose a large ventilation fan motor, a loading machine used for training gun crews, a damaged boat davit, and the ship's motor whaleboat (which was later recovered by the *James E Kyes*).[16]

Once it was safe to do so, *Larson* approached the *Evans* and made her fast alongside. Towing hawsers were rigged in preparation for *Larson* to take *Evans* in tow, if required. However, during the afternoon the fleet tug USS *Tawasa* (AT-92) came alongside *Larson* to take over salvage operations. Upon *Tawasa* assuming responsibility for *Evans*, *Larson* departed. The remainder of that day and part of the next were devoted to preparing *Evans* for towing, and the tug got under way for Subic Bay on 4 June with wreckage in tow. Arriving in Subic Bay on 9 June, she laid the ruined destroyer alongside a pier.[17]

Photo 18-5

Frank E. Evans' after section, made up alongside USS *Everett F. Larson* (DD-830), after she was cut in two in a collision with the Australian aircraft carrier *Melbourne*. Naval History and Heritage Command photograph #NH 98651

AFTERMATH

On 12 June 1969, the chief of Naval Operations ordered that *Frank E. Evans* be decommissioned on 1 July 1969. This took place on the date specified, and she was subsequently sunk by the guided missile destroyer USS *Cochrane* (DDG-21) for target practice.[18]

Following a joint RAN–USN board of inquiry to establish the events of the collision and the responsibility of those involved, the commanding officers of *Melbourne* and *Evans*, and the two junior officers in control of *Evans* at the time of the collision were court-martialed. The three USN officers were charged, and the RAN officer was cleared of wrongdoing.[19]

MEMORIAL SERVICE FOR THE *FRANK E. EVANS*

Years later, a memorial service for the seventy-four officers and men of the USS *Frank E. Evans* who perished in the South China Sea, was held in Long Beach, California.

> *They shall grow not old, as we that are left grow old:*
> *Age shall not weary them, nor the years condemn.*
> *At the going down of the sun and in the morning*
> *We will remember them.*

> —Stanza of the poem "For the Fallen" by Robert Laurence Binyon
> (1869-1943), which was included in a brochure given to attendees
> at the first annual Memorial Service for the USS *Frank E. Evans*
> (DD-754), held in Long Beach, California, on June 3 2005.[20]

The identities of these men may be found in Appendix C, as well as others who were killed in action, or who died by natural causes or as a result of accidents at sea or ashore, while assigned to ships that served on the gunline in the Vietnam War.

19

Turnover to the Vietnamese

Don't you people realize what's happening?... There is no longer a consensus of support for the war back in the United States. I have a letter in my pocket from the president [Lyndon B. Johnson] that tells me to turn the war over to the Vietnamese.... You tell me that we'll be all turned over by 1976. That's out of the question! The country will not sit still for that kind of commitment. The president wants to get the war turned over as soon as possible. We have to make that happen.

—Gen. Creighton W. Abrams Jr., commander, U.S. Military
Assistance Command, Vietnam, addressing his chief
advisors at a meeting on 2 November 1968[1]

A decline in Seventh Fleet operations during the post-Tet years from late 1969 to early 1972, reflected a diminishing American role in the war. The prohibition against bombing North Vietnam, effective on 1 November 1968, limited the number of lucrative targets available to Task Force 77 to those in South Vietnam, Laos, and Cambodia. Additionally, beginning in 1970, the U.S. Navy enacted stringent measures to conserve fuel, ammunition, and aircraft to cut operating costs. As a result, the monthly average during 1968 of three aircraft carriers on Yankee Station decreased to two from 1969 to 1971. Similarly, the 1968 monthly average of 5,000 to 6,000 aircraft sorties in Southeast Asia dropped to between 3,000 and 4,000 from November 1968 to mid-1970. This level dropped further through the end of 1971, as naval air averaged 1,000 to 2,500 sorties in Laos and South Vietnam.[2]

The changing U.S. role in the war and the relatively low level of enemy combat activity in the coastal regions also resulted in a reduced need for naval gunfire support in the post-Tet years. Accordingly, fewer ships were made available to the Naval Gunfire Support Unit, and the Navy withdrew many ships with large-caliber guns. Immediately prior to the battleship *New Jersey*'s return to the United States in early 1969, generally, one battleship, one cruiser, four to ten destroyers, and two rocket ships were providing Naval gunfire support. By 1971, only three ships, on average, steamed offshore; one assigned in support of I-Corps, and the others Vietnamese operations in the Ca Mau and U Minh areas of the southernmost reaches of South Vietnam.[3]

VIETNAMIZATION COMPLETED

Photo 19-1

Activities associated with MARKET TIME operations: inspection and boarding of junks and sampans suspected of smuggling arms and ammunition to the Viet Cong. USS *Camp* (DER-251) Western Pacific 1967-1968 cruise book

During this period, responsibility for Operation MARKET TIME was turned over the South Vietnamese, as part of the ACTOV program of the U.S. Navy and the Coast Guard's SCATTOR (Small Craft Assets, Training, and Turnover of Resources) plan. The term Vietnamization, used by the Nixon administration, and the Navy acronym ACTOV (Accelerated Turnover to the Vietnamese) meant the same thing. President Richard M. Nixon had promised Americans that if elected to the highest office, he would get the United States out of the war, and he meant to do so, as soon as possible.[4]

In September 1970, Task Force 115 turned over the last of the PCFs and WPBs assigned to the Market Time inner barrier to the Vietnamese Navy. Through the following year, 1971, the U.S. Navy transferred seagoing ships, harbor control and mine craft, and logistic support craft of many types, including the Coast Guard cutters *Yakutat* (WHEC-380), *Bering Strait* (WHEC-382), *Castle Rock* (WHEC-383), and *Cook Inlet* (WHEC-384), each equipped with 5-inch guns.[5]

Among the Navy ships handed over were the former tank landing ship *Garrett County*, reconfigured as a small craft tender, and the radar escort picket ship *Camp* (DER-251). *Camp* was one of the ships assigned to Market Time to serve on the gunline, due to an immediate threat to allied troops ashore.[6]

Photo 19-2

Photograph used on the cover of the destroyer escort USS *Camp*'s (DE-251) Western Pacific 1967-1968 cruise book

As one example, while *Camp* was deployed as a unit of the Seventh Fleet from 6 July 1967 to 26 February 1968, she was assigned on an alternating basis: duties as SOPA, Hong Kong, to the Taiwan Patrol, and to Market Time operations. (SOPA is a fleet shorthand for Senior

Officer Present Afloat.)   About seventy percent of her deployment involved duty with Market Time forces.[7]

Her first such commitment began on 26 July, when *Camp* relieved the *Wilhoite* (DER-397) and took up her patrol off Vietnam's northern coastline.   Day and night her crew watched artillery fire and air strikes as the Army and Air Force pounded the tenacious Viet Cong. Frequently, while on patrol, *Camp* provided fuel and fresh water for PCFs ("Swift boats") operating in the area.[8]

On 7 August, *Camp* was notified that Viet Cong were overrunning the Vietnamese Naval Junk Base 16 on the Song Tra Khuc River, in Quang Ngai Province.   The motor-propelled and sail junk boats of the Coastal Junk Force (manned by Regional Irregular Forces personnel and local fishermen recruited for the occasion) kept watch along the 1,200-mile coastline. The original name Coastal Junk Force was later changed to Regular Forces and came to be known as Coastal Groups.[9]

The destroyer escort sped to the aid of the Vietnamese and an American advisor.   Arriving on the scene within an hour, it was learned that a spotter was not available and targets were unidentified.   Being tactically infeasible to support a counteroffensive, Comdr. Paul D. Butcher (*Camp*'s commanding officer) directed PCFs to enter the river and evacuate wounded personnel.   *Camp* used her guns for the next three nights to provide star shell illumination, as base personnel braced themselves against further attack and adequately rebuilt their defenses.[10]

The 306-foot *Camp*, a Fairbanks-Morse diesel-propelled, 1,590-ton *Edsall*-class destroyer escort was commissioned on 16 September 1943. Following war service, she was decommissioned at the New York Navy Yard on 1 May 1946, after 2.6 years of service. Recommissioned on 31 July 1956 as DER-251, she was assigned to Newport, Rhode Island, as a unit of Escort Squadron 16.   In August 1965, *Camp* received orders changing her homeport to Pearl Harbor. Subsequent duty in Vietnam included her serving as an escort for the battleship *New Jersey*.[11]

On 13 February 1971, *Camp* was decommissioned, transferred to South Vietnam, and renamed *Tran Hung Dao* (HQ-1). She escaped with South Vietnamese forces to the Philippines in 1975 as part of Operation FREQUENT WIND. Chapter 21 provides details of this operation. *Tran Hung Dao* subsequently became the destroyer escort BRP *Rajah Lakandula* (PS-4) of the Philippine Navy, and was still in use as a stationary barracks ship in Subic Bay as of 1999.[12]

HMAS *VENDETTA*'S VIETNAM SERVICE

The remainder of the chapter is devoted to the deployment of HMAS *Vendetta* in 1969-1970. Her duties were akin to those of other USN and RAN ships during the post-Tet period. The Australian destroyer (captained by Comdr. Eric Eugene Johnston) departed Sydney Harbor on 15 September 1969. She was bound for Subic, where she was to replace HMAS *Brisbane* in the Seventh Fleet on the 28th. The *Daring*-class destroyer, like USS *Carronade*—an inshore fire support ship, and the subject of Chapter 12—was unique amongst ships ordered to duty on the gunline during the war.[13]

Photo 19-3

HMAS *Vendetta* (D08) departing Sydney Harbor, Australia.
Courtesy of Commodore Hector Donohue, AM RAN (Retired)

The four Royal Australian Navy warships that served in Vietnam were supplied with fuel, ammunition, food and other stores by ships of the Seventh Fleet Mobile Logistic Support Force. These ships ranged in size from the 53,000-ton fast combat support ship *Sacramento* (AOE-1) to smaller oilers, ammunition ships, and store ships.[14]

The three sister ships *Hobart*, *Perth* and *Brisbane* (modified *Charles F. Adams*-class destroyers built in the United States) were well suited to integration with the Seventh Fleet. Minimal modification of logistic procedures was required as these ships, with their U.S. Navy-type armament and fire control system, used standard USN ammunition, electronic components and other spare parts. *Vendetta*, with her British armament, required special accommodations.[15]

To keep her rearmed, HMAS *Jeparit* (an Australian National Lines bulk carrier operated by the Royal Australian Navy between 1969 and

1971) carried ammunition for her 4.5-inch guns from Australia to Subic
Bay. At Subic, it was put aboard U.S. Navy ammunition ships for
delivery to *Vendetta* on the gunline. To ensure compatibility and enable
the Australian-built destroyer to replenish at sea from U.S. Navy oilers,
ammunition, and supply ships, some adaptations were required. These
included the installation of modified "housefall" kingposts fore and aft,
and being fitted with four probe-fueling points for rapid refueling.[16]

Photo 19-4

The aircraft carrier USS *Hancock* (CVA-19) and the guided missile destroyer
USS *Robison* (DDG-12) refuel from the USS *Sacramento* (AOE-1), 1 October 1965.
National Archives photograph #USN 1109945

On 2 October 1969, *Vendetta* relieved the *Walke* (DD-723) at Da
Nang as Naval Gunfire Support Ship for I-Corps. Enemy activity in the
area was light for the remainder of the month as North Vietnamese
Army and Viet Cong forces were preparing for the winter-spring
campaign expected to begin in November. Experience had shown that
at such times, enemy units tended to avoid major actions in favor of
consolidating supplies of food and arms.[17]

While operating on patrols from Da Nang (on the South China Sea
at the mouth of the Han River), *Vendetta* first experienced the necessity
to weave through tightly-packed fishing fleets manned by taciturn crews
who declined to acknowledge the presence of the warship zigzagging

her way among them. At night, she had to thread her way through unlit fishing craft, and her propellers were in constant danger of being fouled by their nets, lines and stakes. Such challenges existed at many locations along the Vietnamese coast, as depicted in the following photograph.[18]

Photo 19-5

Tank landing ship USS *Chesterfield County* (LST-551) moving through fishing craft and nets in the Perfume River, near the DMZ, April 1968. Naval History and Heritage Command photograph #NH 82555

Photo 19-6

Vendetta's (D08) divers entering the water in Da Nang Harbor to conduct a bottom search for possible mines. Courtesy of Commodore Hector Donohue, AM RAN (Retired)

While in port at Da Nang, strict precautions were taken against mining of the ship by enemy sappers, although no swimmers had been observed in the harbor for the previous year. (North Vietnamese and Viet Cong swimmer sappers were elite special forces trained in the use of explosives and limpet mines.) *Vendetta*'s divers searched her hull and anchor cable as a precautionary measure every morning, and U.S. Navy harbor patrol craft made anti-swimmer sweeps every night.   Any suspicion of an enemy swimmer near the ship resulted in an immediate evacuation of the mess decks and lower compartments, and the ship assuming an advanced state of damage control readiness.[19]

SUPPORT FOR THE U.S. 23RD INFANTRY DIVISION

By 7 October 1969, *Vendetta* had moved south to waters off Quang Tin Province, to provide gunfire support for the 23rd Infantry Division, which was operating in the area of Chu Lai, an important military supply post and major airbase. In the destroyer's first spotted mission, her guns shifted rapidly and accurately from one target to another, destroying a Viet Cong storage area and troop concentration.[20]

Photo 19-7

Chu Lai Peninsula, Vietnam, in January 1966.
Naval History and Heritage Command photograph #NH 74192

SUPPORT FOR KOREAN/VIETNAMESE TROOPS

Following her spotted missions and harassment fire in the vicinity of Da Nang, *Vendetta* proceeded to northern II-Corps to conduct naval gunfire in support of the Korean Capital "Tiger" Division, near its base at Qui Nhon. (In response to U.S. President Johnson's desire to have "more flags" supporting the war, the Republic of Korea had sent the "Tiger" division to South Vietnam in October 1965.) The division was then engaged in operations against elements of the 18th North Vietnamese Army Regiment. On 24 October, *Vendetta* departed for Singapore for a maintenance and leave period.[21]

The Australian destroyer returned to the gunline on 9 November, off Phuoc Tuy Province in III-Corps, where the enemy had initiated the winter-spring campaign on the 3rd. Mid-month, she fired illumination and spotted fire missions for South Vietnamese and Korean troops operating inland of Tuy Hoa in Phu Yen Province (about sixty miles south of Qui Nhon.) The "White Horses" of the Korean 9th Infantry had a larger area of responsibility (AOR) than did the Tigers to the north—and within the AOR were important cities, ports, and military bases at Tuy Hoa, Nha Trang, Cam Ranh, and Phan Rang.[22]

Photo 19-8

Troops of the Korean 9th "White Horse" Infantry Division march under a huge sign welcoming them to South Vietnam. The 5,500-man unit arrived in September 1966 and took up positions along the central coast at Nha Trang, Tuy Hao, and Cam Ranh. U.S. Information Agency photograph #66-3171

On 19 November, three Korean regiments moved into position to make a sweep against four Viet Cong battalions to the west of Tuy Hoa.

Vendetta fired fifty-eight starshells to illuminate the area as enemy forces attempted to break through the cordon. Later, increasing gales, rain and fog of a monsoon made accurately spotted gunfire impossible, and she set a course for Taiwan on the 29th. After visiting Keelung and Kaohsiung for crew liberty, *Vendetta* proceeded southward to Subic for rebarreling and boiler cleaning.[23]

BACK ON THE GUNLINE

The destroyer returned to the gunline on 21 December, taking up her NGFS station near Phan Thiet in southern II-Corps. Harassment fire against Viet Cong positions ceased the evening of 24 December, when the Christmas ceasefire began. *Vendetta* withdrew to seaward, six miles off the coast, but remained on patrol in a two-watch defense posture. (At this condition of readiness, half the crew was on watch, with at least one gun mount manned.)[24]

Vendetta's guns went back into action the day after Christmas, when she took under fire Viet Cong camp fires observed in the hills southwest of Phan Thiet. Harassment firings on enemy positions in the vicinity of Phan Thiet continued unabated until the three-hour New Year ceasefire on 1 January 1970. For this short interlude, *Vendetta* tracked two craft by radar and, as one neared the beach, she took it under fire, destroying the craft while in the process of landing stores. The Australian sailors were gratified to learn that a Viet Cong defector had told captors that his unit "had become completely demoralized during the past two to three weeks because of the heavy mortars from the sea."[25]

Following a lengthy period in Hong Kong for needed boiler repairs, *Vendetta* was back on station on 18 February, near the Long Hai hills, east of Vung Tau. Her mission involving firing on cave complexes was successful. Australian troops later found the bodies of nineteen Viet Cong, victims of her guns. *Vendetta* relieved the destroyer escort *Bradley* (DE-1041) near Cap Ke Ga south of Phan Thiet on the 21st. While providing long-range fire for a clearing operation near the coast, Viet Cong troops, detected moving through the undergrowth, were a principal target for the destroyer's 4.5-inch guns.[26]

VENDETTA'S COMBAT DUTY NEARS AN END

Vendetta took up station on 2 March near Phan Rang, a coastal town in the southern part of the central lowlands. She shelled a Viet Cong village being built high in the mountains, in an area spared naval gunfire for some time. Thereafter, she bombarded a bunker and cave complex on a headland before proceeding to Subic, where new barrels were fitted to A and X turrets (the forwardmost of her two forward gun mounts, and her after gun mount) on 7 March. *Vendetta*, with three turrets, was always able to respond to a call for fire immediately, unlike the DDGs *Hobart*, *Perth*, and *Brisbane*.[27]

Vendetta's last period of duty on the gunline involved assignment to waters off the notorious U Minh Forest in IV-Corps. The huge mangrove jungle—which for centuries had offered a safe haven for pirates, smugglers, bandits, and more recently the Viet Cong—covered large areas of the Kien Giang and Ca Mau Provinces. These adjacent provinces encompassed the south and southwest areas of IV-Corps. The assignment proved frustrating because, although South Vietnamese troops were engaged in heavy fighting, *Vendetta* was seldom able to obtain clearance to fire in support of the ground forces.[28]

Map 19-1

IV-Corps Tactical Zone in the southernmost part of South Vietnam

On 28 March 1970, HMAS *Hobart* relieved HMAS *Vendetta* of her duties at Subic Bay. During the turnover of responsibility, Comdr. Eric Eugene Johnson presented "the weight" to Capt. Rothesay Cathcart Swan, in the presence of Flag Officer Commanding the Australian Fleet, Rear Adm. Hugh David Stevenson, CBE. As successive destroyers went on the gunline, they were passed "the weight." Comprised of the bases of two 5-inch powder cases, it symbolized the responsibility imposed on RAN destroyers that served with the Seventh Fleet. The lower section was inscribed with the names, dates, and call signs of the destroyers that served with the fleet.[29]

HMAS *Vendetta* arrived back in Sydney on 11 April 1970, the only Australian-built warship to serve as a combatant in Vietnam.[30]

Photo 19-9

Capt. David Leach, commanding officer of HMAS *Perth* (on the right) handing over "the weight" to Capt. Alan Willis, commanding officer of HMAS *Brisbane*. Courtesy of Commodore Hector Donohue, AM RAN (Retired)

CHALLENGES ASSOCIATED WITH "GUNS UP"

It would be easy after reading about gunline results to believe that dropping rounds on target was relatively easy, absent bad weather hindering spotting, or encounters with enemy shore battery fire. Such was not the case, as accurately and humorously portrayed in the poem CIC AND THE GUNS by Edwin J. McKinley, a Radarman First Class Petty Officer assigned to the destroyer escort USS *Bradley* (DE-1041).

Photo 19-10

Destroyer escort USS *Bradley* (DE-1041) under way in July 1965. Naval History and Heritage Command photograph NH 96757

Breakdowns of gun mounts occurred as a result of the stresses of endless hours of firing, and the associated effects of heavy vibrations on interrelated mechanical, electrical, and hydraulic systems. When the guns were up (most of the time) the bridge-combat information center-gun plot-fire control director-and ammunition handling room team had to work perfectly in concert. If not, spotters, in this case, call sign Two Six Charlie, would provide the ship and her captain "direct feedback"—particularly if that individual had to duck for cover.

CIC AND THE GUNS

Gunline aboard the BRADLEY is a hell'va life,
    Be you short timer, lifer, or observer with "wife."
Reveille goes at 0438,
    Gotta be on station, don't be late.
You're up in the morning before the sun,
    Fire mission is called, man the damn gun.
Break out the hoses, charge 'em well,
    In case of fire, run like hell.

We're on station, ready to go,
    The gun craps out, wouldn't you know.
You grab your tools and work for a spell,
    Every bolt frozen tighter than hell.
You beat with a hammer' til you're ready to cuss,
    Gun boss in CIC makin' a helluva fuss.

You get it fixed, everyone's glad,
    Fog rolls in, radar goes bad.
Radar up and the fog goes away,
    Hot Damn, shouts the gun boss, we're ready to play.

On station and ready we finally report
    We bet ten to one, the rounds won't fall short.
We crank in bearing, a range – height are all right.
    Plot set, Shoot. Boom, Boom, Boom.
    "Shot," Hey, what's time-of-flight?

Ivory Coast, Ivory Coast this is Two Six Charlie
    One gun, One salvo, not a whole damn volley.
Two Six Charlie this is Ivory Coast, Did spots take effect?
    Damned if I know, I'm on the deck.

Gun Control, 51 has a foul bore,
    Unload 51, point to the rear,
Make sure all bores are clear.
    Gun Control, Captain, What's the score?
    Well, All rounds fell short sir, but we'll try once more.

Wait' til we turn, we're way outta range,
  Combat, Conn, Try aiming this time, just for a change.

Captain, The magazine's empty, there are no more.
  Don't worry, tonight we'll pick up 4,000 more.
But Sir, Why are we getting so few?
  The Exec said we could hold field day if
  we don't find something better to do ......[31]

ABRUPT END TO RELATIVE LULL ON THE GUNLINE

Between near the end of 1968—when SEA DRAGON operations were terminated by direction of President Lyndon B. Johnson—and early 1972, less than a handful of U.S. Navy ships serving on the gunline earned combat action ribbons. This same phenomenon held true for Royal Australian Navy destroyers, as may be deduced from the table:

Summary of Royal Australian Navy Ships' Efforts on the Gunline

Ship	Total Rounds Fired	No. Times Enemy Fire Received
HMAS *Hobart* (D39)		
1st Deployment (7 Mar - 27 Sep 67)	9,204	9
2nd Deployment (22 Mar - 11 Oct 68)	16,270	3
3rd Deployment (16 Mar - 17 Oct 70)	16,901	0
Totals:	42,375	12
HMAS *Perth* (D38)		
1st Deployment (2 Sep 67 - 10 Apr 68)	13,351	4
2nd Deployment (19 Sep 68 - 20 Apr 69)	7,648	1
3rd Deployment (14 Sep 70 - 8 Apr 71)	9,712	0
Totals:	30,711	5
HMAS *Brisbane* (D41)		
1st Deployment (20 Mar - 13 Oct 69)	7,891	0
2nd Deployment (16 Mar - 15 Oct 71)	7,760	0
Totals:	15,651	0
HMAS *Vendetta* (D08)		
1st Deployment (15 Sep 69 - 11 Apr 70)	13,709 (4.5") 414 (40mm)	0
Totals:	14,123	0[32]

However, the almost three-and-a-half years of relative safety for ships serving on the gunline came to an end at noon on 30 March 1972. Midday that date, the North Vietnamese Army launched a coordinated invasion of South Vietnam, the so-called "Easter Offensive."

North Vietnam's Easter Offensive

Every minute, hundreds of thousands of people die on this earth. The life or death of a hundred, a thousand, tens of thousands of human beings, even our compatriots, means little.

—Remark attributed to Vo Nguyen Giap after defeating the French at Dien Bien Phu in May 1954, forcing France from Indochina. The relentless and charismatic North Vietnamese general was from the early 1960s to the mid-1970s, perhaps second only to his mentor, Ho Chi Minh, as the face of a tenacious, implacable enemy.[1]

In early March 1972, the relatively calm state of the South Vietnamese countryside seemed to vindicate the Nixon administration's "Vietnamization" policy—withdrawal of U.S. ground combat forces from the country while also improving the capability of the armed forces of the Republic of Vietnam. Richard M. Nixon had succeeded Lyndon B. Johnson as president on 20 January 1969 amidst much dissent and unrest throughout the nation, resulting from the long war that had taken many American lives. During his campaign, Nixon had pledged to get the United States out of Vietnam and, after taking office, he directed additional actions to expand, equip, and train Vietnamese military forces, steadily reduce American troops, and give South Vietnam greater responsibility for fighting the war.[2]

This lull in warfare, however, would prove illusionary. In Hanoi, the senior North Vietnamese general, Vo Nguyen Giap, was planning a massive invasion designed to destroy the South Vietnamese armed forces and capture South Vietnam. Giap hoped for a conclusive outcome, or at least to seize enough territory for North Vietnam to improve its negotiating position in Paris. At noon on 30 March 1972, the North Vietnamese 308th Army Division plus two independent regiments struck the ARVN (Army of the Republic of Vietnam) fire support bases along the DMZ. Concurrently, the 304th Division rolled out of Laos striking past Khe Sanh toward Quang Tri City.[3]

The "Easter Offensive" mounted by the North Vietnamese Army, and led by Soviet-built tanks moving across the DMZ into South Vietnam's Quang Tri province, was the first major assault since the Tet Offensive in January 1968. The difference between the Tet '68 and Easter '72 offensives was that in 1968 the United States had been escalating its operations. In 1972, military action was phasing down and the North Vietnamese knew it. Most of the major U.S. ground forces had already left Vietnam, Nixon had just made his historic visit to Peking, and Secretary of State Henry Kissinger was in Paris negotiating with the North Vietnamese for an end to the Vietnam War.[4]

The destroyer *Bausell* (DD-845) had been operating along the coast from Quang Tri province northward. She was in close to shore and able to visually observe Soviet-built amphibious tanks crossing at the mouth of the Cua Viet River. U.S. Army front line troops, including the 101st Airborne Division, had been withdrawn from South Vietnam, leaving behind only a few advisors. Several of these individuals functioned as spotters, calling in shore bombardment in support of retreating South Vietnamese troops. A few brought fire on their own positions in order to create chaos so they could escape.[5]

Photo 20-1

Naval Gunfire Support mission at "Point Allison," a gunline position just off the coast of Quang Tri Province, but very close to the DMZ.
USS *Bausell* (DD-845) Western Pacific 1971-1972 cruise book

Bausell took the enemy under direct fire, not needing any spotters. Several destroyers started ranging up the North Vietnamese coast in an attempt to slow down and blunt the enemy advances. This operation was called FREEDOM TRAIN. A key choke point to the southern movement of the NVA was the infamous Thanh Hoa Bridge. (Earlier in the war, American pilots had been shot down in considerable numbers while attacking targets like the bridge at Thanh Hoa in North Vietnam.) It was relatively far inland but within range of the destroyer's guns. She hit it at night, but it would be rebuilt the next day. After several of these cycles, *Bausell* continued north, shelling the islands of Hon Ne and Hon Matt, both heavily fortified with shore guns.[6]

OPERATION FREEDOM TRAIN/LINEBACKER

> *USS* Buchanan *has been my "Ace" of FREEDOM TRAIN NGF Operation. Commodore Johnson, ComDesRon 31 in* Buchanan, *has led almost every movement of Naval gunfire since the operation started.* Buchanan, *his flagship, has been in the forefront of this series of operations all the way. It is unfortunate indeed that this outstanding ship was the first to meet tragedy in FREEDOM TRAIN. We all knew that eventually even the poor marksmanship of NVN would find their target. In this case,* Buchanan, *who has defied coastal defense guns on so many occasions, was hit, causing the death of one crewman and injury to seven.* Buchanan *will be repaired and back with us as soon as possible. But we all mourn the loss of a comrade in arms and will miss the services of this gallant ship. Although hit,* Buchanan *still has more to say to the enemy.*

> —Vice Adm. James L. Holloway III, USN,
> commander, U.S. Seventh Fleet.[7]

As South Vietnamese artillery posts fell like dominoes during the first forty-eight hours of the attack, and heavy cloud cover grounded most tactical air, naval gunfire support became the only reliable source of supporting arms along the highway leading to Quang Tri City. U.S. Marine gunfire observers flying with Air Force forward air controllers directed naval gunfire by the *Buchanan* (DDG-14), *Joseph Strauss* (DDG-16), *Waddell* (DDG-24), and *Hamner* (DD-718). The destroyers, under Capt. Theodore R. Johnson Jr., commander, Destroyer Squadron 31, hurled gun rounds day and night at North Vietnamese targets moving anywhere in the coastal region and around the town of Dong Ha.[8]

On 2 April, naval gunfire from the *Buchanan* destroyed four PT-76 amphibious tanks attempting to cross the Cua Viet River, after two American servicemen slowed the advance of the enemy south by blowing up the Dong Ha railroad bridge, the main link over the river to Quang Tri Province. The bridge lay at the intersection of Highway QL-1 and Route 9, north-northwest of Quang Tri. To the south of Quang Tri City, QL-1 was referred to as the "highway of horrors" by refugees fleeing toward Hue during the Easter Offensive.[9]

By mid-day Easter Sunday, 2 April, no resistance existed on the QL-1 axis between advancing enemy forces and the coveted Quang Tri City except a river, a bridge, and a battalion of Vietnamese Marines and tanks. Intelligence reports estimated that three NVA mechanized divisions were involved in the assault into the south with approximately 10,000 infantry, 150 T-54 and PT-76 tanks, 75 tracked anti-aircraft vehicles, one artillery regiment of 47 130mm guns, and anti-aircraft missile units. The 3rd VNMC (South Vietnamese Marine Corps) Battalion, with Capt. John W. Ripley as its sole American advisor, was spreading along Route 9 from Cam Lo to Dong Ha.[10]

With the report of approaching tanks, Maj. Le Ba Binh, the South Vietnamese battalion commander, received orders to "hold Dong Ha at all costs." Ripley was told to expect the worst: a column of PT-76 and T-54 tanks were approaching, refugees were clogging the roads out of Dong Ha, and no further units were available to help. As the Marines and their tanks approached the railroad bridge, a large red North Vietnamese flag was sighted flying over it and NVA infantrymen storming across both spans. Enemy tanks appeared on the horizon, kicking up rooster tails of dust as they sped down QL-1.[11]

Naval gunfire from destroyers in the Tonkin Gulf had some effect on the enemy advance, but not enough to stop them. At noon, M-48 battle tanks of the 20th ARVN Tank Battalion began firing at the NVA tank column, knocking out six Communist vehicles. At 1245, Maj. James E. Smock, the U.S. Army advisor with the tank battalion, received orders to blow the Dong Ha Bridge immediately—a double-lane highway bridge constructed by a U.S. Navy construction battalion in 1969. Smock had blown up, on his own, its single-lane predecessor, originally used as a railway bridge.[12]

Smock, on an ARVN tank, upon sighting Ripley, called "Hey Marine, climb aboard and let's go blow a bridge." The two officers dismounted fairly near the bridge, shielded from enemy view by an old bunker. They then ran across the open space to find ARVN engineers placing 500 pounds of TNT and C-4 plastic explosives at the juncture of the bridge and the approach ramp. Using this method, upon detonation, the bridge would merely "flap" in place and not drop into the river. Ripley quickly determined that the explosives would have to be placed along the girders under the bridge. This action required Ripley to scramble over a high chain-linked fence topped by concertina wire, designed to prevent access to the underpinnings of the bridge. As Ripley swung hand-over-hand and dropped down from one beam and swung over to the next, he positioned the ammunition crates, in which the explosives had been packed, in a staggered pattern. Smock muscled each of the 50lb boxes from near the fence, and placed them within Ripley's reach, who was able to slide them out under the span suspended between the flanges of the adjoining girders.[13]

As the Marine laboriously positioned each crate of TNT, Smock became impatient with Ripley's meticulous manner. Concerned about small-arms fire from the north bank, 50 meters away, he called, "Hey, you dumb jarhead, that isn't necessary... What are you waiting for?" Ripley responded, "You tankers don't know anything," explaining that the charges had to be placed diagonally in order to torque the span from its abutment. When the explosives and electric blasting caps were in place and wired, Ripley tried to detonate the charge from the battery of a burned-out jeep but nothing happened. Fortunately, he had rigged a back-up system of conventional safety-fuse using his teeth to crimp the caps. This was successfully used to detonate the charge after the fuse had been lit and had burned for its prescribed period. When the bridge blew, the span, curling in the predicted twisting manner, was severed from the berm and settled into the river. At 1630, Ripley reported to division headquarters that the bridge had been destroyed.[14]

Air strikes by South Vietnamese A-1 Skyraiders struck the enemy armored column backed up north of the bridge. The enemy was, however, determined to cross. NVA tanks shifted their positions to make room for PT-76 amphibious tanks to come forward to the river's edge. Upon sighting four preparing to cross, Ripley called a naval gunfire mission. *Buchanan* quickly closed the shore to inside the five-fathom curve (30-foot water depth) to decrease the range, and fired off a salvo. All four amphibious tanks were destroyed on the riverbank.[15]

With their armored thrusts thwarted at the Dong Ha and Cua Viet areas, the NVA attempted a crossing at the Cam Lo Bridge to the west. The destroyers squelched enemy movement all night long, as hundreds of gun projectiles were called in upon the enemy. Although the battle for Dong Ha was still in doubt, the Communist armored-assault had been halted on Easter Sunday by the efforts of "a few good men." For their actions that day, Captain Ripley was awarded the Navy Cross, and Major Smock, the Silver Star Medal.[16]

BOMBARDMENT IN SUPPORT OF SOUTH VIETNAM

While providing naval gunfire support in defense of South Vietnam during the Easter Offensive, *Waddell, Buchanan, Joseph Strauss,* and *Hamner* received 58 rounds of counterbattery fire from positions near the mouth of the Cua Viet, but sustained no damage.[17]

By 6 April, *Waddell* had joined *Lockwood* (DE-1064), *Lloyd Thomas* (DD-764), and *Everett F. Larson* (DD-830) in providing naval gunfire support south of the DMZ. *Joseph Strauss, Richard B. Anderson* (DD-786), *Buchanan,* and *Hamner,* in turn, began striking targets in North Vietnam south of the 20th parallel as part of a combined air and naval operation called FREEDOM TRAIN. On the first day of Freedom Train, the cruiser *Chicago* (CG-11) fired a missile at a North Vietnamese radar site for a probable kill. South of the DMZ, Navy destroyers struck the Ben Hai bridge and eight other targets between the DMZ and the Cua Viet. *Waddell* fired on a previously engaged coastal defense site at 18,000 yards and immediately encountered extremely accurate counter fire. Shrapnel was later found strewn on her weather decks.[18]

HAIPHONG HARBOR RAID

> *The cruiser* Oklahoma City, *in company with the Seventh Fleet destroyers* Buchanan, Bausell, Hamner, *and* McKenzie *Sunday shelled targets on the Do Son Peninsula, eight miles from North Vietnam's major port city of Haiphong. While steaming at high speeds in formation and guns blazing, the five ships made a classic display of naval gunfire operations ... the first ever undertaken this far north in Vietnam. The naval gunfire strike operations followed the massive early morning raids from the* Coral Sea, Kitty Hawk, *and* Constellation. *Aircraft from the three carriers again struck targets in Haiphong in conjunction with the shelling attack by* Oklahoma City *and accompanying destroyers. The strike was marked by a dramatic rescue by the* Hamner *which recovered a downed Naval aviator in close proximity while continuing to fire her guns at the enemy shore battery.*

> —United States Seventh Fleet press release describing a raid by U.S. Navy ships on Haiphong Harbor on 16 April 1972.[19]

In mid-April (following a stint of plane guard duty for *Kitty Hawk* and *Coral Sea* at Yankee Station in the Tonkin Gulf), *Bausell* was directed to rendezvous with the cruiser *Oklahoma City* (CLG-5) and several other destroyers about forty miles east of Haiphong Harbor. She joined the *Oklahoma City, Buchanan* (DDG-14), *Hamner* (DD-718), and *George K.*

MacKenzie (DD-836) on the night of 15 April and formed a line-abreast, 1,000 yards apart and slowly approached the coast.[20]

Just prior to first light, when about fifteen miles from Haiphong, the ships set General Quarters and increased speed to 25 knots. The next signal was "break out your BATTLE ENSIGNS." This referred to the practice of hoisting a very large American flag atop the mast before going into battle. *Bausell*'s position was third ship to the right of the *Oklahoma*, which now sported a flag which almost dwarfed the cruiser.[21]

Photo 20-2

Sunrise in Da Nang Harbor, North Vietnam.
USS *Oklahoma City* Western Pacific 1971-1972 cruise book

It was a beautiful cloudless day, with not a hint of a breeze or a ripple on a glassy smooth sea. *Bausell*'s radar screen showed a cluster of hundreds of small contacts, fishing sampans whose number increased as the warships approached the Haiphong Harbor entrance. About twelve miles east of Haiphong Harbor, the formation encountered a long line of merchant ships departing the harbor. They were all Eastern bloc ships—mostly Soviet—and amazingly they dipped their ensigns to the cruiser and destroyers. Convention would have been for the USN ships to dip their flags in kind. On this day, with much more important business pending, the merchantmen were ignored.[22]

About eight miles from Haiphong, but only a few miles from the Do Son Peninsula (an arm of the harbor), all five ships commenced firing their forward guns—rapid, continuous fire—at pre-designated targets. The targets were anti-aircraft missile sites, which were then firing at U.S. fighters supporting bombers. Three aircraft carriers on Yankee Station had emptied their decks and scores of Navy and Marine Corps aircraft were overhead and diving at their targets. The closer the surface strike group got to Haiphong, the more intense the hostile fire became. Water geysers were erupting all around the group, plus black puffs of airbursts above it. *Bausell*'s executive officer was mesmerized by what he was witnessing, until instructions from the commanding officer brought him out of his daze:

> XO! Get off the [bridge] wing and get here under shelter! Better yet, get back to secondary con [located aft] in case the bridge gets a direct hit. We can't both be disabled.[23]

Photo 20-3

Cruiser USS *Oklahoma City* (CLG-5) firing an 8-inch salvo off her port beam.
USS *Oklahoma City* Western Pacific 1971-1972 cruise book

When about two miles from the peninsula, the five ships executed a 90 degree turn to port. This maneuver unmasked the after guns, so that all the ships' guns were firing rapid, continuous fire. It was an amazing display of firepower. In opposing action, a U.S. fighter was hit by a missile directly overhead *Bausell*. The flight of the missile was like a slow-moving telephone pole that increased in speed and then arced to intercept the aircraft. The ejection seat shot up from the aircraft, the parachute deployed, and the empty seat crashed into the sea alongside *Bausell*. She swung out of formation as the parachute drifted aft, but was ordered to resume station. The destroyer behind her, *Hamner*, was directed to pick up the downed pilot.[24]

After depleting their magazines, the strike force did another "9-turn" and returned to Yankee Station. There they rearmed and refueled from an ammunition ship and a tanker. *Oklahoma City* required about 300 crewmen when rearming under way, because 6-inch projectiles, weighting over 100 pounds each, and powder cases, up to 70 pounds, had to be moved and stowed by hand.[25]

Photo 20-4

USS *Oklahoma City* receiving 6-inch projectiles from an ammo ship.
USS *Oklahoma City* (CLG-5) Western Pacific 1971-1972 cruise book

BUCHANAN SUFFERS MEN KILLED AND WOUNDED

The following day, 17 April, *Buchanan* moved north to shell vital bridges around the city of Vinh in North Vietnam, in company with *George K. Mackenzie* and *Hamner.* Around midday, *Mackenzie* shifted her fire to an observation tower on the island of Hon Matt, not far from the coast. Soon after, two enemy patrol boats, believed to be *Shanghai*-class, were sighted in the vicinity of Dao Bien Island. *Mackenzie* quickly took them under fire causing the boats to reverse course and retreat.[26]

Just over ten minutes later, *Buchanan* began receiving incoming fire believed to be from a 120mm or 130mm shore battery. A hit on her 01-deck, starboard side at frame 160, blasted a two-and-half-foot hole in the destroyer, killing Seaman Leonard R. Davis. Seven other members of ship's company were wounded. Seaman Apprentice Shropshire was transferred to the guided missile cruiser *Chicago* for further treatment of a foot wound, as was the body of Seaman Davis.

Buchanan Crewmembers Killed/Wounded by Enemy Fire

SN Leonard D. Davis KIA	GMG3 Danny K. Hammond
Lt. Robert S. Nemmers, Supply Corps	CS3 Frank S. Musiol
SD3 Primicitis J. Beltran	EMC Frederick J. Shortreed Jr.
SA Vincent G. Guerrero	SA Gary D. Shropshire[27]

HIGBEE BOMBED BY NORTH VIETNAMESE MIG-17

In a desperate attempt to defend its coastline from continued Navy shore bombardment, North Vietnam struck back on 19 April. On that day, *Oklahoma City* and destroyers *Higbee* (DD-806) and *Lloyd Thomas* were shelling targets near Dong Hoi while the guided missile destroyer *Sterett* (DLG-31) provided air cover and spotting services for the naval gunfire support ships. *Oklahoma City* carried a Talos missile battery, but *Sterett* was assigned to provide additional anti-aircraft cover with her longer-range Terrier system. She also had her LAMPS (Light Airborne Multi-Purpose System) helicopter aloft to serve as an aerial spotter for the bombarding ships.[28]

Late in the afternoon, *Oklahoma City, Higbee,* and *Lloyd Thomas* began a bombarding run steaming south, parallel to the coast. Counterfire from North Vietnamese shore 'bracketed' the ships, but made no hits. Around 1700, *Sterett*'s radars picked up three hostile aircraft in the vicinity of Dong Hoi just as the naval gunfire support ships were beginning to withdraw from the area. One of the planes, a North Vietnamese Air Force MiG-17 piloted by Nguyen Van Bay, came out of the mountains, went "feet wet" and bored in on *Higbee*. The MiG dropped one 250kg bomb, but the near miss caused no damage. The persistent MiG then circled back and, on this attack run, scored a direct hit on *Higbee*'s after five-inch gun mount.[29]

Photo 20-5

Destruction of USS *Higbee*'s (DD-806) after gun mount resulting from a direct hit by a 250kg bomb dropped by a North Vietnamese Air Force MiG-17.
Courtesy of NavSource and Ty Martin

Photo 20-6

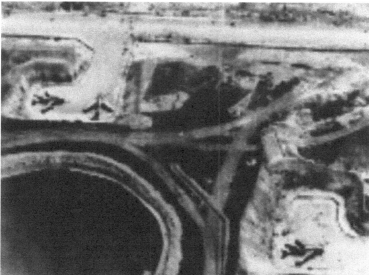

North Vietnamese Air Force Russian-made MiG-17 jet aircraft parked in protective shelters at the Phuc Yen Airfield northwest of Hanoi.
U.S. Information photograph #66-3189

Photo 20-7

Two enemy MiG-17 jet fighters approaching the destroyer USS *Higbee* (DD-806) and two other naval gunfire support ships off Dong Hoi, North Vietnam, on 19 April 1972. USS *Lloyd Thomas* (DD-764) Western Pacific 1972 cruise book

The Soviet-built MiG-17 was not designed to function as a fighter-bomber, but in 1971 Hanoi had ordered that U.S. Navy warships be attacked by elements of the North Vietnamese Air Force. Carrying out this directive required the MiG-17 to be fitted with bomb mountings and release mechanisms for a ground attack role. A short time earlier, two pilots from the 923rd Fighter Regiment had taken off in their modified, bomb laden MiG-17s. Their mission marked the first time that North Vietnamese aircraft actually attacked U. S. fleet units. Each of the planes was armed with two 250kg (550lb) bombs.[30]

The bomb blast, combined with exploding ready ammunition, peeled back the sides of the mount like a sardine can—destroying the gun, but inflicting no fatalities. The gun crew had vacated the turret earlier, following the misfire of a powder case. When a powder case failed to ignite after the firing key was closed, and a hot gun (caused by prolonged firing) could result in a projectile "cooking off" in the barrel, the standard procedure was to evacuate the mount and allow it to cool down before any attempt was made to remove the gun round. Because of this action, the only injuries were those to four men assigned to the upper ammunition handling room below the mount.[31]

Photo 20-8

Terrier missiles aboard DLGs berthed in San Diego, California, 19 May 1961. Naval History and Heritage Command photograph #NH 124079

Sterett fired a Terrier missile at the attacking MiG, but missed the target. Her second one did not miss. Soon after the downed MiG had begun its attack, a second MiG flown by Le Xuan Di had turned around and headed back inland. *Sterett* fired two additional Terrier missiles and, when the plane and the missiles disappeared from radar simultaneously, a second MiG kill was assumed.[32]

Photo 20-9

Soviet *P-6* class motor torpedo boats in formation at high speed.
National Archives photograph #USN 1095067

However, the battle was not yet over. As the four ships left the area heading northeast, *Sterett*'s radar picked up two small surface targets heading at high speed toward the formation. The destroyer locked her five-inch gunfire control radar on the nearest target and at the same time began maneuvering to allow her forward missile fire control radar to lock on to the same target. Suddenly, the missile fire control radar lifted off the surface target and began tracking something in the air coming toward them. (The Terrier fire control system was programmed so that if any new target appeared to separate upward from a surface target, it assumed that a missile had been fired, and would automatically lock on to the air target.)[33]

Sterett's electronic countermeasures operators detected a signal they identified as a Soviet-built SS-N-2 'Styx' anti-ship missile homing radar. The destroyer fired two Terriers at the suspected incoming missile and *Sterett*'s bridge watch saw the two missiles enter a cloud bank and seconds later heard two explosions, although they never saw the actual impact. At the same time, the missiles and the target disappeared from radar. They had every reason to believe they had killed a Styx missile.[34]

In the meantime, the surface contacts were nine miles away, paralleling the missile destroyer's course and speed of 32 knots. *Sterett* took them under fire with her 5-inch guns, and the targets (identified as P-6-type boats) disappeared from radar and were presumed destroyed.[35]

The reported Styx missile kill was the subject of much investigation and study. Analysts concluded that if *Sterett* had shot down another air target it was most likely not a Styx. This assessment was based primarily on a belief that the North Vietnamese did not have a Soviet-supplied anti-ship missile until 1974. In his analysis of the Battle of Dong Hoi, Stuart Slade, a senior aerospace and defense analyst, concluded, "I think the USN had good reason to disallow the claimed shoot-down. This does not change the fact that the CIC crew did a fantastic job in a very confused environment. They had an air action to fight, a crippled ship to protect and also a potentially lethal surface threat developing. Even if they didn't kill a missile, they still deserve a salute for jobs well and skillfully done."[36]

DESTROYER GUNFIRE SUPPORT FOR THE MINING OF HAIPHONG HARBOR

I have determined that we should go for broke.... We must punish the enemy.

—President Richard M. Nixon expressing in a memorandum to
Secretary of State Henry Kissinger, his desire to resume a
broad air interdiction campaign against North Vietnam,
and a naval blockade of the entire North Vietnamese
coast, including mining actions against Haiphong
and other major harbors.[37]

Despite the efforts by carrier air and destroyers to stem the invasion of the Republic of Vietnam by North Vietnamese troops, on 1 May 1972 South Vietnam's military situation was extremely bleak. Following a month of hard fighting, the NVA occupied the country's northernmost province and was threatening Hue, Kontum, and An Loc. Moreover, a continuous stream of refugees, including many deserters, flowed into Hue, making the situation more desperate for the city's defenders. The deteriorating military situation, especially in Military Region I, threatened not only the peace negotiations in progress but the entire Vietnamization program and the survival of South Vietnam as an independent country.[38]

North Vietnam's invasion of South Vietnam violated the Geneva agreements and justified strong retaliatory action by the United States. President Nixon favored two responses: the resumption of a broad air interdiction campaign against North Vietnam, and a naval blockade of the entire North Vietnamese coast, including the mining of Haiphong and other major harbors. The latter action was intended to starve North Vietnam of war materiel and supplies which had been arriving regularly at its ports up to this point in the protracted war, aboard Chinese and Soviet merchant shipping.[39]

The Johnson administration had opposed a mining campaign, doubting its usefulness and fearing that using sea mines to close ports to Communist shipping could trigger Chinese or Soviet intervention. However, the Navy had received authorization to mine key supply routes in North Vietnam as part of Rolling Thunder. Air Force planes loaded with mines targeted ferry crossings, bridges, storage areas, fuel dumps, and truck parks. Carrier aircraft assisted in this effort by sowing rivers and roads used to transport munitions into Laos and South Vietnam with Mk 36 destructors. These mines, containing 500 pounds of explosives, detonated when trucks, tanks, or other metal objects disturbed their magnetic fields.[40]

Per the president's wishes, the chairman of the Joint Chiefs and former chief of Naval Operations Adm. Thomas Moorer asked the Navy's Mine Warfare Office to develop a plan for a Haiphong mining operation. In considering how best to address the numerous challenges that such an operation would present, the staff decided to employ Mk 52 magnetic mines. In addition to being the most effective against large oceangoing, steel-hulled merchant ships, these type mines offered other advantages. They would allow for a longer arming delay than other mines, providing thirty-six neutral vessels in Haiphong Harbor a grace period in which to leave after the mines were sown. (In the end, only one British and four Soviet vessels took advantage of the delay and escaped the harbor.) Magnetic mines would also be the easiest for U.S. forces to later sweep, as part of an eventual peace settlement.[41]

To protect the *Coral Sea* (CVA-43), and A-6 and A-7 bombers launched from her deck, from air and surface threats while they carried out the mission, the cruisers *Chicago* (CG-11), *Long Beach* (CGN-9), and *Sterett* (DLG-31) took up positions between the port of Haiphong and the carrier.   A group of destroyers—*Berkeley, Myles C. Fox, Richard S. Edwards,* and *Buchanan*—shelled coastal anti-aircraft sites on the Do Son Peninsula west of the Haiphong channel. Concurrently, *Kitty Hawk*'s planes struck diversionary targets at Thanh Hoa and Phu Qui.[42]

COMMENCEMENT OF MINING OPERATIONS

In early morning on 8 May, the *Coral Sea* launched three Marine A-6 Intruders and six Navy A-7 Corsair attack planes toward the coast of North Vietnam. Arriving over enemy waters, the aircraft laid strings of thirty-six 1,000-pound Mk 52 mines in the approaches to Haiphong, through which most of North Vietnam's war materiel and all of its fuel supply passed. In succeeding months, other carrier aircraft dropped thousands of mines and Mk 36 destructors in the seaways of secondary ports and "reseeded" the Haiphong approaches.[43]

Photo 20-10

Navy A-7 Corsair aircraft of Attack Squadron VA 22 loaded with Mk 52 mines.
Courtesy of Ron Swart

The strikes against targets on the Do Son Peninsula by *Berkeley, Fox, Edwards,* and *Buchanan* was followed up by another operation to suppress hostile shore batteries, enabling mining of the Haiphong Harbor entrance. On the night of 10 May, *Buchanan,* in company with the *Newport News, Providence, Oklahoma City,* and *Hanson,* returned to the Do

Son Peninsula to carry out additional naval gunfire missions. These five ships, with *Newport News'* nine 8-inch guns, and twelve 6-inch guns aboard both *Providence* and *Oklahoma City* (in addition to the three cruisers' smaller 5-inch guns and those of the destroyers), constituted the most formidable cruiser-destroyer strike group assembled in the Western Pacific since World War II.[44]

LOSS OF *WARRINGTON* TO U.S. NAVY MINES

> *When you are a soldier or even a pilot in battle, you see the targets that you aim at and sometimes even witness the result of your actions. Not so for the Navy Minemen that assembled the mines planted in Vietnam. Even though our fingerprints were still fresh on the mine cases, we were never present when the mine got its prey, whether it be friend or foe. This was not the case concerning the Navy destroyer, USS* Warrington. *We knew she hit two of our MK 36 Destructors off the coast of Vietnam, in mid July 1972.*

> —Michael Gonzales Jr., Mineman Chief Petty Officer, USN (Retired), in his article, "The *Warrington* Incident (a true account)."[45]

Photo 20-11

Destroyer USS *Warrington* (DD-843) under way, location and date unknown.
Naval History and Heritage Command photograph #NH 107115

On 16 July 1972, the Atlantic Fleet destroyer *Warrington* relieved the *Hamner* on Linebacker duty, and took up her principal mission involving the destruction of North Vietnamese small craft and observation of communist Chinese merchant shipping. The following morning, while operating with *Hull* (DD-945) and *Robison* (DDG-12), *Warrington* came under heavy fire of enemy shore batteries, but took prompt evasive action and avoided damage.[46]

Later that day, luck abandoned her when, at 1316, two underwater explosions close aboard her port side rocked the destroyer—resulting in severe damage to her after fireroom and after engine room. Damage control efforts by her crew enabled *Warrington* to depart the area at 10 knots under her own power. However, the damage incurred soon forced her to secure her boilers and main engines and ask *Robison* for a tow.[47]

Photo 20-12

Guided missile destroyer USS *Robison* (DDG-12) towing the destroyer
USS *Warrington* (DD-843) out of mined waters.
USS *Robison* Western Pacific 1972 cruise book

Throughout the night of 17 July, *Warrington*'s crew struggled to control flooding, and the destroyer remained afloat. *Robison* turned her over to the salvage ship *Reclaimer* (ARS-42) for transit to Subic Bay. On the 20th, the fleet tug *Tawakoni* (ATF-114) took over the tow from *Reclaimer* and brought *Warrington* into port on the 24th.[48]

An inspection of the gaping hole in the side of the destroyer found debris from Mk 82 general bomb casings imbedded in her hull. Navy minemen had converted some of these type 500lb bombs into Mk 36 destructors, to mine North Vietnamese waterways and most recently, Haiphong Harbor.[49]

Photo 20-13

Destructors staged aboard the USS *Constellation* (CV-64) off Yankee Station in 1971. Courtesy of Ron Swart

Pilots returning to their carriers had orders to release unexpended munitions in the "unarmed" configuration in specified areas, which Navy ships were advised were dangerous and to be avoided. In this case, experts believed that stray Mk 36 destructor mines, dropped due to a navigational error of an aircraft attempting to jettison its load of weapons in an area used to get rid of bombs and destructors, might be the source of the explosions.[50]

The end of October found the ocean minesweeper USS *Inflict* (MSO-456) lying off the North Vietnamese coastline. She was sent to hostile waters to conduct a magnetic environmental conditions survey of the "*Strauss-Warrington* area" to determine if conditions conductive to minesweeping existed. This area off Dong Hoi was so-called because in it on 4 June the guided missile destroyer USS *Joseph Strauss* (DDG-16) had been rocked by two underwater explosions, followed by the ones that damaged the *Warrington* on 17 July.[51]

On 5 September, the Navy had considered the possibility of sweeping the area with ocean minesweepers. Because it was located in the open sea, ten to twenty miles northeast of Dong Hoi with adequate water depths of sixty to eighty feet, MSOs pulsing electricity through their magnetic cables ("magtails") were considered the best method of clearance. However, the unintentional minefield was never cleared, except perhaps through self-destruction of the destructors. During the next three weeks, *Inflict* endured hostile shelling, a fire on board, and a typhoon; the latter she evaded, seeking safety first in Da Nang and then in Cam Ranh Bay, South Vietnam.[52]

Photo 20-14

Ocean minesweeper USS *Inflict* (MSO-456) off the Virginia Capes, 27 October 1981. U.S. Navy photo DN-SC-87-05384

Leaving Cam Ranh Bay in the middle of November, *Inflict* proceeded to Subic Bay to join the other units of Mine Flotilla 1 in preparation for possible mine clearance operations off North Vietnam. Operation END SWEEP, a U.S. Navy and Marine Corps operation to remove mines from Haiphong Harbor and other waterways in North Vietnam, would take place from 6 February to 27 July 1973.[53]

Warrington was not as fortunate as the *Strauss*, which earlier had detonated two mines in the same area—one about 100 feet ahead of the ship and the other 95 feet on her starboard beam, with no hull damage and only light equipment degradation. Following *Warrington*'s arrival at the Subic Bay Ship Repair Facility, work was begun to improve habitability and restore her watertight integrity. However, at the end of August, a board of inspection and survey found the destroyer unfit for further service. She was decommissioned at Subic Bay on 30 September 1972, and struck from the Navy list. *Warrington* was sold on 24 April 1973 to the Taiwanese Navy for cannibalization and scrapping.[54]

LINEBACKER AND MINING OF HAIPHONG HARBOR

Operation LINEBACKER grew—from air attacks and naval shore bombardment in response to the March 1972 North Vietnamese offensive—to a concerted campaign to isolate North Vietnam from its outside sources of supply by destroying railroad bridges and rolling stock in and around Hanoi and northeastward toward the Chinese frontier. Linebacker, which ended on 23 October, helped cut short the enemy's "Easter Offensive" in South Vietnam. Its bombing and shore bombardment, in concert with the mining of Haiphong Harbor, was instrumental in bringing the North Vietnamese back to the negotiating table in the Paris cease-fire talks that August.[55]

Photo 20-15

The Vietnam Peace talks begin on 25 January 1969. The U.S. delegation is in foreground with chief negotiator Henry Cabot Lodge, facing camera.
U.S. Information Agency photograph #69-526

Final Duty on the Gunline

On 27 January 1973, U.S., South Vietnamese, North Vietnamese, and Viet Cong representatives finally signed the long-sought cease-fire agreement at Paris. Under its provisions, the Communists agreed to release all American prisoners of war within a space of two months in exchange for U.S. military withdrawal from South Vietnam and the U.S. Navy's clearance of mines from North Vietnamese waters.

—From Edward J. Marolda's book, *By Sea, Air, and Land:*
An Illustrated History of the U.S. Navy
and the War in Southeast Asia [1]

As a result of Operation LINEBACKER—a massive aerial offensive by U.S. Navy and Air Force bombers, in conjunction with naval shore bombardment and interdiction of North Vietnamese shipping—by the end of September 1972, the North Vietnamese diplomats in Paris were much more amenable to serious negotiation to end the war than they had been at the end of March 1972.[2]

Believing that a negotiated settlement was possible, on 11 October the Nixon administration ordered U.S. Pacific forces to cease bombing in the vicinity of Hanoi. In a related move, on the 23rd, Washington restricted allied strikes to targets below the 20th parallel. Nevertheless, negotiations with the North Vietnamese again bogged down in Paris while the enemy strengthened the air defenses of Hanoi and Haiphong and restored rail lines to China destroyed by American air squadrons. Moreover, the Communists once more stockpiled war reserves.[3]

LINEBACKER II

On 13 December, North Vietnamese negotiators walked out of secret talks with National Security Advisor Henry Kissinger. President Nixon then issued an ultimatum to Hanoi to send its representatives back to the conference table within 72 hours "or else." The North Vietnamese rejected Nixon's demand and on 18 December, Nixon ordered

Operation LINEBACKER II, a full-scale air campaign against the Hanoi area. White House Press Secretary Ronald Ziegler stated that the bombing would end only if all U.S. prisoners of war were released and an internationally recognized cease-fire were in effect.[4]

On the night of 18 December, and succeeding nights of the operation, wave after wave of B-52 bombers and supporting aircraft struck Hanoi, hitting command and communication facilities, power plants, rail yards, bridges, storage buildings, open stockpiles, truck parks, and ship repair complexes. The North Vietnamese met this bombing campaign with 1,250 surface-to-air missiles, which brought down fifteen of the big bombers and three supporting aircraft; anti-aircraft defenses and MiG interceptors destroyed another four carrier planes. In concert with the bombing, ships on the gunline carried out shore bombardment against enemy targets.[5]

To spread thin North Vietnamese defenses, the target area was broadened to include not only Hanoi, but Haiphong, Thai Nguyen, Long Dun Kep, and Lang Dang. The expanded effort succeeded. LINEBACKER II concluded on 29 December 1972, and by year's end the North Vietnamese had resumed serious discussions in Paris. On 15 January 1973, Nixon suspended military action in North Vietnam, giving peace talks between Kissinger and North Vietnamese leader Le Duc Tho a chance to succeed.[6]

PEACE TREATY SIGNED

On 27 January 1973, The Paris Peace Accords, officially titled the Agreement on Ending the War and Restoring Peace in Vietnam, was signed to establish peace in Vietnam and end the Vietnam War. United States, Democratic Republic of Vietnam (North Vietnam), the Republic of Vietnam (South Vietnam), and Viet Cong representatives signed the long-sought cease-fire agreement at Paris. Under its provisions, North Vietnam agreed to release all American prisoners of war within a span of two months in exchange for U.S. military withdrawal from South Vietnam and the clearance of mines from North Vietnamese waters.[7]

LAST COMBAT ACTION RIBBONS TO BE AWARDED FOR DUTY ON THE GUNLINE IN THE VIETNAM WAR

Between when Linebacker II ended in late December, and word reached all the belligerents of the signing of the Paris Peace Accords in late January, Navy destroyers continued to serve on the gunline and shell targets ashore, with some missions opposed by enemy shore batteries. Sixteen Navy ships which earned combat action ribbons (CR) in January 1973 for duty on the gunline, are identified in the table:

U.S. Navy Destroyers/Destroyer Escorts
Awarded Combat Action Ribbons in January 1973

Ship	CR Date(s)	Ship	CR Date(s)
Bausell (DD-845)	24-27 Jan 73	*O'Callahan* (DE-1051)	18 Jan 73, 26 Jan 73
Blandy (DD-943)	1 Jan 73	*O'Hare* (DD-889)	18 Jan 73
Bordelon (DD-881)	13 Jan 73	*Paul* (DE-1080)	27 Jan 73
Cochrane (DDG-21)	12-13 Jan 73	*Preble* (DLG-15)	24 Jan 73, 26 Jan 73
Epperson (DD-719)	27 Jan 73	*Rich* (DD-820)	24 Jan 73
John King (DDG-3)	18 Jan 73	*Richard E. Kraus* (DD-849)	13-14 Jan 73
Leonard F. Mason (DD-852)	29 Dec 72- 8 Jan 73	*Rogers* (DD-876)	27 Jan 73
McCaffery (DD-860)	5 Jan 73, 13 Jan 73	*Turner Joy* (DD-951)	8-16 Jan 73, 16-28 Jan 73[8]

DUTY OF THE DESTROYER *LEONARD F. MASON*

Photo 21-1

Destroyer USS *Leonard F. Mason* (DD-852) under way off Oahu, Hawaii, 5 May 1974.
Naval History and Heritage Command photograph #NH 107131

USS *Leonard F. Mason*'s (DD-852) service, from late December 1972 to late February 1973, illustrates nicely the transition from Linebacker II, through final duty on the gunline and signing of the peace treaty, to the commencement of Operation END SWEEP. End Sweep was the name given the U.S. Navy's mine clearance efforts at Haiphong and in other North Vietnam coastal waters and inland waterways.[9]

Mason departed San Diego on 24 October 1972 in company with the *Orleck* (DD-886), bound for the Western Pacific via port visits in the South and Southwest Pacific and a joint exercise with New Zealand, Australian, and Canadian units. The two *Gearing*-class destroyers stopped briefly at Pearl Harbor, and then continued their transit. On 3 November, they crossed the equator, involving for most of the crew of the *Mason*, a Shellback Initiation. Following this interlude, the two ships continued on to Pago Pago, American Samoa, arriving on 6 November. Departing the following day, *Mason* and *Orleck* arrived at Auckland, New Zealand, on the 11th and berthed at Calliope Dock West.[10]

Photo 21-2

Naval Station, Pago Pago Bay, American Samoa, 1932.
Naval History and Heritage Command photograph #NH 122275

The destroyers left Auckland on 14 November for the first portion of the New Zealand-sponsored joint convoy protection exercise LONGEX 72. The fleet ships participating in the exercise arrived at

Wellington, New Zealand, on 19 November, anchoring in the harbor for the night before departing the next day for the second part of the exercise. *Leonard Mason* returned with the *Orleck* to Auckland on the 26th. *Mason* left there on 28 November for Tauranga in the Bay of Plenty on New Zealand's North Island, arriving later that day. She was the first U.S. Navy ship to visit the harborside city for many years.[11]

Mason stood out of Tauranga on 1 December and rendezvoused with the *Orleck* for passage to Australia. The two ships arrived at HMAS Moreton, a Royal Australian Navy Depot located in Brisbane, on 4 December. Their stay was cut short when a fight broke out between members of *Mason*'s crew, aided by some SEALs, and sailors of the Australian Navy on the evening of 5 December. A group of Navy SEALs in Australia for R&R at Sydney, met the *Mason* in Brisbane for transport to Subic Bay. Since the SEALs were attired in dress uniforms, they were recognized for what they were and where they had been. After a few beers, a fight broke out between the American and Australian sailors. (Apparently, the Aussies weren't intimidated by the presence of Navy Special Forces members.) The two ships left Brisbane on 6 December, made a brief stop on the 11th at Manus Island (the largest of the Admiralty Islands in northern Papua New Guinea), and arrived at Subic Bay on 16 December.[12]

PARTICIPATION IN LINEBACKER II

Mason and *Orleck* departed Subic Bay on 20 December 1972. *Mason* detached from *Orleck* the following day and proceeded to the Gulf of Tonkin. Arriving there, she relieved the destroyer *Shelton* (DD-790) in performing search and rescue missions. During U.S. Air Force and U.S. Navy night air raids on missile battery positions in the vicinity of Haiphong and Hanoi, the ship's crew watched the nightly 'fireworks' show. In late December, *Mason* joined one of several Naval Surface Action Groups (Task Unit 77.1.1) operating off the coast of North Vietnam, relieving the *Bordelon* (DD-881).[13]

Mason operated in company with the *Cone* (DD-866) and *Lawrence* (DDG-4). Except for a brief Christmas break, the ships carried out two or three strike missions nightly. Occasionally, *Mason* came under intense hostile fire. Fortunately, she received only minor damage (shrapnel damage topside from close air bursts), and minor injuries to some crewmembers. During one mission, the destroyer launched a chaff cannister (missile decoy) that malfunctioned. Instead of leaving the launcher, blooming at height, and forming an alternate radar target drifting away from the ship, the chaff streamed out from the launcher, creating a line pointing straight to the ship. Drawing heavy enemy fire as a result, *Mason* zigzagged away at high speed to make targeting more difficult, with guns blazing.[14]

A *Leonard F. Mason* crewmember later described this period:

> The ship's chaff display and survival during that mission were the "talk of the gulf" that evening. The particular chaff device involved was no longer used after that (even though it had been used successfully in previous missions). Unofficially, *Mason* set a Tonkin Gulf record for most coastal battery rounds received and most failing to hit their intended target. At times, the enemy fire was so intense and so near its intended target that, from within the ship's Combat Information Center, the sound of the exploding shells around the ship were almost as loud as the ship's own guns firing - prompting the gunfire control seaman to call out "that's us... that's them... that's us."[15]

POST-LINEBACKER/PRE-PEACE TREATY PERIOD

During the early part of January 1973, *Mason* was part of a three-ship strike unit that included the *Cochrane* (DDG-21) and the *McCaffery* (DD-860). This unit shelled enemy targets along the Vietnam coast north of the DMZ, usually coastal defense batteries and supply storage areas. The unit encountered heavy hostile fire during a mission on 1 January 1973. After the strike unit disbanded, *Mason* operated independently. She shelled coastal targets on 9 and 16 January, receiving hostile fire during the former mission, and also operated on the gunline at Quang Tri, South Vietnam.[16]

Following a stint of search and rescue duty with the nuclear-powered, guided-missile destroyer leader *Truxton* (DLGN-35), she returned to the gunline, joining the destroyers *Bausell* (DD-845), *Henderson* (DD-785), *Horne* (DLG-30), *McCaffery* (DD-860), *Morton* (DD-948), and *O'Callahan* (DE-1051).[17]

OPERATION END SWEEP

On 12 February 1973, *Mason* made a mail stop at Da Nang, South Vietnam, with a number of the ship's crew going ashore. With the ebbing tide of warfare in Vietnam, the Fleet Activities Support Unit at Da Nang was being phased out. *Mason* shared the pier with only a barge, and just a handful of Vietnamese workers and guards watched as the destroyer, the final U.S. warship to call at Da Nang, departed the harbor. *Mason* then proceeded to rendezvous with the *Morton* and *Bradley* (DE-1041) for various operations.[18]

Mason joined the *Worden* (DLG-18) and Task Force 78 (under the command of Rear Adm. Brian McCauley) on 20 February, relieving

Epperson (DD-719) of her duties in Operation END SWEEP. *Mason* rode 'shot gun' for the minesweepers clearing Haiphong Harbor, as part of the mine clearance effort in North Vietnamese waters. The ocean minesweepers *Engage* (MSO-433), *Force* (MSO-445), *Fortify* (MSO-446) and *Impervious* (MSO-449) had left Subic for the Tonkin Gulf on 27 January, coincident with the signing of the agreement. END SWEEP commenced on 6 February with the four MSOs sweeping the areas in which the amphibious ships (LPHs and LPDs) carrying minesweeping helicopters were to anchor. Marine CH-53 helicopters had been modified at Subic to tow the Magnetic Orange Pipe minesweeping device employed against magnetic mines.[19]

Photo 21-3

Ocean minesweeper USS *Force* (MSO-445) off Oahu, Hawaii, 18 October 1971. Naval History and Heritage Command photograph #NH 84418

Minesweeping helicopters had many limitations not shared by the ocean minesweepers. They could not sweep in inclement weather or at night, nor sweep to as great water depths as the ships. However, their crews were much safer than those of MSOs during the performance of minesweeping duties. A mine detonated by a device pulled by a low-flying helicopter would not blast the aircraft out of the sky, while the explosion of a magnetic mine close aboard might well damage or sink a minesweeping ship. For this reason, the Navy used helicopters—

towing a Mk-105 magnetic sled, the Mk-104, and the AMK-2G acoustic devices, the MOP or the triple MOP (three in tandem)—to conduct precursory sweeps before sending in the MSOs. Helicopters also swept shallow waters that precluded ship operations.[20]

Photo 21-4

A CH-53 helicopter towing a magnetic orange pipe minesweeping device during sweep operations in Haiphong Harbor, 20 June 1973.
National Archives photograph #USN 711574

Photo 21-5

The special minesweeper USS *Washtenaw County* (MSS-2, formerly *LST-1166*) carrying out operations in Haiphong Harbor during Operation End Sweep, 20 February 1973.
Naval History and Heritage Command photograph #USN 711573

The surface mine sweeping force grew to ten ocean minesweepers, used principally in the deep-water approaches and as helicopter control ships. In addition, a surface support force was made up of two destroyers, two fleet tugs (later reduced to one), a submarine rescue ship, a tank landing ship (LST) for MSO support, and a specially configured LST—the USS *Washtenaw County*—to transit the Haiphong channel after sweeping had been completed in order to demonstrate confidence in the thoroughness of the sweep. The "guinea pig" performed pressure mine and check sweeping, and made several passages through the main Haiphong Channel to demonstrate the effectiveness of mine clearance efforts, with the last runs on 20 June 1973.[21]

During the initial sweeping when the amphibious ships were still in Subic, the *Worden* served as flagship for McCauley and as an alternate site for meeting the North Vietnamese. On the night of 27 February, because of difficulties over the second POW exchange, Task Force 78 was withdrawn. Within twelve hours, the issues were resolved and the task force was ordered back into North Vietnamese waters.[22]

Photo 21-6

Col. Robinson Risner, USAF (waving), and Capt. James Stockdale, USN, two American prisoners of war released by Hanoi, arriving at Clark Air Force Base, Philippines, in February 1973.
National Archives and Records Administration photograph #USN 1155662

On 17 April 1973, because of difficulties in Laos and Cambodia, the force was once again withdrawn. The period of inactivity lasted until 13 June when the Paris Joint Communique was signed, implementing the agreement and protocols of 27 January on ending the war and restoring peace in Vietnam. Having completed sweeping in the Haiphong area the task force moved south to the Hon Lai coastal area. Final sweeping in this area was performed on 5 July and, after the North Vietnamese refused to allow sweeping of the remainder of the fields, the task force left Vietnamese waters on 18 July 1973.[23]

DESTROYER *LEONARD F. MASON* LAUDED

Following duty with END SWEEP force, the *Mason* visited Hong Kong during the first week of March, while en route to Sasebo, Japan. At Sasebo, she was drydocked two weeks for repair of combat damage. Both her port and starboard rudders had holes punched in them by the explosions of enemy shells close aboard. There was also additional damage to the ship caused by shrapnel from numerous airburst rounds from coastal batteries and by the recoil of *Mason*'s guns from all the rounds she had fired during the various missions.[24]

In recognition of her exemplary accomplishments, USS *Leonard F. Mason* was awarded the Combat Action Ribbon and Meritorious Unit Commendation, in addition to the Vietnam Service Medal, which every officer and man aboard could display proudly on their uniform blouses.

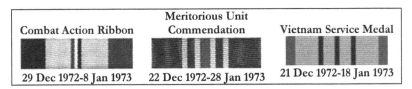

Combat Action Ribbon	Meritorious Unit Commendation	Vietnam Service Medal
29 Dec 1972-8 Jan 1973	22 Dec 1972-28 Jan 1973	21 Dec 1972-18 Jan 1973

Commander Robert Leon Warren, USN, brought the *Mason* home to San Diego, California, on 2 May 1973, concluding her six-month deployment. Three-and-a-half years later, the now thirty-year-old ship was decommissioned on 2 November 1976, and struck from the Naval Register. The destroyer was sold to Taiwan on 10 March 1978, and renamed ROCS *Shuei Yang* (DDG-926).[25]

22

Naval Magazine, Subic Bay

The primary munitions of the DDs, 5" projectiles, were being produced in the U.S., airlifted to the red label area of Cubi Point NAS, transported by truck to the pier for loading aboard a waiting AE [ammunition ship], and thence to the combat zone. We estimated that less than two weeks after manufacture, a 5" projectile was out the bore of a DD 5" gun mount and on its way into Vietnam.

—Capt. Philip M. Palmer, USN (Retired), former commanding officer, Naval Magazine, Subic Bay, remarking on the high consumption of gun rounds by destroyers on the gunline.

Photo 22-1

Naval Magazine, Subic Bay (on Camayan Point), Philippine Islands, September 1965.
Naval History and Heritage Command photograph #NH 74182

Capt. Philip M. Palmer, USN (Retired) authored this chapter which, written in the first person, provides a very interesting and compelling account of the many interrelated actions and hard work that were necessary to keep the ships on the gunline supplied with ammunition, and naval aircraft with bombs and mines.   During his tour as commanding officer, Naval Magazine, Subic Bay, Palmer witnessed first-hand, three phases of the war; the buildup, the naval bombardment and mining campaigns, and the drawdown. They all presented their own unique challenges as the following several pages illustrate.

LINEBACKER OPERATIONS SUPPORT

When I arrived in July 1971, the tempo of operations in South Vietnam was building and so were the naval force levels in Southeast Asia. To interdict coastal supply trains into the South from North Vietnam, the Navy established a coordinated coastal shore bombardment from destroyers, cruisers, the battleship *New Jersey*, and carrier-based aircraft. All of the ordnance to support these operations flowed through NAVMAG Subic. The firing rates were such that the supply train could barely keep up with the expenditures. More logistic support force ships were ordered to the area, many deployed from the East Coast.

We were short of manpower and ordnance handling equipment (called "yellow gear" because of its color) and so an augmentation was begun. Our SeaBee sailors (naval construction battalion personnel) who operated and maintained the yellow gear were increased in number, and every piece of yellow gear not required either ashore or afloat elsewhere in the Navy was relocated to Subic. Our gear all had to be certified for handling explosive material so we got the very best. We also received additional sailors and U. S. civilians and hired additional Filipino nationals.

By early 1972 we were operating at a full wartime tempo. We had installed an additional pontoon pier at Camayan Wharf for use by ordnance-transporting LSTs (tank landing ships). We routinely were servicing five ships simultaneously; two at the wharf, one at the pontoon pier, and two at anchor. This went on around the clock even though handling ammunition after dark is not supposed to be done. Subic Bay looked like a scene in WWII movies. Ships were at piers and at anchor throughout the Bay. We had 1,000,000 pounds net equivalent high explosive weight on Camayan Wharf at all times. How do I know that? Because that's all the explosive handling regulations permitted. So, that's what we said we had.

Ordnance demand was so heavy that the ammunition ships (AEs) were being used just as shuttles to carry ammunition to the multicommodity ships (AOEs) which stayed on station in the Gulf of Tonkin servicing the combatants around the clock.

In July of 1972, we had a series of typhoons pass over Luzon and stack up to the east of the island. The result of this meteorological phenomenon was torrential tropical rain. It rained without letup for 31 days and nights. When it finally ended, 103" of rain had fallen. I remember the number because, coincidentally, during that period, the Magazine moved a record 103,000 tons of ordnance under nearly impossible conditions.

The Central Luzon plain was flooded to the second story level in many places and you could go from the foothills of the mountains below Baguio to Manila by Banca boat. You could not get from Subic to Manila by vehicle. The main road from Cubi down to Subic washed away carrying the main waterline with it and left us in all that rain with no water. The sailors in the Magazine lived down the hill in Subic so they had to come to work via a circuitous road that remained intact. We got water in buckets from tanker trucks we called "water buffalo" that were parked on Captain's Circle, senior officer housing.

I was proud of the officers and sailors and also of the Filipinos who had no national stake in this war but were willing to work hard for their pesos. A stevedore earned $1.15/day. 15 cents of that went back to the stevedore company for a lunch of fish heads and rice. They were an interesting group. Every morning a large contingent of day laborers would assemble at the union hall in Olongapo. LUSTEVCO, the stevedore contractor, would announce the numbers required for the day. That number would be trucked down to the Magazine piers.

During my tour we had an excellent explosives safety record. The water tower that stood in the middle of Nabasan Wharf had a message written in bold letters on its sides and visible at some distance. It was the byword of explosives safety, "ORDNANCE SAFETY PRECAUTIONS ARE WRITTEN IN BLOOD."

We exercised safe operations as rigorously as we could while operating at a wartime tempo. The one exception I know we made was in staging ammo on Nabasan Wharf for loading aboard waiting and incoming ships. The pier explosive limit was 1,000,000 net equivalent pounds of TNT (NET). That limit would not permit us to keep up with the tempo of operations required to support the peak of the naval war. When asked how much ordnance we had on the wharf I always responded 1,000,000 NET. We probably had more than double that but I never really knew. I couldn't allow myself to worry about it.

EXPLOSION OF *NEWPORT NEWS'* GUN TURRET

USS *Newport News* (CA-148) was a heavy cruiser of the *Des Moines*-class. She carried 9 - 8"/55 caliber guns in 3 turrets, 12 - 5"/38 caliber guns in 6 dual mounts, and 12 - 3"/50 caliber guns in 6 twin mounts. On 1 October 1972, while in action off the Demilitarized Zone in Vietnam, she suffered an in-bore explosion in her center 8" gun of number two turret. Twenty sailors were killed and thirty-six injured. The accident required an inquiry to determine the cause before the ship could be allowed to fire her 8" guns again; a survey of the ordnance to determine its safety; and repairs to the ship. These activities necessitated that *Newport News* come into Subic Bay. (When I entered the Navy, all major bore naval weapons were called "rifles." However, the use of "rifle" passed from the lexicon being replaced by "gun" early in my career.)

The ship operated for three years after repairs with the barrel removed and the turret locked in train. She did return to the gunline prior to cessation of hostilities and fire again. More about how this came to pass in what follows.

Photo 22-1

Heavy cruiser USS *Newport News* (CA-148) after repairs. The center barrel of turret #2 has been removed and the port barrel has been blanked off.
Courtesy of Capt. Philip M. Palmer, USN (Retired)

Newport News came to Subic carrying a lot of political baggage in addition to the sorrow and shock of the incident and loss of life. There was tremendous pressure being brought to bear by various technical and professional groups to do several things simultaneously. There was a sense of urgency to get *Newport News* back on the gunline so the safety of her ordnance could be demonstrated in combat. This priority was not necessarily compatible with sound ship repair, thorough investigation and understanding of the incident, and ordnance safety. In fact, it was based on a giant assumption that this was a random event or easily correctable situation. As is the usual case, the operational commanders had more clout than the logistics and administrative chain.

The ship came first to anchor for a quick look by EOD personnel to determine if it was safe to come to the Magazine for download of ordnance and, if not, to render safe or remove any unsafe ordnance. They removed some damaged rounds and the ship proceeded to Nabasan Wharf. Her commanding officer, Capt. Walter F. Zartman, told me that his chief interest was the safety of his crew and the confidence level he expected in the safety of ordnance on board his ship. Therefore, he said he wanted me to load no ordnance aboard his ship unless I could assure him that it would be safe to fire. This admonition on his part would prove to be prescient.

Two investigations were conducted, one, the formal investigation required for all such significant accidents. It was carried out by Rear Adm. Philip P. Cole, commander, Service Group Three, who was appointed by the operational chain of command. The other was an informal investigation conducted by retired vice admirals Lloyd M. Mustin and Kleber S. Masterson. They were appointed by the chief of Naval Material and were to determine the cause(s) of the in-bore explosion and to make recommendation for corrective action to prevent any recurrence. Mustin and Masterson were known as the M&M boys. They were gunners of the old school with formidable reputations for their knowledge and thorough, no nonsense approach to gunnery and ordnance matters.

The two investigations were conducted cooperatively, smoothly, and without interference. We were required at the Naval Magazine to do a 100 percent inspection of all 8" rounds to be loaded aboard *Newport News*. The rounds were first examined by x-ray. Those believed to be suspect as a result of x-ray inspection were then subjected to disassembly and visual inspection. We had to report the results of rounds inspected daily with data on rejections and causes. Inspection criteria were provided by NAPEC (Naval Ammunitions Production Engineering Center). Material from the explosive incident was rendered safe and then shipped to the Naval Weapons Laboratory and the Naval Ordnance Laboratory. Once the repairs to the ship were done, the Navy did not want the ship sitting around waiting for ordnance.

Finally, on 18 October 1972, the investigations were complete, repairs were done, and we had a sufficient number of certified 8" rounds for *Newport News* to return to the gunline. She received her ordnance at Nabasan Wharf and she sailed for the gunline the next day. She did fire her 8"/55-caliber main battery again.

FINDINGS OF MUSTIN AND MASTERSON

Based on their investigation, Mustin and Masterson concluded that the explosion had been caused by the premature functioning of a projectile auxiliary detonating fuze, while the gun round was still in the barrel. In their concise eight-paragraph report (USS NEWPORT NEWS (CA-148) Turret Explosion, 1 October 1972, 05445 NOV2272), the retired vice admirals described the event, and absolved personnel of the *Newport News* of any blame. The report also emphasized that since 1965, twenty-three in-bore projectile explosions had taken 24 lives, degraded combat readiness, and resulted in millions of dollars of damage to fleet units. The four paragraphs most pertinent to the subject of this book follow:

> 2. The explosion resulted from the high-order detonation of a projectile in the bore of the center gun of turret two, which vented mainly to the inside of the turret. By some mechanism not clearly apparent, this ignited additional powder charges in all three hoists. The resulting high-energy flame propagated downward almost instantly from charge to charge in the hoists, blowing apart the hoist casings between decks in the way of ignited charges, until for some reason also not apparent, the propagation stopped just above the handling room level. Some 720 pounds of powder burned in the hoists. Twenty men died.

> 3. If flame propagation down the hoists had extended a few feet further, into the handling room level below the armor deck, the extent of possible further damage and casualties might have been catastrophic. The loading scuttles at the bottom of the hoists would have been no protection if the hoists themselves had blown apart, as they did in the levels above. Events could then have led to a magazine explosion, from which the survival of the ship herself would have been in question.

> 4. In our judgment this casualty was not caused by inadequate manning, training, experience, maintenance, or operating procedures in NEWPORT NEWS; nor by defective design of the material involved. Rather, we conclude that it was caused by the premature functioning of the projectile's auxiliary detonating fuze,

which resulted from defective fuze manufacture and inadequate product acceptance inspection.

5. The NEWPORT NEWS casualty adds emphasis to what, in our judgment, has become an unsatisfactory present situation with respect to Navy gun ammunition, specifically ammunition safety for fleet users. Since 1965 there have been 23 shipboard in-bore projectile explosions, which have cost millions of dollars, degraded combat readiness, and taken 24 lives. The rate per shot fired at which these explosions have occurred since that date has increased by a factor of more than 25 over the rate for the preceding nineteen years since the close of World War II. The hardware defects which cause such explosions are documented and wide-spread. Statistically, the next fleet in-bore projectile explosion could occur at any moment. It could cost us a ship.

MINING OPERATIONS SUPPORT

On Palm Sunday in 1972, I was in the Chapel at the Cubi Point Naval Air Station with my family. Just as the sermon was about to start, a messenger came down the aisle and told me I needed to come to the Magazine immediately. At the gate I was directed by the Duty Officer to proceed directly to the Mine Shop. When I arrived, I found that Master Chief Mineman Wheelock, his minemen, newly reported LDO (Limited Duty Officer) LCDR Dick Anderson, and the other mine shop CPOs and officers were either there or on their way. We had a TOP SECRET message informing us that the U. S. was about to initiate a naval blockade to interdict all supplies destined for North Vietnam and that a major element of the blockade would be the mining of Haiphong Harbor.

Over the next three weeks, we prepared every mine that went into Vietnam waters; some 8,000 in all including destructor kits for installation aboard aircraft carriers in 500lb bombs to convert them into magnetic influence, bottom mines. Scores of the others were very sophisticated mines which required the minemen to make settings for depth, delays, ship counts, self-neutralization, etc., as called for in the mining plan. It was very complex, exacting work which required meticulous performance and record keeping. This was our proudest moment. We knew we were contributing to an ending of hostilities in a very direct way.

WAR'S END AND RECOGNITION

In early 1973, the release of American POWs and an end to U. S. involvement in the war was negotiated. The first stop of the POWs was at Clark Air Force Base in the Philippines. We watched it with pride and tears over TV.

On 10 December 1973, the Naval Magazine officers and men stood at formation while Rear Adm. Doniphan B. Shelton, USN, commander, Naval Base, Subic Bay, presented NAVMAG Subic with the Meritorious Unit Citation for support of the war effort in 1972. The citation, signed by the Secretary of the Navy, read:

> In the face of extremely adverse climatic conditions and unusually demanding operational commitments, U. S. Naval Magazine, Subic Bay carried out its highly important mission of munitions support to the Seventh Fleet with outstanding skill and dedication and provided a significant and vital contribution to successful naval operations in the Southeast Asian theater during this period. By their hard work, perseverance and unfailing devotion to duty throughout, personnel of the U. S. Naval Magazine, Subic Bay reflected great credit upon themselves and upheld the highest traditions of the United States Naval Service.

During the period noted in the award, the Naval Magazine supported record numbers of fleet units and merchant ships, and handled munitions tonnages, which more than doubled any previous comparable peak period. At the height of operations, the Naval Magazine provided ordnance support to six aircraft carriers, fifty destroyers, four cruisers, and 23 logistics replenishment ships. Merchant ships serviced more than tripled during this period, averaging over 80,500 tons per month for six consecutive months. The magazine normally handled less than 20,000 tons per month.

Operation FREQUENT WIND

This action closes a chapter in the American experience. I ask all Americans to close ranks, to avoid recrimination about the past, to look ahead to the many goals we share, and to work together on the great tasks that remain to be accomplished.

—Statement by American President Gerald Ford on 29 April 1975 as Operation Frequent Wind commenced, the evacuation by airlift of American and "at risk" South Vietnamese personnel from Saigon, ending over twenty years of U.S. involvement in Vietnam.[1]

Photo 23-1

South Vietnamese refugees arrive by helicopter aboard a U.S. Navy aircraft carrier or amphibious ship as part of Operation Frequent Wind, the final evacuation of Saigon, South Vietnam, 29-30 April 1975.
Official U.S. Marine Corps photograph

In the final year of the Vietnam War, a series of offensives by the North Vietnamese led to the fall of the South Vietnamese capital Saigon on 30 April 1975. North Vietnamese troops entered the deserted streets of Saigon just hours after the last Americans were evacuated, airlifted by Marine helicopters to U.S. Navy ships waiting off the coast. As those ships were steaming away from Vietnam, Comdr. Paul Jacobs, USN, the commanding officer of the destroyer escort USS *Kirk* (DE-1087), received a mysterious order to head back to Vietnam. This directive came from Rear Adm. Donald B. Whitmire, USN, commander of the evacuation mission, Operation FREQUENT WIND.[2]

In preceding days, with the fall of Saigon imminent, the U.S. Navy had formed Task Force 76 off the coast of South Vietnam, a massive assembly of aircraft and ships that became the largest helicopter evacuation in history. FREQUENT WIND was the final phase in the evacuation of thousands of Vietnamese who had ardently supported U.S. efforts to stop the Communist takeover of South Vietnam and a dwindling number of American civilians still remaining in Vietnam.

Task Force 76: USS *Blue Ridge* (LCC-19) (command ship)
Movement Transport Groups

TG 76.4 (Alpha)	TG 76.5 (Bravo)	TG 76.9 (Charlie)
USS *Okinawa* (LPH-3)	USS *Dubuque* (LPD-8)	USS *Anchorage* (LSD-36)
USS *Vancouver* (LPD-2)	USS *Durham* (LKA-114)	USS *Denver* (LPD-9)
USS *Thomaston* (LSD-28)	USS *Frederick* (LST-1184)	USS *Duluth* (LPD-6)
USS *Peoria* (LST-1183)		USS *Mobile* (LKA-115)[3]

The task force would be joined by the carriers *Hancock* and *Midway* (carrying Marine and Air Force CH-53 and HH-53 helicopters); the Seventh Fleet flagship *Oklahoma City*, and other surface combatants for naval gunfire, escort, and area defense; additional amphibious ships; and the cargo ship USNS *Sgt. Andrew Miller.*

Seventh Fleet flagship: USS *Oklahoma City* (CLG-5)

Aircraft Carriers	Surface Combatants	Surface Combatants
USS *Hancock* (CV-19)	USS *Bausell* (DD-845)	USS *Kirk* (FF-1087)
USS *Midway* (CV-41)	USS *Cochrane*	USS *Richard B. Anderson*
Cargo Ship	(DDG-21)	(DD-786)
USNS *Sgt. Andrew Miller*	USS *Cook*	USS *Rowan* (DD-782)
(T-AK-242)	(FF-1083)	
Amphibious Ships	USS *Gurke* (DD-783)	USS *Worden* (DLG-18)
USS *Barbour County*		
(LST-1195)		
USS *Mount Vernon*		
(LSD-39)		
USS *Tuscaloosa*		
(LST-1187)[4]		

Photo 23-2

U.S. Navy ships of Task Force 76 staged off Vung Tau, Vietnam in the
South China Sea for the start of Operation Frequent Wind, 29 April 1975.
Official U.S. Marine Corps photograph A7718475

FREQUENT WIND was carried out 29-30 April, during which 71
American military helicopters extracted more than 7,800 evacuees from
the Defense Attaché Office and U.S. Embassy. Such was the speed of
the operation and the number of people involved that the ships became
overwhelmed with evacuees and the helicopters that brought them. Out
of necessity, orders were given to jettison surplus helicopters over the
sides of the ships to make room for more to land.[5]

Photo 23-3

South Vietnamese Air Force UH-1 Huey helicopters landing aboard the aircraft
carrier USS *Midway* (CV-41) during Operation FREQUENT WIND.
USS *Midway* 1975-76 cruise book

Photo 23-4

A South Vietnamese helicopter is pushed over the side of the amphibious assault ship USS *Okinawa* (LPH-3) during Operation Frequent Wind, April 1975.
Official U.S. Marine Corps photograph

The first of the helicopters that participated in the evacuation had carried U.S. Marines to form defensive perimeters at a landing zone at Tan Son Nhut Air Base near Saigon, and at the U.S. Embassy. When the last helicopter departed Vietnam, it radioed, "Swift 22 is airborne with eleven passengers. Ground-security force is aboard."[6]

Vietnamese refugees were taken to Clark Air Base and the naval base at Subic Bay in the Philippines, Andersen AFB in Guam, and Wake Island. In Operation NEW ARRIVALS, Military Airlift Command transports and commercial airliners transported tens of thousands of refugees from the Pacific island camps to reception centers in the continental United States. Refugees landed at one of several military bases, including Fort Chaffee, Arkansas; Camp Pendleton, California; and Eglin AFB, Florida. To reduce the refugee population on Guam, which was becoming increasingly vulnerable as the typhoon season approached, the Department of Defense opened a fourth reception center at Fort Indiantown Gap, Pennsylvania.[7]

ESCAPE OF THE SOUTH VIETNAMESE NAVY

We're going to have to send you back to rescue the Vietnamese navy. We forgot 'em. And if we don't get them or any part of them, they're all probably going to be killed.

—Directive to Comdr. Paul H. Jacobs, commanding officer of the destroyer escort USS *Kirk* (DE-1087) from Rear Adm. Donald B. Whitmire, commander of Operation FREQUENT WIND, embarked aboard the command ship *Blue Ridge* (LCC-19).[8]

The average age of my crew was 23. They were young and new to the Navy and were trained for war, but the situation quickly turned into a humanitarian effort. We had to take care of a large amount of people by providing them food, shelter, and medical care.

—Capt. Paul Jacobs, USN (Retired) describing unique challenges his crew faced during evacuation of the South Vietnamese Navy to Subic Bay, Philippine Islands, in May 1975.[9]

During FREQUENT WIND, as Seventh Fleet ships monitored on radar screens U.S. helicopters loaded with evacuees flying seaward to them, hordes of unknown air contacts began appearing. South Vietnamese army and Air Force Hueys, packed with refugees, were following the American aircraft, in an effort to escape Vietnam as well. Lt. Comdr. Raymond W. Addicott, the USS *Cook*'s (DE-1083) executive officer, later recalled that the image on the radar scope "looked like a swarm of bees," explaining, "I went topside on the bridge and the sky was just full of helicopters. It was an amazing sight." In addition to the

Marine and Air Force helicopters evacuating people from Saigon, there were also hundreds of Vietnam Air Force (VNAF) Bell UH-1 Iroquois helicopters (better-known as "Hueys") flown by south Vietnamese pilots who had fled with their friends, neighbors, and relatives in tow.[10]

The carriers *Midway* and *Hancock* along with the *Blue Ridge* attracted the initial wave, but eventually, smaller ships such as the *Cook* and sister ship *Kirk* had to take on refugees. The 415-foot USS *Kirk* (DE-1087) quickly began to land aircraft on her relatively small flight deck. A *Knox*-class destroyer escort, she had been commissioned at Long Beach, California, on 9 September 1972 (too late for war duty) and assigned to Destroyer Squadron 23 in San Diego.[11]

Photo 23-5

Destroyer escort USS *Kirk* (DE-1087) off Oahu, Hawaii, on 9 February 1973. Naval History and Heritage Command photograph #NH 78236-KN

Kirk had sailed from San Diego in early March 1975, beginning her second Western Pacific deployment since commissioning. During this cruise, she and her crew of 250 sailors had participated in the evacuation of Phnom Penh, Cambodia, in early April. Cambodia fell before Vietnam, and Operation EAGLE PULL, of which *Kirk* had been a part, proved to be a quick, orderly extraction of fewer than 300 Americans. The *Kirk* then proceeded south with *Cook* and the carrier *Midway* and entered Singapore on 16 April for a welcomed visit to that exotic port.

Soon, liberty was summarily cancelled, the crews abruptly recalled, and the three ships ordered north to join the evacuation force off the coast of Vietnam.[12]

First one and then two helicopters were on the *Kirk*'s deck. With several more approaching, Comdr. Paul H. Jacobs, her commanding officer, gave the order to start pushing aircraft over the side once the men, women, and children were safely aboard to make room for more. Then the unthinkable happened, a twin-rotor CH-47 Chinook, the largest helicopter in the South Vietnamese inventory, appeared. As the flight deck crew tried to wave off the massive helicopter, its pilot, with utmost prowess, hovered over the fantail while the refugees jumped or were dropped into the waiting arms of sailors. After everyone was safely aboard, the pilot moved a short distance off *Kirk*'s starboard quarter. Hovering within inches of the sea, he slowly rolled the Chinook over on its right side, and escaped the crash unharmed by diving out the left door in mid-roll. Both main rotors disintegrated on impact, and shattered shards of the blades flew across *Kirk*, splashing into the sea well off her port side. The captain's gig and motor whaleboat were standing by and rescued the pilot in short order. By days end, the DE had landed thirteen aircraft safely without any mishaps.[13]

The refugees were transferred to the Military Sealift Command freighter SS *Green Port* the following morning. The destroyer escort was without refugees, but that wouldn't last long. That night, Jacobs received orders from Rear Admiral Whitmire, sending the *Kirk* by herself to an island off the Vietnamese mainland. Whitmire also informed Jacobs that he would be taking orders from a civilian. Late that afternoon, *Kirk* received orders to rendezvous with the *Blue Ridge*, for a boat transfer of "an important person." That person turned out to be Richard L. Armitage, emissary of the Department of Defense (and future Deputy Secretary of State under Colin Powell in the George W. Bush Administration).[14]

A former naval officer, Armitage had served in the Vietnam War as an advisor, and this experience and acquired fluency in Vietnamese made him useful to the foreign service community after the war. Leaving active duty as a lieutenant commander in 1973, he had joined the State Department. He had been working in Vietnam as of late, planning the extraction of as many South Vietnamese Navy ships as possible. *Kirk* was to deliver Armitage to the South Vietnamese Navy's flagship, RVNS *Tran Nhat Duat* (HQ-03), off Con Son Island, east of the southern tip of Vietnam, early the next morning.[15]

After arrival aboard *Kirk*, Armitage was escorted to the wardroom where he met with Jacobs and Capt. Donald P. Roane, USN, commander, Destroyer Squadron 23, who was embarked aboard the *Kirk*. Roane remarked, 'Young man, I'm not used to having strange civilians come aboard my ship in the middle of the night and give me orders.' Armitage (who'd just turned 30 that week) responded, 'I am equally unaccustomed, sir, to coming aboard strange ships in the middle of the night and giving you orders. But steam to Con Son.' So, the *Kirk* set a course for the largest island in the Con Dao archipelago, off southern Vietnam.[16]

Map 23-1

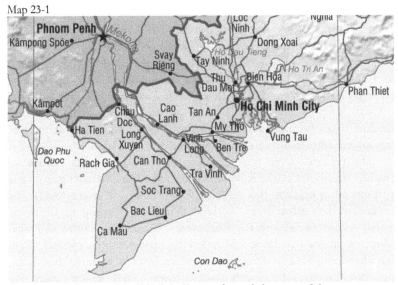

Con Dao Archipelago. Ho Chi Minh City was formerly known as Saigon.

At dawn on 1 May, *Kirk* was greeted by the somber sight of the remnants of the Vietnamese Navy: ships and boats of all sizes and descriptions, either anchored, drifting, or slowly steaming in the vicinity of Con Son Island. Some were empty and had been abandoned, but thirty-two ships considered seaworthy for the 1,000-mile open-ocean transit to the Philippines were overloaded with refugees. Aboard the flotilla were more than thirty thousand Vietnamese men, women, and children, and the entire fleet was well within striking range of North Vietnamese MiGs that were suspected to be operating freely out of the captured Tan Son Nhut airfield. Armitage's task was to quickly move the vulnerable ships and precious human cargo east to the Philippines, with *Kirk* initially the lone U.S. ship, responsible for providing security, engineering support to the damaged and floundering ships, and feeding and providing medical care.[17]

Kirk's engineers repaired what they could on seaworthy vessels and transferred people from the ships that would be left behind. The flotilla of 32 navy ships and 2 fishing vessels sailed the next morning, under escort by the Kirk. The Cook rendezvoused Kirk and the Vietnamese fleet to form a five-mile-long convoy that would safely lead the ships to Subic Bay. They were joined by the amphibious ships Barbour County, Denver, Mobile, and Tuscaloosa; salvage ship Deliver (ARS-23); stores ship Vega (AF-59); fleet tugs Abnaki (ATF-96) and Lipan (AT-85); and the ammunition ship Flint (AE-32). Proceeding only as fast as the slowest ship (about 5 knots), Cook and Kirk brought the flotilla safely into Subic Bay on 7 May 1975, saving an estimated 30,000 evacuees.[18]

Photo 23-6

Former South Vietnamese and Cambodian Navy ships at Subic Bay, Philippines, 31 May 1975. They are (l-r): Vietnamese ships: HQ-471, Dong Da II (07), Chi Lang II (08), Chi Linh (11); Cambodian Ships: P-112, E-312. National Archives photograph #K-109092

Earlier, the Kirk's commanding officer had received some bad news as the flotilla approached the Philippines. President Ferdinand Marcos had been one of the first to recognize the Communist rulers now in control of a single Vietnam, and Jacobs was told the ships should go back. The Philippine government wasn't going to allow the flotilla in, because its ships now belonged to the North Vietnamese, and they didn't want to offend the new country. Armitage and Capt. Kiem Do, deputy chief of staff for the South Vietnamese Navy, quickly came up with a solution that Marcos would have to accept. Do explained:

> We will raise the American flag and lower the Vietnamese flag as a sign of transfer [of] the ship back to the United States, because during the war those ships are given to the Vietnamese government as a loan, if you want, from the United States, to fight the Communists. Now the war is over, we turn them back to the United States.[19]

There was a frantic search to find sufficient American flags, and two personnel from the *Kirk* were sent aboard each Vietnamese ship to take command after a formal flag ceremony. Rick Sautter, one of the *Kirk* officers who took command of a Vietnamese ship, recalled about the occasion, "That was the last vestige of South Vietnam. And when those flags came down and the American flags went up, that was it. Because a Navy ship is sovereign territory and so that was the last sovereign territory of the Republic of Vietnam." (A listing of these ships may be found in Appendix D.)[20]

UNIT AWARDS FOR THE EVACUATION OF SAIGON

The below listed surface combatant ships received the Armed Forces Expeditionary Medal (AE), Humanitarian Service Medal (HS), and Meritorious Unit Commendation (MUC) for Operation FREQUENT WIND. The asterisks denote awards for Operation EAGLE PULL.

Ship	AE Medal	HS Medal	MUC
Bausell (DD-845)	29-30 Apr 75	29-30 Apr 75	22-30 Apr 75
Cochrane (DDG-21)	29-30 Apr 75	29-30 Apr 75	22-30 Apr 75
Cook (FF-1083)	11-13 Apr 75*	12 Apr 75*	12 Apr 75*
	29-30 Apr 75	20-30 Apr 75	
Gurke (DD-783)	29-30 Apr 75	29-30 Apr 75	22-30 Apr 75
Kirk (FF-1087)	11-13 Apr 75*	12 Apr 75*	22 Apr-7 May 75
Oklahoma City (CLG-5)	29-30 Apr 75	29-30 Apr 75	22-30 Apr 75
Richard B. Anderson (DD-786)	29-30 Apr 75	29-30 Apr 75	22-30 Apr 75
Rowan (DD-782)	29-30 Apr 75	29-30 Apr 75	22-30 Apr 75
Worden (DLG-18)	29-30 Apr 75	29-30 Apr 75	22-20 Apr 75[21]

Postscript

On the Gunline closes with a several-page long pictorial tour of leisure activities sailors commonly enjoy aboard ship and ashore. One of the photographs depicts a desperately tired sailor trying to get adequate rest, a most basic form of relaxation. Two other photos provide insight into an activity involving fun only for some. The remaining participants most likely wanted their involvement in a longstanding tradition among mariners—a Line Crossing Ceremony for those who had not previously sailed across the Equator—to end as soon as possible.

The bulk of the photographs are intended to help former sailors to reminisce about runs ashore with shipmates, and provide opportunity for those who were unable to visit one or more of the liberty ports depicted, to do so vicariously. Navy Ships home ported on America's West Coast typically arrived in Vietnam having stopped at Pearl Harbor, Hawaii, and Subic Bay, Philippine Islands, en route. During interludes from duty on the gunline, they typically visited Subic Bay, Hong Kong, Singapore, a port in Japan, or Kaohsiung (if assigned Taiwanese Straits patrol duty) for crew liberty. East Coast-based ships followed a similar pattern which also included stops at Midway Atoll.

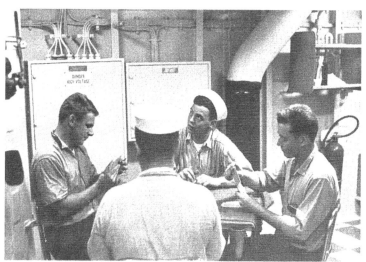

Members of AS (Anti-submarine) Division playing cards in an equipment space aboard the destroyer USS *Edson* (DD-946) after work hours.
USS *Edson* Western Pacific 1967 cruise book

Cookout on the fantail with food barbequed on a pit made from an empty fuel drum.
USS *Du Pont* 1967-1968 cruise book

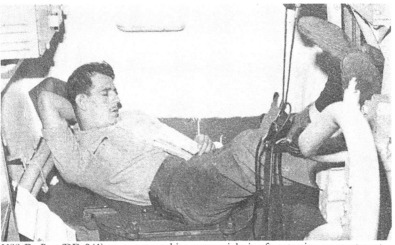

USS *Du Pont* (DD-941) crewman catching some winks in after steering compartment.
USS *Du Pont* 1967-1968 cruise book

USS *Du Pont* (DD-941) sailors providing their own entertainment.
USS *Du Pont* 1967-1968 cruise book

Bill Noteman, a crewmember aboard the destroyer USS *Benner* (DD-807) blowing the blues harmonica in Hong Kong in 1968. Following his naval service, he became a professional musician and lead man in the blues band Bill Noteman and the Rockets. Courtesy of Richard Mathews

Journalist Third Robert J. Kermen (who would retire as Capt., USNR) shooting skeet off the fantail. Trap shooting was a popular activity when the gun cruiser USS *St. Paul* (CA-73) to which he was assigned, was off the gunline.
Courtesy of Robert J. Kermen

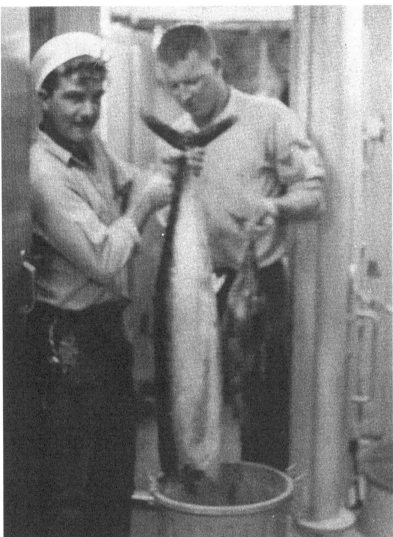

Two *Edson* crewmembers showing off their catch. Fishing off the fantail of one's ship while at anchor was popular, although not necessarily among the deck force members responsible for cleaning up residue from bait or spilled remains of cleaned fish.
USS *Edson* Western Pacific 1967 cruise book

IN THE HIGHEST COURT OF THE RAGING MAIN.

THE DOMAIN OF IMPERIVM NEPTVNI REGIS

SEND GREETINGS TO: __USS BARRY (DD 933)__

YOU ARE COMMANDED TO APPEAR BEFORE THE ROYAL COURT ON   __28 February 1966__

A complaint has been filed with the government of THE DOMAIN OF IMPERIVM NEPTVNI REGIS, STATE OF THE RAGING MAIN, EQUATORIA, against you:

> **WHEREAS:** YOU HAVE CONSPIRED TO ENTER THE ROYAL DOMAIN WITHOUT VISA, PASSPORT OR PROPER AUTHORIZATION.

> **WHEREAS:** YOU HAVE FAILED TO MAINTAIN THE PERSONAL HYGIENIC PERFECTION REQUIRED TO ENTER THIS DOMAIN. TO WIT: YOU HAVE ALLOWED TO COVER YOUR BODY AND ENTER YOUR MIND A CERTAIN AMOUNT OF SLIME THAT IS USUALLY FOUND ON POLLYWOGS AND OTHER LOWER SPECIMEN OF THE REALM.

> **WHEREAS:** YOU ARE FURTHER CHARGED WITH BROWN BAGGERY, MOPERY, DOPEING OFF, CHIT REQUESTING, APPLE POLISHING, SYMPATHY SEEKING, GUN DECKING, PROCRASTINATION, GOLD BRICKING, LIBERTY HOUNDING AND REVEILLE NEGLECTING.

> **WHEREAS:** YOU ARE SPECIFICALLY CHARGED WITH THE HENIOUS CRIMES OF: _____

> **WHEREFORE:** THE PEOPLE OF THE DOMAIN OF IMPERIVM NEPTVNI REGIS, STATE OF THE RAGING MAIN, EQUATORIA, PRAY THAT THE DEFENDENT BE BROUGHT BEFORE THE ROYAL COURT FORTH-WITH AND BE TRIED BEFORE THE BENEVOLENT JUDGES PRESIDING.

Subscribed and sworn to
before me this _26_ day of _February_

NEPTUNUS REX.

Royal scribe in and for THE DOMAIN
OF INPERIVM NEPTVNI REGIS.
DAVY JONES. ROYAL SCRIBE

Guidance from Neptunus Rex concerning an impending Shellback Initiation aboard the destroyer USS *Barry* (DD-933) on the day she crossed the equator.
USS *Barry* 1965-1966 Around the World cruise book

NAVAL MESSAGE
OPNAV FORM 2110-28 (REV. 3-61)

RELEASED BY		DRAFTED BY			PHONE EXT NR		PAGE	PAGES
DATE 25 FEB 1966	TOR/TOD TOR:1300Z/25 FEB		ROUTED BY WU/MU	CHECKED BY SUPV/KO			OF	

MESSAGE NR IN 1324	DATE/TIME GROUP (GCT) 2 5 1 2 3 7 Z	PRECE-DENCE	FLASH	EMERGENCY	OPERATIONAL IMMEDIATE	PRIORITY	ROUTINE	DEFERRED
		ACTION		EEEEE				
		INFO		EEEEE				

FM:DAVY JONES
TO:SLIMY POLLYWOGS OF BARRY
INFO:ALL TRUE & TRUSTY SHELLBACKS OF BARRY

///U N C L A S ///

IT HAS COME TO MY ROYAL ATTENTION THAT CERTAIN BARRY POLLYWOGS ARE
DEMONSTRATING COMPLETE LACK OF CONCERN AND TOTAL DISREGARD OF RESPECT
CONCERNING MY PROPOSED VISIT.THEREFORE I INTEND TO VISIT BARRY TO INSURE
PROPER ATTITUDE IS TAKEN BY THESE MISERABLE FLOATING SCUM BEFORE HIS
MOST SUPREME HIGHNESS KING NEPTUNIS REX ARRIVES SUNDAY 27 FEB.
BE IT HERE UNDERSTOOD THAT SUNDAY 27 FEB 1966 AT MY PLEASURE I AND A
FEW OF MY MOST HIGHLY SELECTED ROYAL AIDS WILL BOARD BARRY FOR AN
INSPECTION OF THE LOWLY POLLYWOGS AND TO INSURE THAT PROPER STEPS ARE
BEING TAKEN SO THAT THEY WILL RENDER THEMSELVES HUMBLE BEFORE HIS MOST
SUPREME HIGHNESS KING NEPTUNIS REX.
FOR PLANNING PURPOSES .I INTEND TO VISIT BARRY 26 FEB.POLLYWOGS REMAIN IN
PRESCRIBED CEREMONIAL UNIFORM UNTIL 27 FEB 1966,THE DAY OF JUDGEMENT.DUE
TO PREVIOUS COMMITMENTS IT WILL BE IMPOSSIBLE FOR KING NEPTUNES REX TO
VISIT BARRY ON ACTUAL DAY OF ENTRY MY DOMAIN.
ARISE SHELLBACKS .PROVE YOUR SEAWORTHYNESS OVER THE SCUM OF THE WAVES.
REGARDS DAVY.

FROM: NEPTUNIS REX
TO: USS BARRY (DD-933) / COURT OF NEPTUNIS / COMEQUATOR INSP
INFO: DAVY JONES LOCKER
         AND BOARDING

...BT...
??.U N C L A S.// INDICATES BARRY WILL ARRIVE MY OP-AREA ABOUT 27
MY OP-SKED 2-66 INDICATES BARRY WILL BOARDING AND INSPECTION
FEB. IAW CURRENT REGS AND CUSTOMS MY BOARDING AND INSPECTION
PARTY WILL BOARD YOU ON ARRIVAL. IT IS UNDERSTOOD THAT PART OF
YOUR CREW ARE POLLYWOGS AND HAVE THE AUDACITY TO TRY TO ENTER
MY DOMAIN UNNOTICED AND UNANNOUNCED. THEREFORE DAVY JONES AND
OTHER HIGH EMMISSARIES OF MY COURT WILL FORM A SPECIAL BOARDING
AND INSPECTING PARTY. THEY WILL BE MET WITH FULL HONORS AND
CEREMONIES AS APPROPIATE. ALL POLLYWOGS WILL BE SHOWN TO THE
PARTY AND WILL BE PREPARED TO ANSWER FOR ALL CHARGES BROUGHT
AGAINST THEM AND SUCH OTHER PUNISHMENT AS MY COURT MAY DIRECT.
DAVY JONES WILL MAKE A REPORT TO ME WHICH MAY NECESSITATE MY
PERSONAL INSPECTION OF CONDITIONS. THIS DECISION WILL BE
PROMULGATED BY LATER MESSAGE.
...BT...

FROM: DAVY JONES
TO: USS BARRY
INFO: COMDESRON 24

...BT...
??.U N C L A S.// INTEND BOARD USS BARRY ABOUT 1530Z FOR PRE-CEREMONY INSPECTION OF
POLLYWOGS. EXPECT POLLYWOGS TO BE IN CEREMONIAL UNIFORM AND
RENDER ALL ROYAL HONORS AS BECOMES THEIR LOWLY STATUS.
...BT...

Naval Message from Davy Jones providing guidance to the Slimy Pollywogs of the
USS *Barry* (DD-933) regarding the impending Shellback Initiation.
USS *Barry* 1965-1966 Around the World cruise book

Officers and men ("pollywogs") aboard the destroyer *Bordelon*, who had not previously crossed the Equator, enduring a Line Crossing ceremony to turn them into "trusty shellbacks."
USS *Bordelon* (DD-881) Western Pacific 1967-1968 cruise book

Pollywogs aboard other Navy ships fared no better, and perhaps worse.
USS *Rowan* (DD-782) Western Pacific 1971 cruise book

Hawaii

Waikiki Beach in Hawaii, with Diamond Head in the background.
USS *Benner* (DD 807) Western Pacific 1966-1967 cruise book

Beach in Hawaii.
USS *Du Pont* (DD-941) cruise book

A picturesque view of Diamond Head wasn't the favorite attraction of most sailors spending time at a beach in Hawaii.
USS *Floyd B. Parks* (DD-884) Western Pacific 1972-1973 cruise book

Attendance at a Hawaiian Luau provided opportunity to enjoy some traditional Polynesian foods such as Poi, Laulau, Kalua pig, Chicken long rice, and fruit (like pineapple and lilikoi), and also wear bright colored garb.
USS *Providence* (CLG-6) Western Pacific 1966-1968 cruise book

Midway Island

Refueling pier at Naval Station, Midway Island.
USS *Lloyd Thomas* (DD-764) Western Pacific 1972 cruise book

Midway Island street.
USS *Cone* (DD-866) Western Pacific 1967-1968 cruise book

Gooney bird on Midway Island.
USS *Du Pont* (DD-941) cruise book

Two of the many other Gooney birds on Midway Island.
USS *Lloyd Thomas* (DD-764) Western Pacific 1972 cruise book

Subic Bay/Olongapo, Philippine Islands

Subic Bay, gateway to the Philippine Islands.
USS *Du Pont* (DD-941) cruise book

Reminders of hard-fought battles in the Philippine Islands in World War II linger
among lush jungle growth and languid summer heat at Corregidor.
USS *Rowan* (DD-782) Western Pacific 1971-1972 cruise book

Guidance for Sailors and Marines embarking on liberty in Olongapo.
USS *Du Pont* (DD-941) cruise book

Olongapo City, Philippine Islands.
USS *Canberra* (CAG-2) 1966-1967 cruise book

A sight typifying the life in Subic Bay was a view of children in small boats begging for coins beneath the Olongapo Bridge. The presence of children at this location day and night made sailors realize how lucky they were to live in America.
USS *Canberra* (CAG-2) 1966-1967 cruise book

The Jeepney was the popular form of public transportation in the Philippines.
USS *Canberra* (CAG-2) 1966-1967 cruise book

Canberra sailors enjoying swimming and snorkeling at Grande Island, Philippines.
USS *Canberra* (CAG-2) 1966-1967 cruise book

Hong Kong, British Crown Colony

The "Pearl of the Orient" as seen from atop Victoria Peak.
USS *Floyd B. Parks* (DD-884) Western Pacific 1972-1973 cruise book

Mary Soo and assistants, renowned for painting the sides of ships.
USS *Du Pont* (DD-941) cruise book

Mary Soo, a legend in Hong Kong for over fifty years.
USS *Rowan* (DD-782) Western Pacific 1971-1972 cruise book

Rickshaw with passenger.
USS *Floyd B. Parks* (DD-884) Western Pacific 1972-1973 cruise book

Lockhart Road, Wanchai, Hong Kong.
USS *Floyd B. Parks* (DD-884) Western Pacific 1972-1973 cruise book

Hong Kong.
USS *Fechteler* (DD-870) Southeast Asian 1967 cruise book

Okinawa, Japan

Very modest dwellings in Okinawa.
USS *Cone* (DD-866) Western Pacific 1967-1968 cruise book

Photo

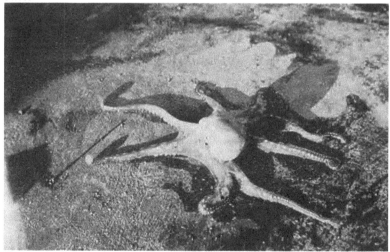

Octopus hard aground at Okinawa.
USS *Cone* (DD-866) Western Pacific 1967-1968 cruise book

Singapore, British Crown Colony

Royal Navy base at Singapore.
USS *Bordelon* (DD-881) Western Pacific 1967-1968 cruise book

Singapore snake charmer.
USS *Bordelon* (DD-881) Western Pacific 1967-1968 cruise book

Singapore Strait from the Tiger Balm Gardens.
USS *Bordelon* (DD-881) Western Pacific 1967-1968 cruise book

The waterway to downtown Singapore.
USS *Oklahoma City* Western Pacific 1971-1972 cruise book

A deserted sailing basin.
USS *Oklahoma City* Western Pacific 1971-1972 cruise book

Kaohsiung, Taiwan

Kaohsiung, Taiwan street market.
USS *Fechteler* (DD-870) Southeast Asian 1967 cruise book

Indigenous craft at Kaohsiung, Taiwan.
USS *Fechteler* (DD-870) Southeast Asian 1967 cruise book

Kaohsiung street scene.
USS *Du Pont* (DD-941) cruise book

Yokosuka, Japan

Yokosuka nightlife.
USS *Du Pont* (DD-941) cruise book

Sailor on liberty at night in Yokosuka.
USS *Du Pont* (DD-941) cruise book

Daytime liberty in Yokosuka.
USS *Fechteler* (DD-870) Southeast Asian 1967 cruise book

Tokyo, Japan

Examples of the architecture in Tokyo.
USS *Providence* (CLG-6) Western Pacific 1966-1968 cruise book

A local "ginza" shopping center.
USS *Oklahoma City* Western Pacific 1971-1972 cruise book

1700-year-old cypress was used in huge torii at Meiji Shrine, Tokyo.
USS *Oklahoma City* Western Pacific 1971-1972 cruise book

Appendix A: Battleship *New Jersey*, and the USN Cruisers, Destroyers/Destroyer Escorts that Served in Vietnam (269 total)

The Combat Action Ribbons (CR), Meritorious Unit Commendations (MUC) and Navy Unit Commendations (NUC) cited in the table were earned during the period covered in this book, 1965-1973. A few of the MUCs or NUCs may not be related to the Vietnam War, but most were.

CR	MUC	NUC	Ship	Ship Class
1			*Agerholm* (DD-826)	*Gearing*
1			*Albert David* (DE-1050)	*Garcia*
2			*Alfred A. Cunningham* (DD-752)	*Allen M. Sumner*
8	2		*Allen M. Sumner* (DD-692)	*Allen M. Sumner*
2			*Arnold J. Isbell* (DD-869)	*Gearing*
1	1		*Ault* (DD-698)	*Allen M. Sumner*
			Bache (DD-470)	*Fletcher*
1			*Badger* (DE-1071)	*Knox*
			Bainbridge (DLGN-25)	*Bainbridge*
3	2		*Barney* (DDG-6)	*Charles F. Adams*
	1		*Barry* (DD-933)	*Forrest Sherman*
	1		*Basillone* (DD-824)	*Gearing*
			Bauer (DE-1025)	*Courtney*
7	1		*Bausell* (DD-845)	*Gearing*
			Beale (DD-471)	*Fletcher*
	1		*Belknap* (DLG-26)	*Belknap*
9	2		*Benjamin Stoddert* (DDG-22)	*Charles F. Adams*
1			*Benner* (DD-807)	*Gearing*
9	2	1	*Berkeley* (DDG-15)	*Charles F. Adams*
	2	1	*Biddle* (DLG-34)	*Belknap*
3	1		*Bigelow* (DD-942)	*Forrest Sherman*
			Black (DD-666)	*Fletcher*
			Blakey (DE-1072)	*Knox*
4	5	1	*Blandy* (DD-943)	*Forrest Sherman*
8		1	*Blue* (DD-744)	*Allen M. Sumner*
6	2		*Bordelon* (DD-881)	*Gearing*
			Borie (DD-704)	*Allen M. Sumner*
14		2	*Boston* (CA-69/CAG-1)	*Baltimore*
			Boyd (DD-544)	*Fletcher*
			Bradley (DE-1041)	*Garcia*

1			*Braine* (DD-630)	*Fletcher*
			Bridget (DE-1024)	*Courtney*
1			*Brinkley Bass* (DD-887)	*Gearing*
1		1	*Brister* (DER-327)	*Edsall*
			Bronstein (DE-1037)	*Bronstein*
			Brooke (DEG-1)	*Brooke*
	1		*Brownson* (DD-868)	*Gearing*
1			*Brush* (DD-745)	*Allen M. Sumner*
7	1		*Buchanan* (DDG-14)	*Charles F. Adams*
			Buck (DD-761)	*Allen M. Sumner*
			Camp (DER-251)	*Edsall*
11	2		*Canberra* (CAG-2)	*Baltimore*
	4		*Carpenter* (DD-825)	*Gearing*
	2		*Charles Berry* (DE-1035)	*Claud Jones*
			Charles H. Roan (DD-853)	*Gearing*
1			*Charles P. Cecil* (DD-835)	*Gearing*
2	2		*Charles R. Ware* (DD-865)	*Gearing*
			Charles S. Sperry (DD-697)	*Allen M. Sumner*
1			*Chevalier* (DD-805)	*Gearing*
1	3	1	*Chicago* (CG-11)	*Baltimore*
	3		*Claud Jones* (DE-1033)	*Claud Jones*
7	3	1	*Cochrane* (DDG-21)	*Charles F. Adams*
			Cogswell (DD-651)	*Fletcher*
3		1	*Collett* (DD-730)	*Allen M. Sumner*
2	1		*Cone* (DD-866)	*Gearing*
			Conway (DD-507)	*Fletcher*
			Cony (DD-508)	*Fletcher*
1		1	*Coontz* (DLG-9)	*Farragut*
		1	*Corry* (DD-817)	*Gearing*
	3		*Dahlgren* (DLG-12)	*Farragut*
			Dale (DLG-19)	*Leahy*
3			*Damato* (DD-871)	*Gearing*
1	2		*Davidson* (DE-1045)	*Garcia*
4	2		*Davis* (DD-937)	*Forrest Sherman*
			Decatur (DDG-31)	*Forrest Sherman*
3		1	*Dehaven* (DD-727)	*Allen M. Sumner*
3	1		*Dennis J. Buckley* (DD-808)	*Gearing*
			Dewey (DLG-14)	*Farragut*
		1	*Douglas H. Fox* (DD-779)	*Allen M. Sumner*
5	1		*Duncan* (DDR-874)	*Gearing*
6	4		*Du Pont* (DD-941)	*Forrest Sherman*
			Dyess (DDR-880)	*Gearing*
			Eaton (DD-510)	*Fletcher*
8	3	2	*Edson* (DD-946)	*Forrest Sherman*
	1	1	*England* (DLG-22)	*Leahy*
4		1	*Epperson* (DD-719)	*Gearing*
1	1		*Ernest G. Small* (DDR-838)	*Gearing*
			Eugene A. Greene (DD-711)	*Gearing*
			Evans (DE-1023)	*Courtney*

6	1		*Everett F. Larson* (DD-830)	*Gearing*
2		1	*Eversole* (DD-789)	*Gearing*
1			*Falgout* (DER-324)	*Edsall*
			Fanning (DE-1076)	*Knox*
3		1	*Fechteler* (DD-870)	*Gearing*
1			*Finch* (DER-328)	*Edsall*
		1	*Fiske* (DD-842)	*Gearing*
1			*Fletcher* (DD-445)	*Fletcher*
2	1		*Floyd B. Parks* (DD-884)	*Gearing*
1	1		*Forrest B. Royal* (DD-872)	*Gearing*
			Forster (DE-334)	*Edsall*
	1		*Fox* (DLG-33)	*Belknap*
1			*Francis Hammond* (DE-1067)	*Knox*
		1	*Frank E. Evans* (DD-754)	*Allen M. Sumner*
1			*Frank Knox* (DD-742)	*Gearing*
1			*Fred T. Berry* (DD-858)	*Gearing*
1			*Furse* (DD-882)	*Gearing*
			Galveston (CLG-3)	*Cleveland*
4	4	2	*George K. MacKenzie* (DD-836)	*Gearing*
1			*Glennon* (DD-840)	*Gearing*
8	2	1	*Goldsborough* (DDG-20)	*Charles F. Adams*
			Gray (DE-1054)	*Knox*
		1	*Gridley* (DLG-21)	*Leahy*
4	1		*Gurke* (DD-783)	*Gearing*
	3	2	*Halsey* (DLG-23)	*Leahy*
7	2	1	*Hamner* (DD-718)	*Gearing*
2	1		*Hanson* (DD-832)	*Gearing*
1	1		*Harold E. Holt* (DE-1074)	*Knox*
			Harold J. Ellison (DD-864)	*Gearing*
4		1	*Harry E. Hubbard* (DD-748)	*Allen M. Sumner*
1	1		*Harwood* (DD-861)	*Gearing*
			Haverfield (DER-393)	*Edsall*
			Hawkins (DDR-873)	*Gearing*
1			*Henderson* (DD-785)	*Gearing*
4	3	1	*Henry B. Wilson* (DDG-7)	*Charles F. Adams*
3	4	2	*Henry W. Tucker* (DD-875)	*Gearing*
			Hepburn (DE-1055)	*Knox*
			Herbert J. Thomas (DD-833)	*Gearing*
2			*Higbee* (DD-806)	*Gearing*
			Hissem (DER-400)	*Edsall*
6	2		*Hoel* (DDG-13)	*Charles F. Adams*
1			*Holder* (DD-819)	*Gearing*
8	1	1	*Hollister* (DD-788)	*Gearing*
			Hooper (DE-1026)	*Courtney*
			Hopewell (DD-681)	*Fletcher*
	1		*Horne* (DLG-30)	*Belknap*
1	1		*Hugh Purvis* (DD-709)	*Allen M. Sumner*
8	3		*Hull* (DD-945)	*Forrest Sherman*
7			*Ingersoll* (DD-652)	*Fletcher*

			Ingraham (DD-694)	*Allen M. Sumner*
			James C. Owens (DD-776)	*Allen M. Sumner*
2			*James E. Kyes* (DD-787)	*Gearing*
			Jenkins (DD-447)	*Fletcher*
			John A. Bole (DD-755)	*Allen M. Sumner*
1			*John King* (DDG-3)	*Charles F. Adams*
6			*John Paul Jones* (DDG-32)	*Forrest Sherman*
6	1	1	*John R. Craig* (DD-885)	*Gearing*
	2		*John R. Perry* (DE-1034)	*Claud Jones*
5	1		*John S. McCain* (DDG-36)	*Mitscher*
	1		*John W. Thomason* (DD-760)	*Allen M. Sumner*
			John W. Weeks (DD-701)	*Allen M. Sumner*
2			*Johnston* (DD-821)	*Gearing*
1			*Joseph Hewes* (DE-1078)	*Knox*
16	1	1	*Joseph Strauss* (DDG-16)	*Charles F. Adams*
			Joseph Daniels (DLG-27)	*Belknap*
	1	1	*Jouett* (DLG-29)	*Belknap*
3			*Keppler* (DD-765)	*Gearing*
2	2		*King* (DLG-10)	*Farragut*
			Knox (DE-1052)	*Knox*
			Koiner (DER-331)	*Edsall*
			Kretchmer (DER-329)	*Edsall*
1			*Lang* (DE-1060)	*Knox*
3	1		*Lawrence* (DDG-4)	*Charles F. Adams*
2	1		*Leary* (DD-879)	*Gearing*
2	2	2	*Leonard F. Mason* (DD-852)	*Gearing*
4	1		*Lloyd Thomas* (DD-764)	*Gearing*
3			*Lockwood* (DE-1064)	*Knox*
1	2		*Lofberg* (DD-759)	*Allen M. Sumner*
1	2	1	*Longbeach* (CGN-9)	*Longbeach*
1			*Lowe* (DER-325)	*Edsall*
		1	*Lowry* (DD-770)	*Allen M. Sumner*
			Lyman K. Swenson (DD-729)	*Allen M. Sumner*
2			*Lynde McCormick* (DDG-8)	*Charles F. Adams*
4		1	*Maddox* (DD-731)	*Allen M. Sumner*
		1	*Mahan* (DLG-11)	*Farragut*
	1		*Manley* (DD-940)	*Forrest Sherman*
5		1	*Mansfield* (DD-728)	*Allen M. Sumner*
1			*Marvin Shields* (DE-1066)	*Knox*
			Massey (DD-778)	*Allen M. Sumner*
4	1		*McCaffery* (DD-860)	*Gearing*
			McKean (DD-784)	*Gearing*
	2		*McMorris* (DE-1036)	*Claud Jones*
	1		*Meredith* (DD-890)	*Gearing*
			Meyerkord (DE-1058)	*Knox*
8	3		*Morton* (DD-948)	*Forrest Sherman*
		1	*Mullany* (DD-528)	*Fletcher*
3	2	1	*Mullinnix* (DD-944)	*Forrest Sherman*
1			*Myles C. Fox* (DD-829)	*Gearing*

	1		New (DD-818)	Gearing
2		1	New Jersey (BB-62)	Iowa
			Newell (DER-322)	Edsall
			Newman K. Perry (DD-883)	Gearing
21	1	2	Newport News (CA-148)	Des Moines
	3		Nicholas (DD-449)	Fletcher
		1	Noa (DD-841)	Gearing
1			Norris (DD-859)	Gearing
1			O'Bannon (DD-450)	Fletcher
1	1		O'Brien (DD-725)	Allen M. Sumner
2			O'Callahan (DE-1051)	Garcia
1	1		O'Hare (DD-889)	Gearing
13	2	1	Oklahoma City (CLG-5)	Cleveland
		1	Orleck (DD-886)	Gearing
2			Ouellet (DE-1077)	Knox
8	3	1	Ozbourne (DD-846)	Gearing
2	2		Parsons (DDG-33)	Forrest Sherman
1			Paul (DE-1080)	Knox
2			Perkins (DD-877)	Gearing
1	1		Perry (DD-844)	Gearing
1			Philip (DD-498)	Fletcher
2		1	Picking (DD-685)	Fletcher
			Porterfield (DD-682)	Fletcher
			Power (DD-839)	Gearing
3	1		Preble (DLG-15)	Farragut
		1	Preston (DD-795)	Fletcher
			Prichett (DD-561)	Fletcher
9		2	Providence (CLG-6)	Cleveland
			Radford (DD-446)	Fletcher
			Ramsey (DEG-2)	Brooke
1	1		Rathburne (DE-1057)	Knox
1		1	Reeves (DLG-24)	Leahy
			Renshaw (DD-499)	Fletcher
4	1		Rich (DD-820)	Gearing
5	2		Richard B. Anderson (DD-786)	Gearing
2			Richard E. Kraus (DD-849)	Gearing
5	1		Richard E. Edwards (DD-950)	Forrest Sherman
			Richmond K. Turner (DLG-20)	Leahy
1			Roark (DE-1053)	Knox
			Robert H. McCard (DD-822)	Gearing
			Robert K. Huntington (DD-781)	Allen B. Sumner
			Robert L. Wilson (DD-847)	Gearing
7	1	1	Robison (DDG-12)	Charles F. Adams
4	1		Rogers (DD-876)	Gearing
3	1		Rowan (DD-782)	Gearing
5	5	4	Rupertus (DD-851)	Gearing
3			Sample (DE-1048)	Garcia
			Samuel B. Roberts (DD-823)	Gearing
1		1	Samuel N. Moore (DD-747)	Allen B. Sumner

2	1		*Sarsfield* (DD-837)	*Gearing*
			Savage (DER-386)	*Edsall*
			Schofield (DEG-3)	*Brooke*
4	1	1	*Shelton* (DD-790)	*Gearing*
1	1		*Somers* (DDG-34)	*Forrest Sherman*
		1	*Southerland* (DD-743)	*Gearing*
1			*Sproston* (DD-577)	*Fletcher*
14	4	1	*St. Paul* (CA-73)	*Baltimore*
1			*Steinaker* (DD-863)	*Gearing*
1		2	*Sterett* (DLG-31)	*Belknap*
			Stickell (DD-888)	*Gearing*
11		2	*Stoddard* (DD-566)	*Fletcher*
	1		*Stormes* (DD-780)	*Allen B. Sumner*
			Stribling (DD-867)	*Gearing*
2			*Strong* (DD-758)	*Allen M. Sumner*
			Taussig (DD-746)	*Allen M. Sumner*
			Taylor (DD-468)	*Fletcher*
5		1	*Theodore E. Chandler* (DD-717)	*Gearing*
			Topeka (CLG-8)	*Cleveland*
4	3		*Towers* (DDG-9)	*Charles F. Adams*
			Trippe (DE-1075)	*Knox*
	1	1	*Truxton* (DLGN-35)	*Truxton*
9	1	1	*Turner Joy* (DD-951)	*Forrest Sherman*
			Uhlmann (DD-687)	*Fletcher*
1			*Vance* (DER-387)	*Edsall*
			Vesole (DD-878)	*Gearing*
	1		*Vogelgesang* (DD-862)	*Gearing*
8		2	*Waddell* (DDG-24)	*Charles F. Adams*
			Wainwright (DLG-28)	*Belknap*
1			*Waldron* (DD-699)	*Allen M. Sumner*
			Walke (DD-723)	*Allen M. Sumner*
			Walker (DD-517)	*Fletcher*
			Wallace L. Lind (DD-703)	*Allen M. Sumner*
			Waller (DD-466)	*Fletcher*
1			*Warrington* (DD-843)	*Gearing*
			Wedderburn (DD-684)	*Fletcher*
1			*Whipple* (DE-1062)	*Knox*
		3	*Wilhoite* (DER-397)	*Edsall*
2			*William C. Lawe* (DD-763)	*Gearing*
			William H. Stanley (DLG-32)	*Belknap*
	2		*William V. Pratt* (DLG-13)	*Farragut*
1	1		*Wiltsie* (DD-716)	*Gearing*
1	1		*Worden* (DLG-18)	*Leahy*

Appendix B: Unit Awards Earned by RAN Destroyers

The Secretary of the Navy takes pleasure in commending
HMAS *HOBART* (D39)
for Services set forth in the following

CITATION:

For Exceptionally Meritorious Service during the period 10th March to 20th September, 1967, while engaged in Combat Operations in direct support of Free World Objectives in South East Asia. As an element of Task Unit 70.8.9 HMAS *HOBART* provided Naval Gunfire Support for United States and Allied Forces ashore in the Republic of Vietnam, and as an element of Task Group 77.1 in the Gulf of Tonkin, supported Naval Operations against North Vietnamese logistics groups and lines of communications. Undeterred by frequent, vigorous, accurate enemy shore fire, *HOBART* was responsible for the destruction of numerous enemy installations, earning an enviable reputation as an Aggressive Eager and Dauntless Member of the US Seventh Fleet. The outstanding Team Work, Courage and Professionalism displayed by *HOBART* Officers and Men reflect Great Credit upon themselves and the Royal Australian Navy and were in keeping with the Highest Traditions of the Naval Service.

Paul R. Ignatius
Secretary of the Navy

The Secretary of the Navy takes pleasure in commending
HMAS *PERTH* (D38)
for Services set forth in the following

CITATION:

For Exceptionally Meritorious Service from 9 September 1967 to 5 April 1968 in the planning and execution of combat missions against enemy aggressor forces in direct support of Free World Objectives. While operating as a unit of the U.S. SEVENTH Fleet, HMAS *PERTH* delivered extensive, destructive naval gunfire against enemy supply routes, coastal defense sites, troop concentrations, and fortified positions in both North and South Vietnam.

The prowess and teamwork displayed by the personnel of *PERTH* were uniformly characterized by personal valor, professional acumen, and individual initiative. Although often within the range of enemy emplacements, and frequently under fire from North Vietnamese coastal defense sites, *PERTH* quickly responded with skill and resourcefulness, silencing enemy batteries while maneuvering adroitly to avoid sustaining any damage or injury to herself.

The tenacity, professionalism, and dedication demonstrated by the officers and men of *PERTH* reflect great credit upon themselves and the Royal Australian Navy.

Paul R. Ignatius
Secretary of the Navy

The Secretary of the Navy takes pleasure in presenting the
Meritorious Unit Commendation to HMAS *PERTH* (D38)
for service as set forth in the following:

For meritorious service from 24 September 1968 to March 1969 while participating in combat operations against enemy aggressor forces in South East Asia.

As a member of the United States SEVENTH Fleet assigned to SEA DRAGON operations, HMAS *PERTH* contributed significantly to SEVENTH Fleet combat operations by conducting numerous successful fire missions against heavily defended enemy logistic installations and lines of communications. When *PERTH* was engaged by enemy shore batteries on two occasions, the combination of her crew members' spirited teamwork and capable leadership produced quick and precise evasive action to spare the ship any material or personnel casualties. *PERTH*'s highly accurate fire inflicted heavy losses on enemy assets and was instrumental in assuring the success of allied operations wherever she was stationed.

The outstanding performance, superlative accomplishments, and inspiring devotion to duty displayed by the officers and men of HMAS *PERTH* throughout her deployment, reflect credit upon themselves and the Royal Australian Navy.

John H. Chaffee
Secretary of the Navy

Appendix C: Personnel Casualties aboard Seventh Fleet Ships

USS *Somers* (DDG-34)

21 May 65	SN Jimmy C. Stinnett	South China Sea

USS *Falgout* (DER-324)

9 Jun 65	FTG2 Edward A. J. Ownby	South China Sea, WIA 8 Jun 65

USS *Turner Joy* (DD-951) Gun Mount Explosion

26 Oct 65	GMG1 Carl W. Deaton	South China Sea
26 Oct 65	GMG2 Glenn M. Lane	South China Sea
26 Oct 65	GMG3 Thomas P. Miller	South China Sea

USS *Taussig* (DD-746)

16 Jun 66	SN Russell G. Darling	South China Sea, WIA 11 Jun 66

USS *Hamner* (DD-718)

27 Aug 66	FTG3 Richard D. Mattson	South China Sea

USS *Philip* (DD-498)

20 Nov 66	SA Daryl E. Smock	Gulf of Tonkin

USS *O'Brien* (DD-725)

23 Dec 66	DC3 Antone Perry Jr.	Gulf of Tonkin
23 Dec 66	FA Thomas L. Tiglas	Gulf of Tonkin

USS *Brister* (DER-327)

14 Jan 67	RM1 Francis J. Zinda	South China Sea

USS *Manley* (DD-940)

9 Mar 67	DK2 John M. Bronkema	South China Sea

USS *Bigelow* (DD-942)

25 Apr 67	GMG2 James W. Hamilton Jr.	South China Sea, Thua Thien Province

USS *St. Paul* (CA-73)

15 May 67	SA Charles D. Hill	South China Sea, MIA

USS *Du Pont* (DD-941)

28 Aug 67	FN Frank L. Bellant	Gulf of Tonkin

USS *Mansfield* (DD-728)

25 Sep 67	MM2 Richard C. Archer	Gulf of Tonkin

USS *William V. Pratt* (DLG-13)

12 Nov 67	SFM2 James D. Roark	MIA Gulf of Tonkin
12 Nov 67	SN John D. Cayce	MIA Gulf of Tonkin

USS *Damato* (DD-871)

22 Nov 67	ETR3 Jeffrey J. Brown	South China Sea

USS *Ozbourne* (DD-846)

4 Dec 67	CS3 Raymond L. Cork Jr.	Gulf of Tonkin
4 Dec 67	SN Edward S. O'Brien	Gulf of Tonkin

USS *Brister* (DER-327)

9 Feb 68	RM1 Loyal B. Doty	South China Sea

USS *Long Beach* (CGN-9)

5 May 68	SN Harry E. Mitchell	South China Sea, MIA
5 May 68	SA Michael J. Kustgian	South China Sea, MIA

USS *New Jersey* (BB-62)

28 Sep 68	MM1 Dan B. Norton	South China Sea

USS *Braine* (DD-630)

26 Oct 68	MM1 Paul T. Schimpf	Pacific Ocean

USS *Mullinnix* (DD-944)

29 Apr 69	BTFN James A. Jensen	South China Sea, WIA 26 Mar 69

USS *King* (DLG-10)

23 May 69	BT2 Kenneth W. Grubb	South China Sea
23 May 69	BT2 Gene L. Ware	South China Sea
23 May 69	BT3 Martin Brown	South China Sea
23 May 69	BT3 Joseph D. Fischer	South China Sea

USS *Frank E. Evans* (DD-754) – Collision with HMAS *Melbourne* (3 June 1969 in the South China Sea)

Lt. (jg) Jon K. Stever	SN Michael K. Clawson
Ens. Alan H. Armstrong	SN Danny V. Clute
Ens. Robert G. Brandon	SN Joe E. Craig
Ens. John T. Norton Jr.	SN James F. Dykes III
Ens. Dwight S. Pattee	SN Francis J. Garcia
BMC Willie L. King	SN Steven A. Guyer

EMC Edward P. Hess
HMC Charles W. Cannington
RDC George J. Laiberte
RD1 Eugene F. Lehman
BM2 Gary L. Sage
BT2 William D. Brown II
IC2 Linden R. Orpurt
RD2 Victor T. Rikall
RD2 Ronald A. Thibodeau
RM2 Ray P. Lebrun
STG2 John R. Spray
YN2 Earl F. Preston
BM3 Patrick G. Glennon
BM3 Frederic C. Messier
BT3 Lawrence J. Reilly Jr.
ET3 James F. Bradley
ET3 Larry W. Cool
ETR3 James W. Davis
GMG3 Steven F. Espinosa
QM3 Gary J. Vigue
RD3 Thomas B. Box
RD3 Christopher J. Carlson
RD3 Terry L. Henderson
RD3 Garry B. Hodgson
RD3 Gregory A. Sage
RD3 Jon W. Thomas
RD3 Con W. Warnock
STG3 Melvin H. Gardner Jr.
STG3 Larry A. Gracely
YN3 James R. Cmelya
SN Andrew J. Botto

SN Thurston P. Smith Jr.
BTFA Robert J. Searle
FA Gerald W. Smith
SA James R. Baker
SA Harris M. Brown
SA Patrick M. Corcoran
SA Leon L. Deal
SA Raymond J. Earley
SA Stephen D. Fagan
SA William D. Fields
SA Alan C. Flummer
SA Henry K. Frye
SA Donald E. Gearhart
SA Kenneth W. Glines
SA Joe L. Gonzales
SA Devere R. Grisson Jr.
SA Dennis R. Johnston
SA James W. Kerr
SA Issac Lyons Jr.
SA Douglas R. Meister
SA Andrew M. Melendrez
SA Timothy L. Miller
SA Michael A. Orlikowski
SA Craig A. Pennell
SA Jerome Pickett
SA Kelly J. Sage
SA John A. Sauvey
SA Thomas F. Tallon
SA John T. Tolar
SA Henry D. West III[1]

USS *Halsey* (DLG-23)

30 Jul 69	SA Cornelius F. Hubbard	South China Sea

USS *Hamner* (DD-718)

2 Oct 69	TN Reynaldo R. Viado	Gulf of Tonkin, C2 Passenger USS *Constellation*

USS *Long Beach* (CGN-9)

2 Oct 69	MM2 William R. Moore	Gulf of Tonkin, MIA, C2A Passenger *Constellation*

USS *Walke* (DD-723)

2 Oct 69	YNC Leonardo M. Gan	C2A Passenger USS *Constellation*
2 Oct 69	PN1 Rolando C. Dayao	C2A Passenger USS *Constellation*

USS *Oklahoma City* (CLG-5)

18 Oct 69	GMG3 Peter E. Gutloff	South China Sea - DMZ

USS *Lloyd Thomas* (DD-764) Gun Mount Explosion

11 Sep 70	GMGSN Dennis J. Bullock	South China Sea
11 Sep 70	SN Alan S. Boor	South China Sea
11 Sep 70	SN Douglas A. Nieboer	South China Sea

USS *John R. Craig* (DD-885)

3 Apr 72	FA Thomas R. Muren	Gulf of Tonkin, MIA

USS *Worden* (DLG-18)

16 Apr 72	BM3 Robert A. Sterling	Gulf of Tonkin

USS *Buchanan* (DDG-14)

17 Apr 72	SN Leonard R. Davis	Gulf of Tonkin

USS *Providence* (CLG-6) – ComCruDesFlot 11 Staff

8 May 72	Rear Adm. Rembrandt C. Robinson	Gulf of Tonkin – SH3G helicopter passenger
8 May 72	Capt. Edmund B. Taylor Jr.	MIA Gulf of Tonkin – SH3G helicopter passenger
8 May 72	Comdr. John M. Leaver Jr.	MIA Gulf of Tonkin – SH3G helicopter passenger

USS *Benjamin Stoddert* (DDG-22)

26 Jun 72	Lt. Comdr. Michael J. Martin	South China Sea
26 Jun 72	GMG1 Robert T. Mills	South China Sea
28 Jun 72	GMCS Gordon R. Uhler	South China Sea

USS *Newport News* (CA-148)

4 Jul 72	SK3 Stephen M. Brumfield	South China Sea, MIA

USS *Benjamin Stoddert* (DDG-22)

8 Aug 72	SN David N. Larson	South China Sea, WIA 26 Jun 72

USS *Newport News* (CA-148)

10 Aug 72	SN James J. Sansone	Gulf of Tonkin, MIA

USS *Robison* (DDG-12)

30 Aug 72	BTCM Charles H. Piper Jr.	South China Sea

USS *Newport News* (CA-148) Gun Turret Explosion

1 Oct 72	GMG1 Tommy M. Hawker	Gulf of Tonkin
1 Oct 72	GMG1 Wesley H. Rose	Gulf of Tonkin
1 Oct 72	BM3 William Clark Jr.	Gulf of Tonkin
1 Oct 72	GMG3 Charles W. Clinard	Gulf of Tonkin
1 Oct 72	SN Jack S. Bergman Jr.	Gulf of Tonkin
1 Oct 72	SN Terry W. Deal	Gulf of Tonkin
1 Oct 72	SN Edward R. McEleney Jr.	Gulf of Tonkin
1 Oct 72	SN Ralph L. Robinson	Gulf of Tonkin

1 Oct 72	SN David L. Scott	Gulf of Tonkin
1 Oct 72	SA Herman C. Acker	Gulf of Tonkin
1 Oct 72	SA Ronald P. Daley	Gulf of Tonkin
1 Oct 72	SA William H. Harrison III	Gulf of Tonkin
1 Oct 72	SA Robert M. Kikkert	Gulf of Tonkin
1 Oct 72	SA Robert T. Moore	Gulf of Tonkin
1 Oct 72	SA Stanley G. Pilot Jr.	Gulf of Tonkin
1 Oct 72	SA Ricky L. Rucker	Gulf of Tonkin
1 Oct 72	SA Jeffrey L. Scheller	Gulf of Tonkin
1 Oct 72	SA Richard C. Tessman	Gulf of Tonkin
1 Oct 72	SR Raymond R. Davis	Gulf of Tonkin
3 Oct 72	SN Joseph Grisafi	Gulf of Tonkin, WIA 1 Oct 72

USS *Henry W. Tucker* (DD-875)

14 Nov 72	FA Douglas T. Manka	South China Sea

USS *Goldsborough* (DDG-20)

19 Dec 72	HTC Donald A. Dix	Gulf of Tonkin
19 Dec 72	BM1 Robert M. Dow	Gulf of Tonkin
1 Jan 73	HT3 Gary L. Boyce	Gulf of Tonkin, WIA 19 Dec 72

USS *William C. Lawe* (DD-763)

3 Jan 73	SA Kenneth D. Scaife	MIA South China Sea

USS *King* (DLG-10)

8 Jan 73	EMC Jose J. Javines	Gulf of Tonkin

Appendix D: Vietnamese Ships that Escaped to the Philippines

Hull#	Ship Name/Formerly	Hull#	Ship Name/Formerly
HQ-01	RVNS *Tran Hung Dao*/ USS *Camp* (DE-251)	HQ-330	RVNS *Loi Cong*/ USS *LSI(L)-699*
HQ-02	RVNS *Tran Quang Khai*/ USCGC *Bering Strait* (WAVP-382)	HQ-400	RVNS *Hat Giang*/ USS *LSM-335*
HQ-03	RVNS *Tran Nhat Duat*/ USCGC *Yakutat* (WAVP-380)	HQ-401	RVNS *Han Giang*/ USS *LSM-110*
HQ-05	RVNS *Tran Binh Trong*/ USS *Castle Rock* (AVP-35)	HQ-404	RVNS *Huong Giang*/ USS *Oceanside* (LSM-175)
HQ-06	RVNS *Tran Quoc Toan*/ USCGC *Cook Inlet* (WAVP-384)	HQ-470	RVNS *HQ-470*/ USS *YOG-80*
HQ-07	RVNS *Dong Da II*/ USS *Crestview* (PCE-895)	HQ-471	RVNS *HQ-471*/ USS *YOG-33*
HQ-8	RVNS *Chi Lang II*/ USS *Gayety* (AM-239)	HQ-474	RVNS *HQ-474*/ USS *YOG-131*
HQ-11	RVNS *Chi Linh*/ USS *Shelter* (AM-301)	HQ-500	RVNS *Cam Ranh*/ USS *Marion County* (LST-975)
HQ-12	RVNS *Ngoc Hoi*/USS *Brattleboro* (PCE(R)-852)	HQ-502	RVNS Thi Nai/ USS *Cayuga County* (LST-529)
HQ-14	RVNS *Van Kiep II*/USS *Amherst* (PCE(R)-853)	HQ-505	RVNS *Nha Trang*/ USS *Jerome County* (LST-848)
HQ-16	RVNS *Ly Thuong Kiet*/ USCGC *Chincoteague* (WAVP-375)	HQ-618	RVNS *Hon Troc*/ USS *PGM-83*
HQ-17	RVNS *Ngo Quyen*/ USCGC *McCulloch* (WAVP-386)	HQ-702	RVNS *Huynh Van Duc*/ USCGC *Point Clear* (WPB-82315)
HQ-228	RVNS *Doan Ngoc Tang*/ USS *LSSL-9*	HQ-800	RVNS *Huynh Van Cu*/ USS *Harnett County* (LST-821)
HQ-229	RVNS *Lu Phu Tho*/ USS *LSSL-101*	HQ-801	RVNS *Can Tho*/ USS *Garrett County* (LST-786)
HQ-230	RVNS *Nguyen Ngoc Long*/ USS *LSSL-96*	HQ-802	RVNS *Vinh Long*/ USS *Satyr* (ARL-23)
HQ-231	RVNS *Nguyen Duc Bong*/ USS *LSSL-129*		Fishing Trawler #1
HQ-329	RVNS *Thien Kich*/ USS *LSI(L)-872*		Fishing Trawler #2[2]

Bibliography/Chapter Notes

Bruhn, David D. *Wooden Ships and Iron Men: The U.S. Navy's Coastal and Inshore Minesweepers, and the Minecraft That Served in Vietnam, 1953-1976.* Westminster, Md: Heritage Books, 2011.

—*Wooden Ships and Iron Men: The U.S. Navy's Ocean Minesweepers, 1953-1994.* Westminster, Md: Heritage Books, 2006.

Cassells, Vic. *The Destroyers: Their Battles and Their Badges.* East Roseville, NSW: Simon & Schuster, 2000.

Grey, Jeffrey. *Up Top: The Royal Australian Navy and Southeast Asian Conflicts, 1955–1972 (The Official History of Australia's Involvement in Southeast Asian Conflicts 1948–1975).* St. Leonards, NSW: Allen & Unwin, 1998.

Halldorson, Michael R. *Navy Daze: Coming of Age in the 1960s Aboard a Navy Destroyer.* Berwyn Heights, Md: Heritage Books, 2016.

Holloway III, James L. *Aircraft Carriers at War: A Personal Retrospective of Korea, Vietnam, and the Soviet Confrontation.* Annapolis, Md: Naval Institute, 2007.

Marolda, Edward J. *By Sea, Air, and Land: An Illustrated History of the U.S. Navy and the War in Southeast Asia.* Washington, DC: Naval Historical Center, 1994.

Parsons, Iain. *The Encyclopedia of Sea Warfare.* New York: Thomas Y. Crowell, 1975.

Petri, Thomas. *Lightning from the Sky, Thunder from the Sea.* Bloomington, Indiana: AuthorHouse, 2009.

Sherwood, John Darrell. *Nixon's Trident: Naval Power in Southeast Asia, 1968–1972.* Washington, DC: Naval History and Heritage Command, 2009.

—*War in the Shallows: U.S. Navy Coastal and Riverine Warfare in Vietnam, 1965-1968.* Washington, DC: Naval History and Heritage Command, 2015.

Shulimson, Jack, Leonard A. Blasiol, Charles R. Smith, David A. Dawson. *U.S. Marines in Vietnam: The Defining Year 1968.* Washington, DC: U.S. Marine Corps History and Museum Division, Headquarters, U.S. Marine Corps, 1997.

Simonsen, Robert A. *Marines Dodging Death.* London: McFarland & Company Inc, 1985.

Stillwell, Paul. *Battleship New Jersey: An Illustrated History.* Annapolis, Md: Naval Institute, 1986.

Sweetman, Jack. *American Naval History: An Illustrated Chronology of the U.S. Navy and Marine Corps, 1775-present.* Annapolis, Md: Naval Institute Press, 2002.

Telfer, Gary L., Lane Rogers, Keith V. Fleming, *U.S. Marines in Vietnam: Fighting The North Vietnamese 1967.* Washington, DC: History and Museums Division, Headquarters Marine Corps, 1984.

Toperczer, István. *MiG-17 And MiG-19 Units of the Vietnam War.* Oxford, UK: Osprey, 2001.

PREFACE NOTES:

[1] ComNavForV Monthly Summary, July 1966.

[2] "Naval Operations in Vietnam" by Jozef Straczek (http://www.navy.gov.au/history/feature-histories/naval-operations-vietnam: accessed 1 October 2018).

[3] Ibid.

[4] Ibid.

[5] Amphibious Operations Naval Gunfire Support (NAVMC-4029) 1945, 5-6 (https://www.ibiblio.org/hyperwar/USMC/ref/phib11/index.html#s1: accessed 1 October 2018).

[6] Ibid, 7.

[7] Ibid, 8.

[8] Ibid, 20.

[9] Ibid, 20-21.

[10] Ibid, 8-9.

[11] "USS *McMorris* History" (http://www.ussmcmorris.org/history.html: accessed 1 October 2018).

[12] Master List of Unit Awards and Campaign Medals, OPNAVNOTE 1650 of 9 March 2001 (http://www.usshorne.net/horne/images/ribbons/opnavnote1650.pdf: accessed 3 November 2018).

[13] "First-Hand: The Naval Tactical Data System in Combat - Chapter 7 of the Story of the Naval Tactical Data System" by David L. Boslaugh (https://ethw.org/First-Hand:The_Naval_Tactical_Data_System_in_Combat_-_Chapter_7_of_the_Story_of_the_Naval_Tactical_Data_System: accessed 28 October 2018).

[14] Ibid.

[15] Ibid.

[16] Iain Parsons, *The Encyclopedia of Sea Warfare* (New York: Thomas Y. Crowell, 1975), 219.

[17] Ibid, 220.

[18] Ibid, 217-218.

[19] "A Tin Can Sailor's Destroyer History USS *George L. MacKenzie* (DD-836)" (http://www.destroyers.org/histories/h-dd-836.htm: accessed 28 October 2018).
[20] Ibid.

CHAPTER 1 NOTES:

[1] James L. Holloway III, *Aircraft Carriers at War: A Personal Retrospective of Korea, Vietnam, and the Soviet Confrontation* (Annapolis, Md: Naval Institute, 2007), 324.
[2] Ibid, 308.
[3] Ibid.
[4] Ibid, 309.
[5] Ibid.
[6] Ibid, 310.
[7] Ibid.
[8] Ibid, 312-313.
[9] Ibid, 309-310, 313.
[10] Ibid, 315.
[11] Ibid.
[12] Ibid, 316.
[13] Ibid, 317.
[14] Ibid.
[15] Ibid, 317-318.
[16] Ibid, 319.
[17] Ibid.
[18] Ibid, 320.
[19] Ibid.
[20] Ibid, 321-322.
[21] Ibid, 322.
[22] Ibid, 323.
[23] Ibid.
[24] Ibid, 310, 323.

CHAPTER 2 NOTES

[1] "Cold War Pickets" (https://www.questia.com/magazine/1P3-140106051/sea-mail: accessed 13 September 2018).
[2] *Vance, DANFS.*
[3] "Modifications of Destroyer Escorts" (ps://www.ussslater.org/history/dehistory/history_modifications.htm: accessed 6 September 2018).
[4] Ibid.

[5] "Modifications of Destroyer Escorts;" "Market Time"
(https://www.history.navy.mil/content/history/nhhc/research/library/onlin
e-reading-room/title-list-alphabetically/m/market-time-u-crc280.html;
"Pacific Barrier, September 1958"
(https://www.willyvictor.com/index.php/squadrons/the-pacificbarrier:
accessed 13 September 2018).

[6] "Radar Picket Ships Stand Watch Far at Sea: Eight Navy vessels operate
out of Seattle on defense, weather-observation duty" by Clark Squire, *Seattle
Times*, July 21, 1957 (http://www.usssavage.org/072157_page_2_and_3.pdf:
accessed 12 September 2018).

[7] "Guarding the Cold War Ramparts: The U.S. Navy's Role in Continental
Air Defense" by Joseph F. Bouchard, *U.S. Navy Naval War College Review
Summer 1999*.

[8] "February 1, 1955: Task Force 43 Commissioned to Plan and Execute
Operation Deepfreeze"
(https://www.navalhistory.org/2013/02/01/february-1-1955-task-force-43-
commissioned-to-plan-and-execute-operation-deepfreeze: accessed 13
September 2018).

[9] Operation Deep Freeze 1961 cruise book
(https://www.history.navy.mil/content/dam/museums/Seabee/Cruisebooks
/postwwiicruisebooks/antarctica-
cruisebooks/DEEPFREEZE%2061%20TASK%20FORCE%2043%20%20
1961.pdf: accessed 13 September 2018).

[10] "Operation Deep Freeze 1961 cruise book;" "McMurdo Station"
(https://www.nsf.gov/geo/opp/support/mcmurdo.jsp: accessed 13
September 2018).

[11] "Operation Deep Freeze 1961 cruise book."

[12] Ibid.

[13] Ibid.

[14] *Vance, DANFS*.

[15] USS *Lansing* (DER-388) 1964-1965 cruise book.

[16] Ibid.

[17] Ibid.

[18] *Vance, DANFS*.

CHAPTER 3 NOTES:

[1] *Vance, DANFS*.

[2] "Market Time"
(https://www.history.navy.mil/content/history/nhhc/research/library/onlin
e-reading-room/title-list-alphabetically/m/market-time-u-crc280.html:
accessed 7 September 2018).

[3] "Modifications of Destroyer Escorts"
(ps://www.ussslater.org/history/dehistory/history_modifications.htm:
accessed 6 September 2018).

[4] *Vance, DANFS*; "Modifications of Destroyer Escorts."

[5] *Vance, DANFS*.

[6] David D. Bruhn, *Wooden Ships and Iron Men: The U.S. Navy's Ocean Minesweepers, 1953-1994* (Westminster, Md: Heritage Books, 2006), 144.

[7] "Market Time."

[8] Ibid.

[9] Bruhn, *Wooden Ships and Iron Men: The U.S. Navy's Ocean Minesweepers, 1953-1994*, 144.

[10] ComNavForV Monthly Summary, April 1966.

[11] Ibid.

[12] Ibid.

[13] ComNavForV Monthly Summary, April, December 1966.

[14] ComNavForV Monthly Summary, May 1966.

[15] Ibid.

[16] Ibid.

[17] "Coast Guard Squadron One" (https://infogalactic.com/info/Coast_Guard_Squadron_One#Point_Welcome_incident: accessed 16 September 2018); ComNavForV Monthly Summary, May and June 1966.

[18] "Coast Guard Squadron One;" ComNavForV Monthly Summary, June 1966.

[19] Ut supra.

[20] ComNavForV Monthly Summary, May 1966.

[21] Ibid.

[22] ComNavForV Monthly Summary, May 1966; "Market Time" by Judith C. Erdheim (https://www.history.navy.mil/content/history/nhhc/research/library/online-reading-room/title-list-alphabetically/m/market-time-u-crc280.html: accessed 16 September 2018).

[23] ComNavForV Monthly Summary, May 1966.

[24] "Coast Guard Squadron One."

[25] Ibid.

[26] "Coast Guard Squadron One;" ComNavForV Monthly Summary, June 1966.

[27] ComNavForV Monthly Summary, June 1966.

[28] "Coast Guard Squadron One;" ComNavForV Monthly Summary, June 1966.

[29] ComNavForV Monthly Summary, June 1966.

[30] Ibid.

[31] Ibid.

CHAPTER 4 NOTES:

[1] "Operation Seamount" by Newt Robinson (http://www.ussdehaven.org/seamount.htm: accessed 20 September 2018).

[2] ComNavForV Monthly Summary, July 1966.

[3] "Operation Seamount" by Newt Robinson; ComNavForV Monthly Summary, August 1966.

[4] Ut supra.

[5] "FRAM Fleet Rehabilitation and Modernization"
(http://www.navsource.org/archives/05/helpers/fram.htm: accessed 20
September 2018).
[6] Ibid.
[7] Ibid.
[8] "History" (http://www.ussdehaven.org/: accessed 21 September 2018).
[9] "Operation Seamount" by Newt Robinson; USS *DeHaven* DD 727 Far East
Tour 1966-1968 cruise book.
[10] ComNavForV Monthly Summary, August 1966.
[11] *Tutuila, DANFS*.
[12] Tom Shropshire, "The Day Calendar: A Baby Boomer's Memoir"
(http://thedaycalendar.com/viet-nam-an-thoi-part-one/: accessed 20
September 2018).
[13] *Tutuila, DANFS*; Shropshire, "The Day Calendar: A Baby Boomer's
Memoir."
[14] ComNavForV Monthly Summary, August 1966; "Don Moore's Run for
the Wall 2011 - In the morning we ride in memory of Specialist Jules T.
Girtanner" (https://bkwaii.org/index.php/13-special-news/14-don-moores-
run-for-the-wall-2011?showall=&start=3: accessed 20 September 2018).

CHAPTER 5 NOTES:

[1] USS *Saint Paul* CA-73 25th Anniversary Book.
[2] *St. Paul, DANFS*.
[3] "US Cruisers List: US Light/Heavy/AntiAircraft Cruisers, Part 2"
(https://www.hazegray.org/navhist/cruisers/ca-cl2.htm); "Baltimore Class
Heavy Cruisers"
(http://www.historyofwar.org/articles/weapons_baltimore_class_heavy_crui
sers.html: accessed 23 September 2018).
[4] "Baltimore Class Heavy Cruisers."
[5] "USS *Columbus* (CA-74)"
(http://www.historyofwar.org/articles/weapons_USS_Columbus_CA74.htm
l: accessed 22 September 2018).
[6] "USS *Northampton* (CA-125)"
(http://www.historyofwar.org/articles/weapons_USS_Northampton_CA125
.html: accessed 22 September 2018).
[7] "Screaming Eagle History"
(https://www.327infantry.org/homescreamingeagles/inside-the-
wire/screaming-eagle-history/: accessed 23 September 2018).
[8] "Highlights June 1966"
(https://www.history.navy.mil/content/history/nhhc/research/archives/digi
tized-collections/vietnam-war/highlights-june-1966.html#deckhouse_map:
accessed 24 September 2018); USS *Saint Paul* CA-73 25th Anniversary Book.
[9] "Highlights June 1966."
[10] Ibid.
[11] Ibid.
[12] Ibid.

CHAPTER 6 NOTES:

[1] "Forrest Sherman Class"
(http://destroyerhistory.org/coldwar/forrestshermanclass/); "Welcome to
USS *Edson* DD946" (http://www.ussedsondd946.org/: accessed 24
September 2018).
[2] "Forrest Sherman Class."

CHAPTER 7 NOTES:

[1] "The Vance Mutiny: Fact Mirrors Fiction" by William Scheck
(http://ussvance.com/Vance/smithg/smithtxt.htm: accessed 15 November
2018)
[2] John Darrell Sherwood, *War in the Shallows: U.S. Navy Coastal and Riverine
Warfare in Vietnam, 1965-1968* (Washington, DC: Naval History and Heritage
Command, 2015), 82
(https://www.history.navy.mil/content/dam/nhhc/research/publications/p
ublication-508-pdf/WITS_508.pdf: accessed 15 November 2018).
[3] Ibid, 82.
[4] Ibid, 82-83.
[5] Ibid.
[6] Ibid, 83.
[7] Ibid, 80-81, 83.
[8] Sherwood, *War in the Shallows*, 83; "The 99 Days of Captain Arnheiter" by
Neil Sheehan, *The New York Times*, August 11, 1968
(http://www.ussvance.com/Vance/AAbook/ny_times_1968.HTM: accessed
15 November 2018).
[9] Ut supra.
[10] Ut supra.
[11] "The 99 Days of Captain Arnheiter."
[12] Ut supra.
[13] "Operation Masher/White Wing/Thang Phong II launched"
(https://www.history.com/this-day-in-history/operation-masherwhite-
wingthang-phong-ii-launched); "USS *Skagit* and Operation Double Eagle
Quang Ngai Province, Vietnam January 28, 1966"
(http://www.ussskagit.org/DE.html: both accessed 19 November 2018).
[14] USS *Barry* (DD-933) 1965-1966 Around the World cruise book.
[15] Ibid.
[16] Sherwood, *War in the Shallows*, 83-84; "The 99 Days of Captain
Arnheiter."
[17] Ut supra.
[18] Ut supra.
[19] "The 99 Days of Captain Arnheiter."
[20] Sherwood, *War in the Shallows*, 84; "The 99 Days of Captain Arnheiter."
[21] "The 99 Days of Captain Arnheiter" by Neil Sheehan.
[22] Sherwood, *War in the Shallows*, 84; "The 99 Days of Captain Arnheiter."
[23] Sherwood, *War in the Shallows*, 83; "The 99 Days of Captain Arnheiter."
[24] Sherwood, *War in the Shallows*, 19; "The 99 Days of Captain Arnheiter."

[25] Sherwood, *War in the Shallows*, 84-85; "The 99 Days of Captain Arnheiter."

[26] Sherwood, *War in the Shallows*, 85; "The 99 Days of Captain Arnheiter."

[27] Ut supra.

CHAPTER 8 NOTES:

[1] "Cruisers and Destroyers in Vietnam," compiled and edited by the Public Affairs Office Cruiser-Destroyer Group, United States Seventh Fleet (http://kman.my.meganet.net/seadrg2.htm: accessed 2 October 2018).

[2] Ibid.

[3] "H-009-3: Significant U.S. Navy Operations and Events in Vietnam Through 1967" (https://www.history.navy.mil/content/history/nhhc/about-us/leadership/director/directors-corner/h-grams/h-gram-009/h009-3.html: accessed 2 October 2018).

[4] "Destroyers" (http://www.navsource.org/archives/05idx.htm: accessed 4 October 2018).

[5] Ibid.

[6] "The Sea Dragon Strikes Again" by Lawrence M. Greenberg, contributing editor of *Vietnam Magazine* (http://dd-692.com/sea1.htm: accessed 4 October 2018).

[7] Ibid.

[8] "Operation Sea Dragon" (http://www.ussmansfield.com/nfseadrg/: accessed 4 October 2018).

[9] "Tom's Sea Tales," Tom Harper (http://www.ussmansfield.com/sea-tales/#Tom: accessed 4 October 2018).

[10] Ibid.

[11] Lawrence M. Greenberg, "The Sea Dragon Strikes Again" (http://www.ussmansfield.com/nfseadrg/: accessed 4 October 2018).

[12] Ibid.

[13] Copy of newspaper article titled "O'Brien Shelled Ships for 2 Days Before Taking Hit" from USS *O'Brien* WestPac 1967 cruise book.

[14] Copies of newspaper articles titled "O'Brien Shelled Ships for 2 Days Before Taking Hit" and "1st Warship Damaged by Shore Guns" from USS *O'Brien* Western Pacific 1967 cruise book.

[15] USS *O'Brien* Western Pacific 1967 cruise book.

[16] Ibid.

[17] "History of the USS *Benner* (DD 807)" (http://www.destroyers.org/uss-benner/history_of_the_uss_benner6.htm: accessed 10 October 2018).

[18] Ibid.

[19] USS *O'Brien* (DD 725) Western Pacific 1965-66 cruise book.

[20] "H-009-3: Significant U.S. Navy Operations and Events in Vietnam Through 1967;" Greenberg, "The Sea Dragon Strikes Again."

[21] Ut supra.

[22] Greenberg, "The Sea Dragon Strikes Again."

[23] Ibid.

CHAPTER 9 NOTES:

[1] "*Perth*-class Guided Missile Destroyer (DDG)"
(http://www.seaforces.org/marint/Australian-Navy/Destroyer/Perth-class.htm: accessed 11 October 2018).
[2] Ibid.
[3] Ibid.
[4] Jeffrey Grey, *Up Top: The Royal Australian Navy and Southeast Asian Conflicts, 1955–1972 (The Official History of Australia's Involvement in Southeast Asian Conflicts 1948–1975)* (St. Leonards, NSW: Allen & Unwin, 1998), 142-146.
[5] Ibid, 125, 130-138, 141, 155.
[6] Ibid, 129, 141.
[7] Ibid, 132.
[8] Ibid, 135, 140-141.
[9] "Operation Rolling Thunder" (https://www.history.com/topics/vietnam-war/operation-rolling-thunder: accessed 11 October 2018).
[10] Grey, *Up Top*, 82-83, 94-95, 144.
[11] Grey, *Up Top*, 82-83, 94-95, 147-149; Edward J. Marolda, *By Sea, Air, and Land: An Illustrated History of the U.S. Navy and the War in Southeast Asia* (Washington, DC: Naval Historical Center, 1994), Chapter 3 (https://www.history.navy.mil/content/history/nhhc/research/library/online-reading-room/title-list-alphabetically/b/by-sea-air-land-marolda/chapter-3-the-years-of-combat-1965-1968.html: accessed 12 October 2018).
[12] USS *Allen M. Sumner* Western Pacific 1967 cruise book.
[13] Ibid.
[14] "Operation Beau Charger - Battle of the Ben Hai River Task Group 76.4 - 18 to 19 May 1967" (http://www.dd-692.com/beau.htm: accessed 12 October 2018).
[15] "H-009-3: Significant U.S. Navy Operations and Events in Vietnam Through 1967" (https://www.history.navy.mil/content/history/nhhc/about-us/leadership/director/directors-corner/h-grams/h-gram-009/h009-3.html: accessed 12 October 2018); *Seminole, DANFS*; "Operation Beau Charger - Battle of the Ben Hai River Task Group 76.4."
[16] Telfer, Rogers and Fleming, *U.S. Marines in Vietnam: Fighting The North Vietnamese 1967*.
[17] "Operation Beau Charger - Battle of the Ben Hai River Task Group 76.4."
[18] Ibid.
[19] "H-009-3: Significant U.S. Navy Operations and Events in Vietnam Through 1967."
[20] Telfer, Rogers and Fleming, *U.S. Marines in Vietnam: Fighting The North Vietnamese 1967*.
[21] "Operation Beau Charger - Battle of the Ben Hai River Task Group 76.4."
[22] Ibid.
[23] Ibid.
[24] USS *Edson* (DD-946) Western Pacific 1967 cruise book.

[25] "HMAS *Hobart*" (http://www.navy.gov.au/hmas-hobart-ii: accessed 11 October 2018).

[26] Grey, *Up Top*, 151.

[27] Ibid, 151-152.

[28] Ibid, 153.

[29] Grey, *Up Top*, 154; Vic Cassells, *The Destroyers: Their Battles and Their Badges* (East Roseville, NSW: Simon & Schuster, 2000), 39.

[30] Account provided authors by Commodore Hector Donohue, AM RAN (Retired).

[31] Donohue

[32] Donohue; "H-019-1: The Mystery of *PCF-19*" (https://www.history.navy.mil/content/history/nhhc/about-us/leadership/director/directors-corner/h-grams/h-gram-019/h-019-1.html: accessed 13 December 2018).

[33] Ut supra.

[34] Ut supra.

[35] Ut supra.

[36] Donohue.

[37] "H-019-1: The Mystery of *PCF-19*."

[38] "The Sinking of *PCF-19* as seen from *PCF-12*" (http://swiftboats.net/stories/pcf19.htm: accessed 13 December 2018).

[39] "H-019-1: The Mystery of *PCF-19*."

[40] "H-019-1: The Mystery of *PCF-19*;" "The Sinking of *PCF-19* as seen from *PCF-12*" (http://swiftboats.net/stories/pcf19.htm: accessed 13 December 2018).

[41] "H-019-1: The Mystery of *PCF-19*."

[42] Ibid.

[43] "H-019-1: The Mystery of *PCF-19*;" "The Sinking of *PCF-19* as seen from *PCF-12*."

[44] Donohue.

[45] "HMAS *Perth*" (http://www.navy.gov.au/hmas-perth-ii: accessed 11 October 2018).

[46] "HMAS *Perth*;" "HMAS *Hobart*" (http://www.navy.gov.au/hmas-hobart-ii); HMAS Perth" (http://www.navy.gov.au/hmas-perth-ii: accessed 11 October 2018).

[47] "HMAS *Brisbane*" (http://www.navy.gov.au/hmas-brisbane-ii); "HMAS *Vendetta*" (http://www.navy.gov.au/hmas-vendetta-ii: accessed 11 October 2018).

CHAPER 10 NOTES:

[1] USS *Edson* (DD-946) Western Pacific 1967 cruise book.

[2] Ibid.

[3] "Compilation of Enlisted Ratings and Apprenticeships, U.S. Navy, 1775 to 1969" (https://www.history.navy.mil/research/library/online-reading-room/title-list-alphabetically/c/enlisted-ratings-in-u-s-navy-1775-1969.html#anchorf: accessed 13 October 2018).

[4] USS *Edson* (DD-946) Western Pacific 1967 cruise book.

[5] Jack Sweetman, *American Naval History: An Illustrated Chronology of the U.S. Navy and Marine Corps, 1775-present* (Annapolis, Md: Naval Institute Press, 2002), 15-16.

[6] "Built to Fight" (https://www.navy.mil/ah_online/constitution/: accessed 14 October 2018).

[7] "Cruisers and Destroyers in Vietnam," compiled and edited by the Public Affairs Office Cruiser-Destroyer Group, United States Seventh Fleet.

[8] Ibid.

[9] Ibid.

[10] Ibid.

[11] Michael R. Halldorson, *Navy Daze: Coming of Age in the 1960s Aboard a Navy Destroyer* (Berwyn Heights, Md: Heritage Books, 2016), 55-56.

[12] Ibid, 56.

CHAPTER 11 NOTES:

[1] USS *Du Pont* (DD-941) 1967-1968 cruise book.

[2] Ibid.

[3] Marolda, *By Sea, Air, and Land By Sea*, Chapter 3.

[4] Ibid.

[5] USS *Du Pont* (DD-941) 1967-1968 cruise book; Marolda, *By Sea, Air, and Land*, Chapter 3.

[6] USS *Du Pont* (DD-941) 1967-1968 cruise book; *Du Pont, DANFS*.

[7] Ut supra.

[8] USS *Du Pont* (DD-941) 1967-1968 cruise book.

[9] "XO's Sea Tales," account by Robert Kesteloot, former executive officer, USS *Mansfield* (http://www.ussmansfield.com/sea-tales/#XO: accessed 18 October 2018).

[10] Kesteloot, "XO's Sea Tales."

[11] Ibid.

[12] Ibid.

[13] "USS *Mansfield* DD-728" (http://www.ussmansfield.com/history-overview/: accessed 18 October 2018).

[14] Marolda, *By Sea, Air, and Land*, Chapter 3.

CHAPTER 12 NOTES:

[1] "USS *Carronade* Fire Support" by Ken Willcox (https://www.mnvietnam.org/story/uss-carronade-fire-support/: accessed 19 October 2018).

[2] USS *Carronade* 1959-1960 cruise book; "USS *Carronade* (LFR-1)" (http://www.navsource.org/archives/10/06/06001.htm: accessed 18 October 2018).

[3] Ut supra.

[4] USS *Carronade* 1959-1960 cruise book.

[5] "USS *Carronade* (LFR-1)."

[6] "USS *Carronade* Fire Support;" "USS *Carronade* (IFS-1)"
(https://www.history.navy.mil/content/history/museums/nmusn/explore/p
hotography/ships-us/ships-usn-c/uss-carronade-ifs-1.html: accessed 19
October 2018).
[7] "USS *Carronade* Fire Support."
[8] Ibid.
[9] Ibid.
[10] "USS *Carronade* (LFR-1)."
[11] "Inshore Fire Suppot Ship (LFR) ex (IFS)"
(http://www.navsource.org/archives/10/06/06idx.htm: accessed 19 October
2018).
[12] Ibid.

CHAPTER 13 NOTES:

[1] "The bloody battle of Khe Sanh: 77 days under siege," *Stars and Stripes*
(https://www.stripes.com/news/special-reports/vietnam-at-50-legacy/the-
bloody-battle-of-khe-sanh-77-days-under-siege-1.314627: accessed 25
November 2018.
[2] "H-017-1: U.S. Navy Operations in Vietnam, January–March 1968"
(https://www.history.navy.mil/content/history/nhhc/about-
us/leadership/director/directors-corner/h-grams/h-gram-017/h-017-1.html:
accessed 25 November 2018).
[3] "The bloody battle of Khe Sanh: 77 days under siege."
[4] "H-017-1: U.S. Navy Operations in Vietnam, January–March 1968."
[5] Ibid.
[6] "VO-67 History" (http://www.vo-67.org/vo67_history.html: accessed 25
November 2018).
[7] "H-017-1: U.S. Navy Operations in Vietnam, January–March 1968."
[8] "VO-67 History."
[9] "H-017-1: U.S. Navy Operations in Vietnam, January–March 1968."
[10] Ibid.
[11] "H-017-1: U.S. Navy Operations in Vietnam, January–March 1968;"
"Khe Sanh and Operation Pegasus: Scenes From Vietnam, 1968" by Ben
Cosgrove (http://time.com/3880754/khe-sanh-and-operation-pegasus-
scenes-from-vietnam-1968/: accessed 26 November 2018).
[12] "H-017-1: U.S. Navy Operations in Vietnam, January–March 1968."

CHAPTER 14 NOTES:

[1] "Remembering North Korea's Audacious Capture Of The USS *Pueblo*"
(https://www.npr.org/2018/01/23/580076540/looking-at-the-saga-of-the-
uss-pueblo-50-years-later: accessed 26 November 2018).
[2] "H-014-1: The Seizure of USS *Pueblo* (AGER-2)" by Samuel J. Cox
(https://www.history.navy.mil/content/history/nhhc/about-
us/leadership/director/directors-corner/h-grams/h-gram-014/h-014-1.html:
accessed 28 November 2018).
[3] Ibid.

[4] Ibid.

[5] Ibid.

[6] Ibid.

[7] Ibid.

[8] "H-014-1: The Seizure of USS *Pueblo* (AGER-2)" by Samuel J. Cox; Bob Chicca email of 29 December 2018.

[9] "H-014-1: The Seizure of USS Pueblo (AGER-2)" by Samuel J. Cox.

[10] "H-014-1: The Seizure of USS Pueblo (AGER-2)" by Samuel J. Cox; Bob Chicca email of 29 December 2018.

[11] "Some Experiences Reported by the Crew of the USS *Pueblo* and American Prisoners of War from Vietnam" (https://www.history.navy.mil/research/library/online-reading-room/title-list-alphabetically/s/some-experiences-reported-crew-uss-pueblo-american-prisoners-war-vietnam.html); "USS *Pueblo* sailors tortured in North Korea see new hope for compensation" (https://www.washingtonpost.com/world/national-security/uss-pueblo-sailors-tortured-in-north-korea-see-new-hope-for-compensation/2016/01/04/a5dbee7e-b2ef-11e5-a842-0feb51d1d124_story.html?utm_term=.3361ce39426f: both accessed 28 November 2018); Bob Chicca email of 29 December 2018.

[12] "Some Experiences Reported by the Crew of the USS *Pueblo* and American Prisoners of War from Vietnam;" Bob Chicca email of 29 December 2018.

[13] Ut supra.

[14] Bob Chicca email of 29 December 2018.

[15] USS *Enterprise* (CVAN-65) 1968 cruise book.

[16] USS *Enterprise* (CVAN-65) 1968 cruise book; "Communist Treatment of Prisoners of War, A Historical Survey" (https://www.loc.gov/rr/frd/Military_Law/pdf/comm_treat_POW.pdf: accessed 29 November 2018).

[17] "Communist Treatment of Prisoners of War, A Historical Survey."

[18] "H-014-1: The Seizure of USS *Pueblo* (AGER-2)" by Samuel J. Cox.

[19] Ibid.

[20] Ibid.

[21] Ibid.

[22] "Medals and awards" (http://www.usspueblo.org/Aftermath/Citations.html: accessed 29 November 2018).

CHAPTER 15 NOTES:

[1] "U.S. Navy Operations in Vietnam, January–March 1968" (https://www.history.navy.mil/content/history/nhhc/about-us/leadership/director/directors-corner/h-grams/h-gram-017/h-017-1.html: accessed 19 October 2018).

[2] "Vietnam War Campaigns"
(https://history.army.mil/html/reference/army_flag/vn.html: accessed 19
October 2018).
[3] Marolda, *By Sea, Air, and Land*, Chapter 3; Jack Shulimson, Leonard A.
Blasiol, Charles R. Smith, David A. Dawson, *U.S. Marines in Vietnam: The
Defining Year 1968* (Washington, DC: U.S. Marine Corps History and Museum
Division, Headquarters, U.S. Marine Corps, 1997), 640
(https://ehistory.osu.edu/books/1968/0641: accessed 30 November 2018).
[4] Shulimson, Blasiol, Smith, Dawson, *U.S. Marines in Vietnam: The Defining
Year 1968*.
[5] "HMAS *Perth* 1st Deployment 2 September 1967-10 April 1968"
(http://www.gunplot.net/main/content/hmas-perth-1st-deployment-2-
september-1967-10-april-1968: accessed 1 December 2018).
[6] Master List of Unit Awards and Campaign Medals, OPNAVNOTE 1650,
9 March 2001. It appears there is an error in this document regarding *Du Pont*,
as her 1968 Vietnam cruise book indicates that she was at Norfolk, Virginia,
on 9 August, and Rodman, Canal Zone on 28 August, the dates cited for
qualification for combat action ribbons.
[7] "Hue City, 1968: Winning A Battle While Losing A War" by Norman L.
Cooling (https://www.mca-marines.org/gazette/hue-city-1968-winning-
battle-while-losing-war: accessed 1 December 2018).
[8] Marolda, *By Sea, Air, and Land*, Chapter 3.
[9] "Hue City, 1968: Winning A Battle While Losing A War."
[10] "Vietnam War Campaigns;" "Hue City, 1968: Winning A Battle While
Losing A War."
[11] USS *Canberra* (CAG-2) 1967-1968 Western Pacific cruise book.
[12] Ibid.
[13] Ibid.
[14] "USS *Canberra* CA 70" (http://www.usscanberra.com/shiphistory.htm:
accessed 30 November 2018).
[15] USS *Cone* 1967-1968 Western Pacific cruise book.
[16] Ibid.
[17] Marolda, *By Sea, Air, and Land*, Chapter 3.
[18] Shulimson, Blasiol, Smith, Dawson, *U.S. Marines in Vietnam: The Defining
Year 1968*, 640.
[19] Robert A. Simonsen, *Marines Dodging Death* (London: McFarland &
Company Inc, 1985), 234.
[20] Shulimson, Blasiol, Smith, Dawson, *U.S. Marines in Vietnam: The Defining
Year 1968*, 359-360.
[21] Ibid, 19.
[22] Ibid, 640.
[23] Ibid.
[24] USS *St. Paul* (CA-73) 1968 cruise book.

[25] "Did the news media, led by Walter Cronkite, lose the war in Vietnam" (https://www.washingtonpost.com/national/did-the-news-media-led-by-walter-cronkite-lose-the-war-in-vietnam/2018/05/25/a5b3e098-495e-11e8-827e-190efaf1f1ee_story.html?utm_term=.da9a56dfd832: accessed 2 December 2018).

[26] "Tet Offensive" (https://www.history.com/topics/vietnam-war/tet-offensive: accessed 2 December 2018).

CHAPTER 16 NOTES:

[1] "H-009-3: Significant U.S. Navy Operations and Events in Vietnam Through 1967" (https://www.history.navy.mil/content/history/nhhc/about-us/leadership/director/directors-corner/h-grams/h-gram-009/h009-3.html: accessed 23 November 2018).

[2] "The Sea Dragon Strikes Again" by Lawrence M. Greenberg (http://www.dd-692.com/sea1.htm: accessed 23 November 2018).

[3] USS *Bordelon* (DD-881) 1967-1968 Western Pacific cruise book.

[4] "History Of Naval (Gun Line) Operations In Vietnam" (http://www.gunplot.net/main/content/gun-line-rans-vietnam-war-detail: accessed 23 November 2018).

[5] Ibid.

[6] Ibid.

[7] Ibid.

[8] "HMAS *Perth* 1st Deployment 2 September 1967-10 April 1968" (http://www.gunplot.net/main/content/hmas-perth-1st-deployment-2-september-1967-10-april-1968: accessed 24 November 2018).

[9] Ibid.

[10] Ibid.

[11] Ibid.

[12] Ibid.

[13] Ibid.

[14] Ibid.

]15] Ibid.

[16] "Operation Sea Dragon" (http://kman.my.meganet.net/nfseadrg.htm: accessed 24 November 2018).

[17] Ibid.

[18] Ibid.

[19] Jim West email correspondence, 2 December 2018.

[20] Ibid.

[21] Jim West email correspondence, 2 December 2018, including a clipping of a newspaper article titled "North Viet Guns Fire Upon US Destroyer After Attack, from an unknown source.

[22] Ibid.

[23] Vince Volk email correspondence of 3 December 2018.

[24] Gregory Roberts email correspondence of 10 December 2018.

[25] "Operation Sea Dragon."

[26] "The Sea Dragon Strikes Again" by Lawrence M. Greenberg.

[27] Ibid.
[28] Ibid.
[29] "Memorial Services Planned For Coronadan, Captain Cedric S. Wallace," *Coronado Eagle*, Volume 6, Number 11, 15 March 1995.

CHAPTER 17 NOTES:

[1] Paul Stillwell, *Battleship New Jersey: An Illustrated History* (Annapolis, Md: Naval Institute, 1986), 201.
[2] Ibid, 202.
[3] "The 99 Days of Captain Arnheiter" by Neil Sheehan, *The New York Times*, August 11, 1968
(http://www.ussvance.com/Vance/AAbook/ny_times_1968.HTM: accessed 15 November 2018).
[4] "Richard Griffiss Alexander 1 August 1922 -"
(https://www.history.navy.mil/content/history/nhhc/research/library/resea rch-guides/modern-biographical-files-ndl/modern-bios-a/alexander-richard-griffiss.html: accessed 21 November 2018).
[5] Stillwell, *Battleship New Jersey*, 202, 204.
[6] Ibid.
[7] Stillwell, *Battleship New Jersey*, 204-205; "The 99 Days of Captain Arnheiter."
[8] Stillwell, *Battleship New Jersey*, 205.
[9] Stillwell, *Battleship New Jersey*, 211; *New Jersey, DANFS*.
[10] Stillwell, *Battleship New Jersey*, 213-214.
[11] Ibid, 214-215.
[12] Ibid, 215-217.
[13] Ibid, 217.
[14] Ibid, 217-218.
[15] Ibid, 218-219.
[16] Ibid, 219-224.
[17] Ibid, 224.
[18] "1969 Chronology of Outstanding Events"
(http://www.ussnewjersey.org/1969_narrative.htm: accessed 22 November 2018).
[19] Ibid.
[20] Stillwell, *Battleship New Jersey*, 226; *Tripoli, DANFS*; "1969 Chronology of Outstanding Events."
[21] "1969 Chronology of Outstanding Events."
[22] Ibid.
[23] "Memories differ on friendly fire and on the night Michael Peterson's marine unit was attacked in Vietnam" by Craig Jarvis
(https://www.heraldsun.com/news/local/crime/article213580889.html: accessed 23 November 2018).
[24] "1969 Chronology of Outstanding Events;" Thomas Petri, *Lightning from the Sky, Thunder from the Sea* (Bloomington, Indiana: AuthorHouse, 2009), 215-219.

[25] "Tet 1969 at Cua Chi" (http://www.historynet.com/tet-1969-at-cu-chi.htm: accessed 23 November 2018); "1969 Chronology of Outstanding Events."

[26] Ut supra.

[27] "1969 Chronology of Outstanding Events."

[28] Ibid.

[29] "Battleship Skipper" by Paul Stillwell, *Naval History Magazine*, April 2008 (https://www.usni.org/magazines/navalhistory/2008-04/looking-back: accessed 23 November 2018).

[30] *New Jersey, DANFS.*

[31] Ibid.

CHAPTER 18 NOTES:

[1] Commander in Chief U.S. Pacific Fleet, Joint USN/RAN Investigation – collision of USS *Frank E. Evans* and HMAS *Melbourne* on 3 June 1969, 21 November 1969 (http://www.jag.navy.mil/library/investigations/HMAS%20EVANS%20AND%20MELBOURNE%203%20JUN%2069.pdf: accessed 3 December 2018).

[2] *Frank E. Evans, DANFS.*

[3] "USS *Frank E. Evans*: Disaster in the South China Sea" by Phil Smith, *Vietnam Magazine*, August 2001 (http://www.historynet.com/uss-frank-e-evans-disaster-in-the-south-china-sea.htm); Australian Government, Department of Veterans Affairs, the Consolidated Library of Information and Knowledge (CLIK) Part 4 Other Relevant Topics and Useful Links, Chapter 4 Collision between USS *Frank E Evans* and HMAS *Melbourne* (http://clik.dva.gov.au/history-library/part-4-other-relevant-tops-and-useful-links/ch-4-collision-between-uss-frank-e-evans-and-hmas-melbourne: both accessed 3 December 2018).

[4] "USS *Frank E. Evans*: Disaster in the South China Sea" by Phil Smith; Commodore Hector Donohue, RAN (Retired), correspondence of 3 March 2019.

[5] "USS *Frank E. Evans*: Disaster in the South China Sea" by Phil Smith.

[6] Rear Admiral [redacted] Jr., U.S. Navy, Board of investigation to inquire into the circumstances surrounding the collision of HMAS *Melbourne* and USS *Frank E. Evans* (DD-754) on 3 June 1969, 8 July 1969 (report).

[7] Ibid.

[8] Ibid.

[9] "USS *Frank E. Evans*: Disaster in the South China Sea" by Phil Smith.

[10] Hector Donahue email correspondence of 4 December 2018.

[11] Hector Donahue email correspondence of 5 December 2018.

[12] "USS *Frank E. Evans*: Disaster in the South China Sea" by Phil Smith.

[13] Hector Donahue email correspondence of 4 December 2018.

[14] "USS *Frank E. Evans*: Disaster in the South China Sea" by Phil Smith.

[15] Australian Government, Department of Veterans Affairs, the Consolidated Library of Information and Knowledge (CLIK) Part 4 Other

Relevant Topics and Useful Links, Chapter 4 Collision between USS *Frank E Evans* and HMAS *Melbourne*.

[16] Ibid.

[17] Ibid.

[18] Rear Admiral [redacted] Jr., U.S. Navy, Board of investigation to inquire into the circumstances surrounding the collision of HMAS *Melbourne* and USS *Frank E. Evans* (DD-754) on 3 June 1969, 8 July 1969 (report).

[19] "Melbourne-Evans Collision" ((http://military.wikia.com/wiki/Melbourne%E2%80%93Evans_collision: accessed 4 December 2018).

[20] "USS *Frank E. Evans* (DD-754)" (http://www.navsource.org/archives/05/754.htm: accessed 3 December 2018).

CHAPTER 19 NOTES:

[1] David D. Bruhn, *Wooden Ships and Iron Men: The U.S. Navy's Coastal and Inshore Minesweepers, and the Minecraft That Served in Vietnam, 1953-1976* (Westminster, Md: Heritage Books, 2011), 195.

[2] Marolda, *By Sea, Air, and Land*, Chapter 4: Winding Down the War, 1968-1973 (https://www.history.navy.mil/content/history/nhhc/research/library/online-reading-room/title-list-alphabetically/b/by-sea-air-land-marolda/chapter-4-winding-down-the-war-1968-1973.html: accessed 7 December 2018).

[3] Ibid.

[4] Ibid.

[5] Ibid.

[6] Ibid.

[7] USS *Camp* (DER-251) 1967-1968 Western Pacific cruise book.

[8] Ibid.

[9] USS *Camp* (DER-251) 1967-1968 Western Pacific cruise book; "Organizations and Progressive Activities of the Republic of Vietnam Navy" by Thong Ba Le (http://www.rivervet.com/vn_navy.htm: accessed 7 December 2018).

[10] USS *Camp* (DER-251) 1967-1968 Western Pacific cruise book.

[11] *Camp, DANFS*.

[12] "USS *Camp* (DE-251)" (https://www.navsource.org/archives/06/251.htm: accessed 7 December 2018).

[13] "HMAS *Vendetta* 15 September 1969 - 11 April 1970" (http://www.gunplot.net/main/content/hmas-vendetta-15-september-1969-11-april-1970: accessed 5 December 2018).

[14] Ibid.

[15] "'On The Gun Line' - The R.A.N's Vietnam War In Detail" (http://www.gunplot.net/main/content/gun-line-rans-vietnam-war-detail: accessed 5 December 2018).

[16] Ibid.

[17] "HMAS *Vendetta* 15 September 1969 - 11 April 1970."
[18] Ibid.
[19] Ibid.
[20] Ibid.
[21] "HMAS *Vendetta* 15 September 1969 - 11 April 1970;" "Capital Division" (http://www.vietnamwar.net/CapitalDivision.htm: accessed 6 December 2018).
[22] "HMAS *Vendetta* 15 September 1969 - 11 April 1970;" "ROKA 9th 'White Horse' Division" (http://www.talkingproud.us/Military/ROKVIetnam/ROKVIetnam/ROK VIetnamWhiteHorse.html: accessed 6 December 2018).
[23] "HMAS *Vendetta* 15 September 1969 - 11 April 1970."
[24] Ibid.
[25] Ibid.
[26] Ibid.
[27] Ibid.
[28] Ibid.
[29] Ibid.
[30] Ibid.
[31] USS *Bradley* (DE-1041) 1970 Western Pacific cruise book.
[32] "'On The Gun Line' - The R.A.N's Vietnam War In Detail."

CHAPTER 20 NOTES:

[1] "Gen. Vo Nguyen Giap, Who Ousted U.S. From Vietnam, Is Dead" by Joseph R. Gregory, *New York Times*, 4 October 2013.
[2] Bruhn, *Wooden Ships and Iron Men: The U.S. Navy's Coastal and Inshore Minesweepers, and the Minecraft That Served in Vietnam, 1953-1976*, 197; John Darrell Sherwood, *Nixon's Trident: Naval Power in Southeast Asia, 1968–1972* (Washington, DC: Naval History and Heritage Command, 2009), 35.
[3] Sherwood, *Nixon's Trident*, 35.
[4] "Cold War Warriors, An Amazing Day, The final major naval battle of the Vietnam War" by Michael Cuseo (http://www.emmitsburg.net/archive_list/articles/misc/cww/2012/amazing _day.htm: accessed 20 October 2018).
[5] Ibid.
[6] "Cold War Warriors, An Amazing Day, The final major naval battle of the Vietnam War" by Michael Cuseo; Stillwell, *Battleship New Jersey*, 204.
[7] "1972 West Pac Vietnam Easter Offensive" (http://www.uss-buchanan-ddg14.org/buchanan72.html: accessed 20 October 2018).
[8] Sherwood, *Nixon's Trident*, 36.
[9] "Ripley at the Bridge: Dong Ha, South Vietnam" by Charles D. Melson (http://kbc3337design.tripod.com/ripley.htm); "Linebacker I" (http://www.geocities.ws/seavet72/LB1/to-charl.htm: accessed 25 October 2018); Petri, *Lightning from the Sky, Thunder from the Sea*, 280.
[10] "Ripley at the Bridge: Dong Ha, South Vietnam."
[11] Ibid.

[12] "Ripley at the Bridge: Dong Ha, South Vietnam;" George Duddy email of 9 November 2018.

[13] Ut supra.

[14] Ut supra.

[15] "Ripley at the Bridge: Dong Ha, South Vietnam."

[16] Ibid.

[17] Sherwood, *Nixon's Trident*, 36.

[18] Ibid, 36-37.

[19] "Cold War Warriors, An Amazing Day, The final major naval battle of the Vietnam War" by Michael Cuseo.

[20] "Cold War Warriors, An Amazing Day, The final major naval battle of the Vietnam War" by Michael Cuseo.

[21] Ibid.

[22] Ibid.

[23] Ibid.

[24] Ibid.

[25] Ibid.

[26] Sherwood, *Nixon's Trident*, 37.

[27] "1972 Vietnam First Line period 63 days" (http://www.uss-buchanan-ddg14.org/Vietnam%20War/buchanan72/72%20first%20line%20period.htm : accessed 28 October 2018).

[28] Sherwood, *Nixon's Trident*, 37; "First-Hand: The Naval Tactical Data System in Combat - Chapter 7 of the Story of the Naval Tactical Data System" by David L. Boslaugh (https://ethw.org/First-Hand:The_Naval_Tactical_Data_System_in_Combat_-_Chapter_7_of_the_Story_of_the_Naval_Tactical_Data_System: accessed 28 October 2018).

[29] "More Vietnam War Navy! This time, USS *Higbee* (DD-806)" (http://cdrsalamander.blogspot.com/2007/04/fullbore-friday_13.html: accessed 28 October 2018); "First-Hand: The Naval Tactical Data System in Combat - Chapter 7 of the Story of the Naval Tactical Data System."

[30] Sherwood, *Nixon's Trident*, 37; István Toperczer, *MiG-17 And MiG-19 Units of the Vietnam War* (Oxford, UK: Osprey, 2001), 54-55, 85-86.

[31] "First-Hand: The Naval Tactical Data System in Combat - Chapter 7 of the Story of the Naval Tactical Data System."

[32] "First-Hand: The Naval Tactical Data System in Combat - Chapter 7 of the Story of the Naval Tactical Data System;" Sherwood, *Nixon's Trident*, 37.

[33] Ut supra.

[34] Ut supra.

[35] Ut supra.

[36] "History and Technology Analysis of the Battle of Dong Hoi" by Stuart Slade (http://www.navweaps.com/index_tech/tech-025.php: accessed 28 October 2018).

[37] John Darrell Sherwood, *Nixon's Trident*, 45 (https://www.history.navy.mil/content/dam/nhhc/research/publications/Publication-PDF/NixonsTrident.pdf: accessed 23 October 2018).

[38] Ibid, 45.
[39] Ibid, 45.

[40] Sherwood, *Nixon's Trident*, 45; "U.S. Mining and Mine Clearance in North Vietnam" by Edward J. Marolda (https://www.history.navy.mil/content/history/nhhc/research/library/onlin e-reading-room/title-list-alphabetically/u/u-s-mining-and-mine-clearance-in-north-vietnam.html: accessed 23 October 2018).
[41] Sherwood, *Nixon's Trident*, 47.
[42] Ibid, 48.
[43] "U.S. Mining and Mine Clearance in North Vietnam."
[44] "1972 West Pac Vietnam Easter Offensive" (http://www.uss-buchanan-ddg14.org/buchanan72.html: accessed 24 October 2018).
[45] "The Warrington Incident (a true account)" by Michael Gonzales Jr. (https://www.angelo.edu/content/files/22070-a: accessed 20 October 2018).
[46] *Warrington, DANFS.*
[47] Ibid.
[48] Ibid.
[49] "The Warrington Incident (a true account)" by Michael Gonzales Jr.
[50] "The Warrington Incident (a true account)" by Michael Gonzales Jr.; Bruhn, *Wooden Ships and Iron Men: The U.S. Navy Ocean Minesweepers, 1953-1994*, 170.
[51] Ut supra.
[52] Bruhn, *Wooden Ships and Iron Men: The U.S. Navy Ocean Minesweepers, 1953-1994*, 170.
[53] Ibid.
[54] *Warrington, DANFS*; page 3-57 of a formerly classified document (https://www.vietnam.ttu.edu/star/images/107/1070416001C.pdf: accessed 3 November 2018).
[55] "A Chronology of the U.S. Navy in Vietnam and Southeast Asia, 1950–75" (https://www.history.navy.mil/browse-by-topic/wars-conflicts-and-operations/vietnam-war0/chronology.html: accessed 20 October 2018).

CHAPTER 21 NOTES:
[1] Marolda, *By Sea, Air, and Land*, Chapter 4.
[2] Ibid.
[3] Ibid.
[4] "Nixon orders the initiation of Operation Linebacker II" (https://www.history.com/this-day-in-history/nixon-orders-the-initiation-of-operation-linebacker-ii: accessed 12 November 2018).
[5] Marolda, *By Sea, Air, and Land*, Chapter 4.
[6] Ibid.
[7] Ibid.
[8] Master List of Unit Awards and Campaign Medals, OPNAVNOTE 1650

of 9 March 2001
(http://www.usshorne.net/horne/images/ribbons/opnavnote1650.pdf:
accessed 3 November 2018).
[9] "History of the *Mason* 1971 to Present"
(https://cosmicshipmedia.net/history2.htm: accessed 11 November 2018).
[10] Ibid.
[11] Ibid.
[12] Ibid.
[13] Ibid.
[14] Ibid.
[15] Ibid.
[16] Ibid.
[17] Ibid.
[18] Ibid.
[19] "History of the Mason 1971 to Present;" "February 6, 1973: Navy Task
Force 78 Begins Operation End Sweep"
(https://www.navalhistory.org/2013/02/07/february-6-1973-navy-task-
force-78-begins-operation-end-sweep: accessed 13 February 2016).
[20] "February 6, 1973: Navy Task Force 78 Begins Operation End Sweep."
[21] Ibid.
[22] "History of the Mason 1971 to Present;" "February 6, 1973: Navy Task
Force 78 Begins Operation End Sweep."
[23] "February 6, 1973: Navy Task Force 78 Begins Operation End Sweep."
[24] "History of the Mason 1971 to Present."
[25] "USS *Leonard F. Mason* (DD-852)"
(http://www.navsource.org/archives/05/852.htm: accessed 13 November
2018).

CHAPTER 22 NOTES:

[1] "April 1975 No room for helicopters with the close of the Vietnam War,
Operation Frequent Wind" by Amanda Uren
(https://mashable.com/2015/05/04/operation-frequent-
wind/#x2.uImn9_8q7); "Vietnam Evacuation: Operation Frequent Wind" by
Daniel L. Haulman (https://media.defense.gov/2012/Aug/23/2001330098/-
1/-1/0/Oper%20Frequent%20Wind.pdf: both accessed 9 November 2018).
[2] Ibid.
[3] "Operation Frequent Wind: April 29-30, 1975"
(https://www.navalhistory.org/2010/04/29/operation-frequent-wind-april-
29-30-1975: accessed 2 November 2018).
[4] Ibid.
[5] "April 1975 No room for helicopters with the close of the Vietnam War,
Operation Frequent Wind" by Amanda Uren; "Vietnam Evacuation:
Operation Frequent Wind" by Daniel L. Haulman.
[6] "Frequent Wind Delivered Thousands to Freedom"
(http://www.navalaviationmuseum.org/history-up-close/frequent-wind-
delivered-thousands-to-freedom/: accessed 9 November 2018).

[7] "Vietnam Evacuation: Operation Frequent Wind" by Daniel L. Haulman.

[8] "At War's End, U.S. Ship Rescued South Vietnam's Navy" (https://www.npr.org/2010/09/01/129578263/at-war-s-end-u-s-ship-rescued-south-vietnam-s-navy: accessed 2 November 2018).

[9] "USS *Kirk* Saigon Evacuation Documentary Premiers at Smithsonian Institute" (https://www.navy.mil/submit/display.asp?story_id=57186: accessed 9 November 2018).

[10] *Cook*, *DANFS*; "USS *Kirk* Saigon Evacuation Documentary Premiers at Smithsonian Institute."

[11] "USS *Kirk* Saigon Evacuation Documentary Premiers at Smithsonian Institute;" "How to Steal a Navy and Save 30,000 Refugees" by Don North (http://www.historynet.com/how-to-steal-a-navy-and-save-30000-refugees-in-the-process.htm: accessed 9 November 2018).

[12] "How to Steal a Navy and Save 30,000 Refugees;" "Frequent Wind" (http://www.kirk1087.org/frequent-wind/: accessed 10 November 2018).

[13] "USS *Kirk* Saigon Evacuation Documentary Premiers at Smithsonian Institute;" "Frequent Wind."

[14] "At War's End, U.S. Ship Rescued South Vietnam's Navy" by Joseph Shapiro and Sandra Bartlett" (http://vnafmamn.com/USS_kirk_VNmission.html: accessed 10 November 2018); "Frequent Wind"

[15] "How to Steal a Navy and Save 30,000 Refugees;" "Frequent Wind."

[16] Ut supra.

[17] "Frequent Wind."

[18] *Cook*, *DANFS*; "At War's End, U.S. Ship Rescued South Vietnam's Navy."

[19] "At War's End, U.S. Ship Rescued South Vietnam's Navy" by Joseph Shapiro and Sandra Bartlett."

[20] Master List of Unit Awards and Campaign Medals, OPNAVNOTE 1650 of 9 March 2001 (http://www.usshorne.net/horne/images/ribbons/opnavnote1650.pdf: accessed 3 November 2018).

APPENDICES NOTES

[1] "Com7th Fleet Vietnam Ship Casualties – US Naval Ships" (http://www.ussmansfield.com/7thfleet/: accessed 5 October 2018).

[2] "Frequent Wind" http://www.kirk1087.org/frequent-wind/: accessed 1 December 2018).

Index

About the Author

Senior Chief Sonar Technician Richard S. Mathews, U.S. Navy (Retired) was destined to be a sailor. His grandfather was a civil engineer in the Navy, and helped to build the Port of Mazatlán, Mexico in the 1920s. His father also served in World War II, finishing his service as a paymaster and Storekeeper First.

Mathews joined the Navy in 1968. Following "boot camp" and sonar school, he was ordered to the destroyer USS *Benner* (DD-807). He made several deployments, spending a good deal of time on the gunline off Vietnam and served as a powderman in one of her 5" gun mounts.

Following decommissioning of *Benner*, Mathews served aboard the *Robison* (DDG-12) and *Maddox* (DD-731). One of the highlights aboard *Robison* was anchoring for five days in Da Nang Harbor while providing Naval Gunfire Support. While assigned to *Maddox*, Gunner's Mate First San Augustine, who was aboard when she was attacked by the North Vietnamese, showed him bullet holes in the fire control director topside.

His next sea duty was aboard the frigate *McCloy* (FF-1038), based in Norfolk, Virginia, aboard which he made two Mediterranean cruises.

Mathews' last three ships were modern *Spruance*-class destroyers, *Leftwich* (DD-984), *Oldendorf* (DD-972), and *Cushing* (DD-985).

Senior Chief Mathews retired from the Navy in 1992. During his career, he had pursued his education while assigned to shore tours at the Fleet Antisubmarine Warfare Training Center, Pacific, San Diego. He earned bachelor's degrees in history from the University of San Diego and in occupational education from Southern Illinois University.

During his post-Navy career, he added a Master of Science degree from Boise State University in Instructional and Performance Technology. His last position was as online professor at the University of Phoenix, teaching writing courses, instructional designed courses, and introducing a course in online education.

Mathews is now fully retired living in Las Vegas with his wife Emma. They have two daughters and four granddaughters.

About the Author

Commander David D. Bruhn, U.S. Navy (Retired) served twenty-two years on active duty and two in the Naval Reserve, as both an enlisted man and as an officer, between 1977 and 2001.

Following completion of basic training, he served as a sonar technician aboard USS *Miller* (FF-1091) and USS *Leftwich* (DD-984). He was commissioned in 1983 following graduation from California State University at Chico. His initial assignment was to USS *Excel* (MSO-439), serving as supply officer, damage control assistant, and chief engineer. He then served in USS *Thach* (FFG-43) as chief engineer and Destroyer Squadron Thirteen as material officer.

After graduation from the Naval Postgraduate School, Commander Bruhn was assigned to Secretary of the Navy and Chief of Naval Operation staffs as a budget analyst and resources planner before attending the Naval War College in 1996, following which he commanded the mine countermeasures ships USS *Gladiator* (MCM-11) and USS *Dextrous* (MCM-13) in the Persian Gulf.

Commander Bruhn's final assignment was executive assistant to a senior (SES 4) government service executive at the Ballistic Missile Defense Organization in Washington, D.C.

Following military service, he was a high school teacher and track coach for ten years, and is now a USA Track & Field official. He lives in northern California with his wife Nancy and has two grown sons, David and Michael.

Printed in September 2021
by Rotomail Italia S.p.A., Vignate (MI) - Italy